THE NECESSARY REFERENCE TO ORGANIZED CRIME

EARTH is an epic publishing feat never to be repeated, proudly created by Millennium House

Western Europe

Locator box indicates location of map within world

Locator box indicates location of map within region

Color-coded bars make identifying each continent easy

Each page is edged with silver gilding to help in the preservation of the book over time

Comprehensive labelling with current data

Specially created state-of-the-art full-color background relief

Colored relief bar indicating elevation

Feature boxes throughout the book focus on milestone events in a country's history or take an in-depth look at a unique feature about a country

Exquisite full-color images are used throughout, with more than 800 images in total

Scale bar and map scale information

A profile of each country provides a snapshot of vital information, including official name, population, area, capital city

A map of each country shows the major cities, highest point, and neighboring countries

Handy map reference information will take you straight to the corresponding map for each country

A locator map pinpoints the location of the country within the region

This limited edition atlas—the world's largest modern atlas—is bound by hand in beautiful custom-dyed leather with silver-gilded pages for preservation and silver-plated corners for protection. *Earth* establishes a new benchmark in the world of atlases, with highly detailed mapping and comprehensive country profiles. With 580 pages, including 355 maps of 194 countries, more than 800 images, 4 breathtaking gatefolds, and information on every country, territory and dependency in the world, *Earth* will appeal to book collectors, libraries and institutions, map lovers, and anyone wishing to enjoy now, and preserve for the future, a record of our world today.

Earth can be ordered from all good book stores or contact Millennium House for your nearest supplier

www.millenniumhouse.com.au

THE NECESSARY
REFERENCE TO
ORGANIZED CRIME

CHIEF CONSULTANT
FRANK SHANTY

MILLENNIUM HOUSE

First published in 2009 as *Mafia* by
Millennium House Pty Ltd
52 Bolwarra Rd, Elanora Heights, NSW, 2101,
Australia
Ph: 612 9970 6850
Fax: 612 9913 3500
Email: info@millenniumhouse.com.au
Website: www.millenniumhouse.com.au

Reprinted 2010

ISBN: 978-1-921209-48-2
ISBN: 978-1-921209-77-2 (Cased)

Authors: Millennium House would be pleased to
receive submissions from authors. Please send brief
submissions to editor@millenniumhouse.com.au

Photographers and illustrators: Millennium House
would be pleased to receive submissions from
photographers or illustrators. Please send
submissions to editor@millenniumhouse.com.au

Color separation by Pica Digital Pte Ltd, Singapore
Printed in China

Photographs on cover and preliminary pages:
Front cover: Digital image of a handgun
with shadow.
Back cover: Car with bullet holes marked by police
Page 1: From left, Michael Bizarro, Joseph Aiello,
Joseph Rubinello, Jack Monzello, and Joseph
Russio face charges over a setup to gun down
Al Capone and Antonio Lombardo, 1927.
Pages 4–5: An Afghan farmer tends his poppy field,
which is situated next to the road from Kabul to
Jalalabad.

Publisher	Gordon Cheers
Associate publisher	Janet Parker
Art director	Stan Lamond
Project manager	Carol Jacobson
Chief consultant	Frank Shanty
Contributors	Jonathan Carlozzi
	Nicolas Giannakopoulos
	David Hompes
	Thomas Hunt
	Lorenzo Picchi
	Frank Shanty
	Charles S. Tumosa
	Andrew L. Urban
	Yue Ma, Ph.D., J.D., LL.M.
Editors	Chris Edwards
	Heather Jackson
	Carol Jacobson
Cover design	Jacqueline Richards
Senior designer	Jacqueline Richards
Designer	Warwick Jacobson
Map Designer	Warwick Jacobson
Picture research	Carol Jacobson
Index	Diane Harriman
Production	Simone Russell
	Bernard Roberts
Production assistant	Michelle Di Stefano

CONTENTS

Mafia and Organized Crime
Threat to Global Security

OPPOSITE Armed Somali pirates such as these are a constant threat to shipping along the east coast of Africa.

Once considered primarily a domestic threat, transnational organized crime now threatens the security of individual states, and relations between states. Many governments today organized crime as a direct threat to national and global security.

Criminals and Terrorists

This evolving global threat, and our collective failure to recognize its scope and reach, has created an international problem which today threatens an already weak global economy and has the potential to undermine the integrity and legitimacy of many governments. Additionally, linkages between violent non-state actors such as terrorists and insurgents pose a direct and growing challenge to the international community.

During the Cold War, relations between nations were relatively stable. The two superpowers, the United States of America and the Union of Soviet Socialist Republics, were able to maintain relative stability within their realms of influence. With the end of the Cold War, borders between nations relaxed allowing for an interchange of people, commerce, and ideas. As tensions between these two nuclear powers abated, a new era in international relations was thought to be on the horizon.

Globalization

As the globalization of trade, commerce, and people began to impact the economies of nation-states, cross-border criminal activity not only increased in intensity but also was transformed into an international phenomenon. Advances in communications technology and transportation also accelerated the evolution of organized crime into a twenty-first century law enforcement nightmare.

Furthermore, the process of globalization has increased the level of cooperation between organized criminal entities. These alliances augment the power and criminal expertise of these groups and make it very difficult for law enforcement to put a stop to their activities or penetrate their operations. Throughout the 1990s, transnational organized crime evolved into a major international security concern that captured the attention of state and federal law enforcement agencies, and now threatens governments, and undermines the economies of developed and developing countries.

BELOW A Bulgarian farmer holds up a poster reading "Stop Mafia," during an anti-government protest in Sofia, in 2009.

Illicit Drugs

The evolving nature of transnational organized crime threatens all facets of global commerce and state security from the subversion of international banking regulations to the smuggling of human migrants, small arms, and nuclear material.

As the number of nuclear-armed countries increases, the threat of nuclear weapon and material proliferation also increases along with the possibility that this technology or its components may be acquired by

violent non-state actors. Moreover the illegal transfer of small arms and light weaponry to such non-state actors sustains ongoing conflicts and increases the likelihood that these conflicts could spread across national borders creating the potential for regional or international hostilities on a grand scale.

Nowhere has the transnational character of organized crime manifested itself more than in the global trade of illicit drugs, a major source of financing for many transnational criminal organizations. Monetary estimates of the size of this activity range from $100 to $400 billion USD annually.

Alliances

Transnational criminal organizations often operate in mutually beneficial alliances and in concert with other national and internationally based groups. Sometimes these relationships are born of necessity and a shared need that serves to further the objectives of both groups. These arrangements can be short-term tactical alliances or longer-term, based on the collective needs of each organization and the perceived benefits of such cooperation.

Organized crime groups thrive in countries which lack a unified political structure, or one in which the existing government has little control over its territory, its law enforcement apparatus is weak or ill-trained and equipped, and its borders are porous. Such countries are open to corruption, extortion, and bribery through government and law enforcement officials, and the general desire of poorer populations to increase their wealth and lifestyle—all of which are consistent with the success of organized crime.

ABOVE Customs officials destroy a massive haul of illicit drugs confiscated in Afghanistan.

What is Organized Crime?

Critical to an understanding of the problem of organized crime is a clear and concise definition of the term. Definitions of organized crime vary depending upon specific laws of individual states and jurisdictions. While much disagreement exists on what constitutes organized crime and how it should be defined, the general consensus is that the term "organized" denotes that there is a consistent pattern and *modus operandi* at work which involves some form of criminal conspiracy which is carried out over a long period of time and may involve many actors, state as well as non-state.

"Organized" can also refer to a group's ability in establishing influence with the governing body to curtail efforts at attempts to impede their activities. Finally, the term "organized" can be applied to those criminal groups that have established and maintained a monopoly over a particular service or commodity.

Operations

Organized crime groups operate similar to legitimate business enterprises by providing goods and services to their customers. However, the services and products that they provide fall outside what is classified as legal. Organized crime engages in activity that generates the highest revenue potential while attempting to minimize risk as much as possible.

Structures

There is no specific organizational structure which criminal groups adopt. They work within various organizational frameworks, many of which are extremely complex, involving many diverse individuals and sub-groups. The organizational structure of any specific group is determined by their specific needs and operational goals and is subject to change according to the changing realities of their operating environment.

Traditional criminal groups such as the Sicilian Mafia operate in a top-down hierarchical structure, similar to legitimate business organizations. Modern day organized

criminal groups tend to operate in a network-type structure. Many of the very large organizations such as those examined here are capable of operating internationally and therefore pose a danger to global security. These organizations are clandestine in nature and depend on operational secrecy and trust for their existence. They are also well educated in the use of modern information technology to facilitate their day-to-day operations and communications.

State and Business Relationships

Major criminal organizations are territorial and adept at utilizing and developing symbiotic relationships with existing state and government apparatus to serve, promote, and further their organizational and operational objectives. Indeed, organized crime cannot successfully conduct operations without some political accommodation.

When their objectives cannot be advanced through extortion, intimidation, and bribes, they often resort to violence, thus threatening public order and endangering the integrity and authority of the state. Organized criminal groups infiltrate legitimate business enterprises through bribery and coercion. They also establish "front companies" to facilitate operations and hide the proceeds from their illegal activities.

Indeed the principal motivating factor and operational concern which drives organized crime is profit. The ability to launder huge amounts of cash is critical to the survival of organized criminal groups. States which lack proper financial oversight of their banking system are conducive to money laundering and also to revenue transfers through the global financial system.

Targets and Allies

Criminal groups engage in targeted violence in an attempt to protect their interests, or influence a person or group of people who threaten their operations. Many of these targets are members of the political establishment and law enforcement community. Civilians are not usually targeted but do encounter violence if they happen to get caught in the crossfire. Since the groups operate internationally, this characteristic makes them difficult to penetrate. There is a growing concern that organized criminal groups are so powerful and financially sound that they have the capability to undermine legitimate governments, and, as in the case of present-day Mexico, can alter relations between states and existing allies.

Critical Response

In the twenty-first century, as states are being threatened by many transnational criminal groups and other armed non-state actors, it is critical that our response be multilateral and that nation-states cooperate in areas which impact their collective security.

Organized crime is one such area that requires a concerted and broad international effort to enact legislation that addresses financial regulation, facilitates information exchange between state law enforcement agencies, and formulates agreements regarding mutual legal assistance, particularly regarding the arrest and extradition of dangerous criminals.

Alongside terrorism, organized crime and how it is fought will be the defining characteristic of this century.

BELOW Al Capone's cell in Eastern State Penitentiary, Philadelphia, holds a few home comforts including artwork, an armchair, and a favorite desk.

1 ORIGINS

Origins The First Mafia

ABOVE Sicilian men and boys line the sea wall in Palermo, the home of the first recorded Mafia.

What is the difference between organized crime and Mafia? When can the word Mafia be used to define a criminal organization? To put it simply, when organized crime acquires a considerable political and social power, it is referred to as Mafia.

Guarduna

In the tale *Riconete Y Cortadillo,* by Spanish poet Miguel De Cervantes, there is a reference to a criminal organization called *Guarduna,* a confraternity founded in Seville in 1417 that is the first documented criminal organization. The *Guarduna* was specialized in organizing homicides on commission and in collecting bribes on any sort of economic activity.

According to their statute, the structure was headed by a *hermano mayor.* This was usually a powerful man well known in the political world who gave orders to the *capatazes*—bosses of the provinces. The army was formed by the *guapos*—also

called *punteaderos*—and by the *floreadores*—assaultmen—usually people escaped from prison. Extra information on which crimes to commit was supplied by the *fecelles*—nobles and members of the *Inquisizione* Tribunal. The organization also used children and teenagers aged between 10 and 15—*chivatos* (*capriole*)—who then had the possibility to move up the criminal social scale after one or two years.

Sicilian Mafia

The first and the most important criminal organization that acquired a strong social and political role that transformed it into a Mafia began in Sicily. The Sicilian Mafia can therefore be considered the model for all the criminal organizations that have developed across the world—each of which then went on to develop its own particular characteristics.

Sicilian aristocrats used criminals to control their feuds, with the complicity of weak and inefficient political institutions. Sicilian landowners nominated the most successful, brutal, and intelligent criminal operating in their territory as "godfather," introducing him to those with political power. In this way, the criminals were integrated into the political system.

Although it is not possible to pinpoint the exact beginning of this Sicilian Mafia, but we do know that when Sicily was under Spanish domination, organized crime there had both the political and social power that defines the Mafia.

ABOVE This engraving of Miguel de Cervantes, author of the tale that first refers to a criminal organization.

Sicilian Mafia
Cosa Nostra

The word *mafia* appeared for the first time as an adjective in the title of the play *I Mafiusi Di La Vicaria*, written in the vernacular by Giuseppe Rizzotto and Gaspare Mosca and first performed in 1863.

The Word

In 1862, according to a most informative account written by one of the actors, the theater company of Rizzotto and Mosca participated in local festivities to celebrate St Rosalia, the patron saint of Palermo. The company was barely making a living, and the landlord of the tavern where they were staying, a certain Iachinu Funciazza, head of the local crime organization, suggested that they should stage something that would be of more interest to the public—based perhaps on the lives of the prisoners in the Vicaria, Palermo's prison.

　　The play that was subsequently written and performed tells the story of a criminal association inside the prison, an association with its own hierarchical organization which operates a system of extortion against other prisoners, offering protection and safety in exchange for compliance. The account of the actor, Natale Cirino, relates that the play did not portray the crime gang in a good light: The actors ridiculed the vulgarity and boorish behavior of the criminals. Audiences were amused, and the play was highly successful. The Honored Society, however, was offended, and to remedy the situation and ensure that future performances would go unhindered, Rizzotto—whose partner, Mosca, left the company—was obliged to add a third act to save the face of the Mafia boss, the inn-keeper Iachinu Funciazza himself.

> *The Mafioso is someone who always wants to give and receive respect. If someone offends him, he does not turn to the law.*
>
> Giuseppe Pitré (1841–1916), Italian folklorist and ethnographer

Spreading the Word

The success of the play was eclipsed by the even greater success of the word *mafia*, the use of which spread very rapidly. By the 1880s it had made its way to America. The link established early between the Mafia and the media would re-emerge in various forms in the future, helping to create damaging and misleading stereotypes and myths. It should be noted that the term only appears in the title of the play. In fact, in the text the organized criminals are referred to as *camorra*, a term now used to refer to the criminal organization active in Naples and other areas in the region of Campania.

Etymology

The etymology of the word *mafia* is unclear. According to one school of thought, it derives from *Ma fia*, meaning "my daughter," which legend claims was the cry of a mother whose daughter was raped by a French soldier on the first day of the Sicilian Vespers in 1268. Another suggestion is that *mafia* is the acronym of the slogan *"Morte ai Francesi Italia Anela"*—Italy calls for death to the French. These proposals are the product of popular imagination and are certainly not based on any methodological approach or verifiable facts.

A third and more reliable theory attributes the word to Arab origins and provides several possibilities, the two most feasible being *mahias*, the Arab word for bravado, and *Mu afah*, meaning protection and safety.

According to the widely accepted definition by Sicilian scholar Umberto Santino, the word *mafia* refers to a *"group of criminal organizations, the most important being Cosa Nostra [Mafia], the purpose of which is to accumulate capital and positions of power through violence and illegal activities. Such organizations operate via a vast system of relationships, have a cultural code and enjoy some degree of social consensus."*

Power System

Clearly, there is a difference between the Mafia and organized crime. The Mafia has a social and political standing that other criminal groups are denied. Just as significant, especially in understanding the characteristics and criminal sophistication of the Sicilian and Italian Mafia, is the nature of its power system. A Mafia-style system comes into being only when organized crime is institutionalized and left unpunished, integrated as part of the broader social and political power system.

ABOVE Mafia operatives? Perhaps. In Palermo, c. 1898, the Mafia was well entrenched in all social institutions and across all social strata.

The Origins

The Mafia did not suddenly appear with the Unification of Italy in 1861. On the contrary, it had always been part of Sicilian history. Existing as a system long before the name *mafia* emerged, it developed through an historic process of evolution spanning centuries.

Early Influence

As early as the early thirteenth century, the Sicilian aristocracy recruited, protected, and occasionally directed groups of bandits to such an extent that political banditry was a fact of life. However, the impunity offered by such a lifestyle was precarious and ceased to function when a bandit turned out to be useless or inconvenient.

Documents dating from the sixteenth century describe the practice of extortion at Palermo market, a tactic fundamental to gaining control of the territory and still a vital aspect of Mafia organizations.

Land Jurisdiction

The Mafia phenomenon had one of its most fundamental origins in the method of administering justice in Sicily, if justice could be said to exist. The barons, politically united and represented in the Sicilian parliament, exercised jurisdiction on their own lands as one of their feudal prerogatives.

In 1569 in Sicily, a reform was introduced whereby judges of the tribunals of the High Court and the Consistory—chosen from the ranks of lawyers—remained in office for only two years. Since in practice only landowners could afford the expense of a court case, the lawyers, who were only temporary judges, could have no interest in opposing the employers on whom they were completely dependent.

The Inquisition

Further complicating the various local systems of justice was the Tribunal of the Inquisition, a repressive political structure in the service of the Spanish government, officially responsible for repressing heresy against the Catholic Church.

ABOVE The forced unification of Italy in 1861, which brought Sicily into the Italian fold, heralded the emergence of the Mafia in its modern form.

OMERTÀ

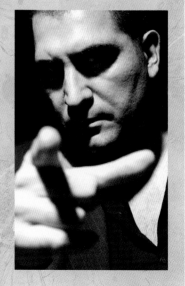

The *omertà* can be defined as a guilty silence. Whoever dares to write or talk about the Mafia, or about anything associated with the Mafia, is exposed to retaliation, intimidation, exclusion from society, and eventually violence. The *omertà* is a silence that furthers the cultural acceptance of the Mafia codes of behavior.

The term has its origins in the word "*umiltà*," or humility, signifying subordination to the wishes of the organization. The conversion of "l" into "r" which is typical of Sicilian dialect would have led to the word "*umirtà*," and then eventually to "*omertà*."

Nowadays, the *omertà* has adjusted to contemporary society and the Italian media complies with this code. Italian newspapers and television stations are largely under the control of government, political parties, banks, or large industrial groups—organizations very often if not always involved with the Mafia. Thus, the media avoid talking about the Mafia. Or if they do, they describe it as a folkloric phenomenon, giving a skewed representation of its influence in society, continuing the code of silence that has existed in Italy for years.

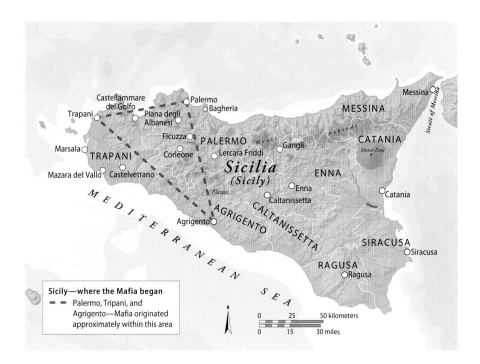

Sicily—where the Mafia began
- - Palermo, Trapani, and Agrigento—Mafia originated approximately within this area

1860 Palermo becomes an Italian city after Garibaldi's invasion.

1869 Chief of Police of Palermo, Guiseppe Albanese, is stabbed by *Mafioso* in a piazza as he tries to blackmail his attacker.

1872 The first persecution by the Mafia is recorded by a surgeon Gaspare Galati in a dispute over a lemon grove.

1898–1900 Report by Chief of Police of Palermo, Ermanno Sangiorgi, recounts a complete picture of Sicilian Mafia.

Associated with this Tribunal were the *familiari*—familiars—who were exempted from paying taxes and had the right to carry arms. The *familiari* were not subject to the *ex abrupto* procedure which allowed a nobleman to make use of false witnesses to show his innocence.

It would have been inopportune for the Spanish government to stand against the aristocracy of Sicily since, with their "private police," they kept discontent and the possibility of rebellion by the rest of the population under control. Consequently criminals and members of the nobility who commissioned murders were regularly absolved.

Even the police forces that came into being over time, the *Compagnie D'Armi*—Armed Troops—and the *Gendarmeria Reale*—Royal Police—were far from immune to corruption as they consisted mainly of delinquents. These "policemen"—in practice criminals—organized their policing according to a system of transactions: They would arrange for a partial return of the stolen goods to the victim, collect a reward for their mediation, then share the rest of the booty with the thieves and bandits who came from their own social background.

Part of the System

In addition to organizing violence, the Mafia's main activities consisted of land management, cattle stealing—a complex crime involving detailed organization and an extensive network of relationships—kidnapping, and theft. Under the land management system, Mafia tax-collectors were the tenants of land belonging to the nobility; they sub-let this land to peasants long inured to poverty and hunger.

It was from this system that the Mafia evolved. In practice a society without state, the Mafia was based on the complicity of the nobility, criminals, the Church, and other social institutions. It is easy to understand why, even today, it thrives in countries where the institutions are weak, corrupt, and inefficient.

ABOVE Police protecting residents, late nineteenth century. In and around Palermo, it was said, no traveler was safe from robbery and the knife.

American Mafia
The Emergence

ABOVE The magnificent architecture of the French Quarter in New Orleans, belies its use as a common battleground of early Mafia in the United States.

New Orleans, Louisiana, was the Mafia's first home in America, when, just a few years after the end of the American Civil War, the city erupted in gang violence as two criminal organizations in its young Sicilian colony vied for underworld dominance.

The Ideal Climate

New Orleans was a bustling cosmopolitan port, located near the mouth of the Mississippi River. Immigrants with the desire for work could find it on the city wharves. Opportunities to generate modest incomes also could be found at sugar and cotton plantations and vegetable farms in the region. Newcomers able to arrange the use of a boat could earn money harvesting oysters and shrimp from nearby waters.

Born to an affluent family in Palermo, Sicily, in 1829, Raffaele Agnello crossed the Atlantic when he was thirty. Like many of his fellow countrymen, he found the climate and opportunities ideal in the "Crescent City." Agnello had little interest in honest work. As a *Mafioso*, his trade was preying upon his more industrious countrymen. Taxing immigrants for protection and reacting harshly to any opposition, Agnello grew wealthy and powerful. By 1868, his only obstacle within the Sicilian community was a stubborn rebellious gang from the Sicilian city of Messina.

Gang Conflict

BELOW The dockyards of New Orleans were a breeding ground for bribery and corruption by Mafia families.

While Messinian leader, Litero Barba, was walking home through the city's French Quarter on the evening of October 28, 1868, an unseen gunman ended his life with a shotgun blast. Mafia boss Agnello momentarily deflected blame from himself by announcing that the local African-American politician and businessman, Octave Belot, was responsible. However, when Belot was able to prove that he had been out of town at the time of Barba's killing, suspicion fell upon Agnello.

Despite efforts by Agnello's brother, Peppino, to ease gang tensions, Barba's chief lieutenant Joseph Banano directly accused Agnello gangster, Alphonse Mateo, of killing Barba. Mateo responded with a knife and, without hesitation, Banano drew a pistol and killed Mateo.

Agnello moved aggressively in the following weeks, ordering armed raids on Messinian homes and businesses. By the end of March 1869, the rebel gang looked beaten. However, on April 1, as Agnello took a victory stroll around the French Quarter, the Mafia boss was shot dead and his organization began to fall apart.

Who kill-a the Chief?

Anti-Italian phrase used after the acquittal of those accused of killing Police Chief Hennessy in 1890.

Peppino's Exit

Peppino Agnello attempted to carry on his brother's war, killing Banano and his companion, Pedro Allucho. The Messinian gang repeatedly targeted Peppino, but he was a difficult man to kill. Peppino escaped injury during an attack in 1869 at Lafayette Square, and the next year he took a stab wound to the chest but recovered. He suffered what doctors believed was a mortal bullet wound on September 13, 1871. However, he rebounded from that as well.

In April 1872, a gunman named Joseph Maressa spotted Peppino at the Picayune Pier. The two men engaged in a fistfight as Maressa allies carrying shotguns swarmed the pier. Surrounded, Peppino jumped to the deck of the moored schooner, *Mischief*, but Maressa fired once and Peppino collapsed onto the schooner's deck and died there a short time later.

Stuppagghieri

Without the Agnellos, the traditional Palermo-based Mafia faded from New Orleans. In its place sprang up a new underworld society rooted in a more radical Mafia tradition from Monreale, Sicily. Under Matranga Crime Family leadership and with the endorsement of Louisiana businessman and political organizer, Joseph Macheca, the Stuppagghieri society eventually dominated the Crescent City underworld.

ABOVE Overcrowded Canal Street, New Orleans, was the hub of the city at the turn of the century, allowing the infiltration of racketeering.

Mafia's first US battleground
⊕ New Orleans

ABOVE This engraving depicts the riot
and assault by citizens on the New
Orleans prison after the verdict in the
Hennessy assassination trial.

Crescent City Vengeance

The rule of the Stuppagghieri Mafia in New Orleans was interrupted with the 1879
arrival of fugitive Sicilian gang boss, Giuseppe Esposito. Accused of kidnapping,
banditry, and murder in his native land, Esposito eluded Italian police until 1877.
On the way to trial, he escaped and slipped onto a ship bound for the United States.
In New Orleans, he adopted the alias of Vincenzo Rebello and became leader of the
local Sicilian underworld, reviving the old Agnello Mafia.

Italian authorities learned of Esposito's whereabouts from an informant and worked
through private investigators to contact two New Orleans detectives, cousins David
and Mike Hennessy. Without the knowledge of their superiors in the police force, the
Hennessys agreed to apprehend Esposito. On July 5, 1881, the cousins waited along
a route Esposito took each day. As the crime lord passed, they drew handguns and
ordered him into a police wagon. Before *Mafiosi* in the city realized what happened,
Esposito was on his way by steamship to extradition hearings in New York.

Provenzano-Matranga Feud

Esposito's supporters, led by the Provenzano Crime Family, openly accused the
Stuppagghieri and its Matranga Crime Family of betraying their leader. Years of
violence followed, as the factions competed for criminal rackets and for legitimate
business contracts. Benefiting from the friendship of businessman Joseph Macheca
and an alliance with a corrupt political machine, the Stuppagghieri surpassed their
rivals. In 1890, the now newly appointed Chief of Police, David Hennessy, tried to
work with Joseph Macheca to end the bloody rivalry. Hennessy achieved only an
intermission. He later discovered Macheca was encouraging Stuppagghieri leader,
Charlie Matranga, toward violence.

Trials and Corruption

On May 5, 1890, a group of Matranga dock supervisors on their way home from work,
were ambushed by Provenzano gunmen. Three men were seriously wounded, including Charlie Matranga's brother Antonio.

Hennessy personally conducted the investigation and arrested Provenzano gang
leaders for ambush and attempted murder. The Stuppagghieri broke with Mafia tradition by cooperating with authorities. Three trials were scheduled for the Provenzanos,
one for each wounded man. Though the Provenzanos offered convincing alibis, they

1868 Joseph Macheca
and his gang conduct raids
on African-Americans living
in New Orleans

1888 David Hennessy
rejoins the police force as
Chief, after being dismissed
in 1882 through Mafia
influence.

1891 Charles Matranga
becomes head of the Mafia
in New Orleans.

1895 Frank Costello, born
in Italy in 1891, moves to New
York with his family.

1899 Alphonse Capone
is born in Brooklyn, in the
midst of the Five Points
Gang territory.

were convicted in the first trial. Afterward, officers from Hennessy's own department came forward to support the Provenzano alibis. As a result, the guilty verdict was thrown out, infuriating the Matrangas.

As the second trial date approached, Hennessy started investigating the Matranga faction. Macheca learned of the chief's investigation and confronted him. He warned Hennessy to stay out of the matter or he would be put "in a box." Unconcerned, Hennessy continued his probe.

Assassination

Late on the night of October 15, 1890, just half a block from his home, Chief Hennessy was struck by shotgun blasts. A man rushed to Hennessy's aid and asked who attacked him. Hennessy whispered an ethnic slur, "Dagos." He was taken to Charity Hospital, where he died the next morning.

Nineteen men were indicted as assassins or conspirators in the assassination. Nine of those, including Joseph Macheca and Charlie Matranga, went to trial early in 1891. A jury found none guilty after prosecutors disclosed evidence that the defense had offered bribes to prospective jurors.

Lynchings

Though not convicted, the defendants remained overnight in Orleans Parish Prison with the other 10 indicted men who were not yet tried. Early the next morning, an angry community turned out for a rally on Canal Street. Incited by fiery speeches, the crowd—thousands strong—marched to the prison and broke into the building through a side door. Execution squads were sent in.

The squads shot nine prisoners to death and brought two more out to be hanged. The squads claimed to be fighting the corruption of the Mafia. However, Charlie Matranga and his top lieutenant were unharmed.

Political Influence

During the latter half of the nineteenth century, corrupt political party leaders encouraged the influence of immigrants, particularly those who would help win elections. Those with Mafia connections, such as the Matrangas, were helpful in turning the tide of voters by discouraging the opposition. This strategy spread quickly throughout the major cities and was influential in the establishment of the Mafia in the United States.

BELOW Cartoon depiction of the jury intimidation by the Mafia in New Orleans, after the assassination of Chief of Police, David Hennessy.

ETHNIC SLUR

The origins of the word "Dago" are varied. One school of thought is that it was derived from the Spanish word "Diego" meaning a person of Spanish descent. Another thought is that it was a derivation of the term "day laborers" or "Day-os," as spoken by Italian immigrants who could barely speak English. Either way, the term spread to become an international offensive ethnic slur for persons of Italian descent.

Italian laborers stop work for a feast of traditional spaghetti. Italian immigrants flooded the United States around 1900, forming close-knit communities with old family feuds.

Yakuza The Origins

1603 The famous Tokaido Highway is built joining Kyoto and Tokyo allowing gangs to operate at way stations along the route.

1735–1740 Feudal authorities recognize official status of the tekiya bosses.

1893 Jirocho of Shimizu, an early Yakuza, dies, after commanding the largest gambling gang in Japan while becoming a folk hero to the nation.

Organized crime groups in Japan are known as the *Yakuza*. *Ya-ku-sa* in Japanese means 8-9-3, which stands for a worthless hand in a traditional Japanese card game.

By the Rule

As the name signifies, the origins of organized crime in Japan can be traced to the gambling gangs that emerged in the mid-eighteenth century. *Hanafuda* (flower cards) is a traditional Japanese card game. Three cards are dealt per player and the player who can accumulate most points wins the game. By the rule, the last digit of the total of the three cards counts as the number of the hand. A sequence of 8-9-3, which adds up to 20, makes up a worthless hand in the game.

    The early gambling gangs used the losing combination to denote something useless. They later applied the term to themselves to mean they were useless to society. They were, however, proud to be outcasts from society.

BELOW Three armed *samurai* pose outside a traditional tea house. After the civil war, many *samurai* were left unemployed and formed gangs.

Give the peasants neither life nor death.

Ieyasu Tokugawa (1543–1616), first *shogun* of the Tokugawa era of Japan.

Spiritual Ancestors

From the twelfth to the nineteenth century, Japan was ruled by the feudal military dictators known as *shogun*. During the *shogun* rule, an aristocratic class of knights called *samurai* gained considerable power as they were hired by local lords to protect their lands during the constant warfare.

    The civil war—brought to an end by the great shogun, Ieyasu Tokugawa, in 1604—left as many as 500,000 *samurai* unemployed. While many became successful merchants or civil bureaucrats, some turned to banditry to make the best use of their skills in the martial arts. These discontented *samurai* soon turned into gangs of roving bandits, swaggering through the streets, committing frequent outrages against defenseless townspeople.

    While these *samurai* bandits appeared to be the forebears of the Japanese underworld, today's Yakuza refuse to identify with them but assert that they are the descendants of those who stood up against the *samurai* bandits—the young men who banded together to protect the townspeople as town servants. They became folk heroes and stories about these chivalrous commoners still remain among the most popular tales of Japan's past. The modern Yakuza look upon these chivalrous commoners as their spiritual ancestors, regarding themselves as compassionate outlaws, useless to mainstream society but willing to stand up for the common people.

Gamblers and Street Peddlers

Although today's Yakuza claim the town servants as their ancestors, the direct connection is hard to make, for both *samurai* bandits and the town servants were eradicated by the shogunate government by the late seventeenth century. The Yakuza's true ancestors were enterprising members of two distinct groups. The *bakuto* were gamblers, and the *tekiya* were street peddlers that came into existence in the eighteenth century.

The *tekiya* were the masters in selling shoddy goods by deceptive salesmanship. The *tekiya* boss controlled the market extortion, determining the allocation of stalls and even the availability of certain goods. He demanded protection money from the peddlers and those who refused to pay would find their goods stolen and customers driven away. They would also risk physical assault for not cooperating with the gang.

To reduce fraud among vendors and to prevent gang turf wars, the government appointed some gang bosses as "supervisors" and granted them status near that of *samurai*. The tolerant approach taken by the government was an early illustration of a unique aspect of organized crime in Japan. That is, the government's willingness to make use of and cooperate with criminals.

BELOW From the novel *Suikoden*, the outlaw hero Kumonryu (Nine Dragons) is tattooed with the elaborate dragons of his nickname.

Gambling

The government played a more pernicious role in the development of gambling gangs as the government officials were among the first to recruit gambling gangs. Under the shogunate administration, local vassals had the responsibility of providing labor for construction, irrigation, and other public-work programs. The local lords turned to labor brokers—in most cases bosses of gambling dens—for supply of laborers. The betting served to attract potential workers and allowed the bosses to retrieve a portion of the salaries paid to workers. Government officials also joined in, hiring gamblers to gamble with the workers.

The hired gamblers were composed of all sorts of people ranging from farmers, laborers, outlaws, to *sumo* wrestlers, merchants, and *samurai*. These gamblers gradually organized themselves into disciplined gangs and became the kernel of organized crime groups in Japan. They gave the country's underworld not only its name Yakuza but also its central tradition of gambling and its customs of tattoos and fingercutting.

Triads Secret Societies

Throughout China's history its people have formed secret societies to find protection against thieves, bandits, and their nation's leaders.

Criminal Fraternities

Although Chinese emperors ruled their empire with an iron fist and suppressed the people, they could never control them. So, although most of these secret societies were honest, others were not and these became criminal fraternities.

China's First Triad Society

Operating in the Chinese provinces of Fujian and Guangdong, the Tiandihui (*T'ien-ti Hui*), or Heaven and Earth Society—also known as the Hung Society—started out as a secret society providing help to Chinese who needed it most. Peasants who lost their land or could not find work were among those people who came to the Tiandihui to ask for help and assistance during these hard times. The requirements to become a member of the Tiandihui were less strict than they were with other secret societies, but the Tiandihui provided the same services, thus making it a very attractive group to join.

Initiation

Once a person became a member of the Tiandihui, he agreed to protect his society brothers and help expand the society by introducing new members. After an initiation ceremony, the new brother was given a membership certificate and the society's secrets, which consisted of hand signs, esoteric prayers, and passwords.

Blanket of Security

As a member, he could call upon his society when he was in trouble. For instance, when a member was out of money he could turn to his brothers for help. But his society also helped out when thieves robbed him, or if criminals were trying to extort his business. When that happened, Tiandihui's enforcers were sent out to avenge their brother and make things right. Eventually this blanket of security became the primary reason for

BELOW The bustling streets of Shanghai at the end of the nineteenth century were the proving ground for early crime gangs.

Chinese to join this secret society. With everybody turning to their society for revenge, it wasn't long before members of the different societies were at war with each other and causing bloodshed. These wars where members sought revenge were called *xie dou* and are very similar to the Italian Mafia's "vendetta."

Sponsorship

The Tiandihui made a fortune by enrolling new members. Each new member had to pay an entrance fee, subscription fees, and a tribute fee to his sponsor for introducing him into the society. In certain provinces men also had to pay an extra fee on top of the normal fees to join. It is clear members enjoyed the security the society brought, but it also became a wise career move when so much money could be made as a sponsor by introducing new members.

Robbery

Other moneymaking operations the societies ran were collecting rent from properties they owned, and loan sharking. With the ability to exercise a lot of power through its growing number of members, the Tiandihui went from loan sharking to robbery. Nobody was safe. The society robbed both civilians and members of rival societies with equal ferocity. Because of this, even more men joined the Tiandihui hoping it would keep them safe from robbery and attacks. All these operations were done in the open, until the Qing Dynasty attempted to eradicate "secret" societies, driving them underground.

ABOVE Chinese gamblers on the way to execution were confined with *cangue* (portable stocks), engraved with the nature of their crime.

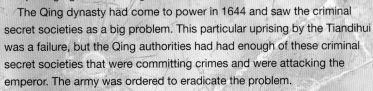

SECRET SOCIETIES AND THE IMPERIAL POWERS

The secret societies have always posed a huge threat to the political powers of China. There are numerous accounts of uprisings led by societies that had amassed a large enough following to undertake such an enormous task.

During the 1760s, Tiandihui leader, Lu Mao, ordered the newly initiated members to rob an official warehouse and treasury, and the homes of the upper class. He told the would-be robbers that the loot would be used to organize an uprising against the Qing authorities.

The Qing dynasty had come to power in 1644 and saw the criminal secret societies as a big problem. This particular uprising by the Tiandihui was a failure, but the Qing authorities had had enough of these criminal secret societies that were committing crimes and were attacking the emperor. The army was ordered to eradicate the problem.

After a large-scale military operation, army commanders claimed they had suppressed the societies. They lied. The societies had grown in such a dramatic way that it had become impossible to eradicate them. They had hundreds of thousands of members; entire villages were owned by the societies. And their power stretched across China into neighboring countries. The attack by the imperial army only drove the secret societies more underground than before, increasing crime and extortion.

LEFT Painting of Chien-lung Ti, fourth Qing emperor of China. The Qing Dynasty was particularly fearful of secret societies. The campaign to eradicate these groups only drove them underground creating a more dangerous form of secret society.

1711 British East India Company begins trading in Guangzhou

1839 First Opium War begins between Britain and China

1856 The Second Opium War begins

1898 The Qing emperor orders social reforms after the defeat in the First Sino-Japanese War

Birth of a Name

The name "Triad" stemmed from the fact that members of these secret societies (*huis*) saw the world as a unity of the three main powers of nature—heaven, earth, and man. And their flags bore a triangle. The name Triad seems to have been first used around the time of British control of Hong Kong. To this day the Triads use old rituals and traditions to maintain discipline within the organization and create an air of mythical powers around them. They even have their own version of how they were formed.

There are many different Triad groups, all of which have their own slightly different version of Triad history. Over the course of decades these versions have changed and adapted new themes. The Triads have combined real historic events in China with Chinese folklore in order to create a very heroic story about their origins. This is all done to impress new members. The story of the First Five Ancestors is how the Triads view their history.

Folklore

Their story begins in the seventeenth century during the Ming Dynasty. In 1644, the Ming dynasty fell when the Manchu forces defeated the imperial forces. The Manchus crowned Shun Chi as the first Manchu Qing emperor. During the reign of the second Qing emperor tribes from the state of Silu started an uprising. The Qing army was not equipped to deal with the rebels and called upon its emperor for reinforcements. The emperor started a recruiting campaign in which he offered high honors, favors, and official employment to men who joined his army and defeated the Silu rebels.

Five Ancestors

At a Shao Lin monastery an assembly of monks decided to offer their services to the emperor. The monks had two reasons for helping out—they wanted to stop the invasion of foreign troops into China and they also wanted to put in use their knowledge of kung fu, which they had been practicing at the monastery. They hoped their martial arts abilities would lead other men to join their monastery.

An elite force of 128 monks joined the imperial army in battle against the Silu and defeated them in three months. The monks were hailed as heroes and were offered their promised honors from the emperor. They declined his offers, saying they had done their civic duty.

However, a nephew of one of the monks—Cheng Kwan-tat—accepted the position of commander of the Qing garrison in the Wuchow district.

Wong Chun-mei, grand secretary of the Qing council, was envious of the post offered to Cheng Kwan-tat and began manipulating the emperor into believing the monks were about to start an uprising themselves.

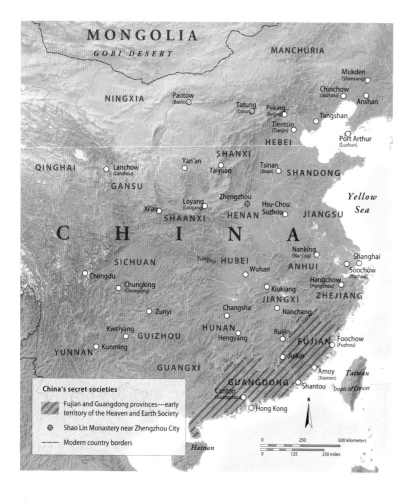

China's secret societies

- Fujian and Guangdong provinces—early territory of the Heaven and Earth Society
- ⊕ Shao Lin Monastery near Zhengzhou City
- — Modern country borders

LEFT Although opium was illegal, opium dens existed all over China. They supplied and sold opium and supplies with which to use opium. Here two wealthy merchants enjoy the opulence of a high society den.

OPIUM

From the time of the Qing dynasty's effort to eradicate Tiandihui, the society became deeply embedded in the underworld.

Opium had become the drug of choice by the late eighteenth century, and thus had a business appeal for any society member. Opium was illegal in China and was smuggled into the country by British, European, and American traders.

Society members bought opium from these traders and from there it went down the distribution ladder until it reached the drug addicts on the streets of China's major cities and villages.

The secret societies had now made the transformation from benevolent organizations to full blown profit-making criminal organizations.

The Triads were born.

To violate the law is the same crime in the emperor as in the subject

Chinese proverb

The emperor then ordered an attack on the Shao Lin monastery. Qing troops set fire to the monastery causing the deaths of 110 monks. Eighteen monks survived, but were presumed dead. These remaining 18 monks fled the ruined monastery by walking down the burning hill on which it was situated. Once in a safe place, 13 monks died from their wounds and lack of food. The five monks who survived—Tsoi Tak-chung, Fong Tai-hung, Ma Chiu-hing, Wu Tak-tai, and Lee Shik-hoi—became the First Five Ancestors mentioned in all Triad history.

These five men traveled the rugged lands of China and met up with several Ming loyalists who joined their cause, and became known as the Second Five Ancestors. Their cause was the overthrow of the Qing dynasty. The men formed several secret societies and used their army of men to fight against the Qing dynasty.

Russian Mafia
Peasant Outlaws

If organized crime means coordinated criminal activities defined by the ruling class, organized crime can find its roots in Tsarist Russia.

Bandits

In the seventeenth and eighteenth centuries, banditry became an extremely serious concern in Russia. Banditry consisted of peasant outlaws who were labeled criminals by the state but heralded as heroes and fighters for justice by peasants. Among many bandit leaders the most famous were Emelyan Pugachev (1726–1775) and Stenka Razin (1630–1671). Proclaiming freedom and equality to all men, they led Don Cossacks in popular uprisings against the landlords and demanded they change the harsh conditions imposed upon the peasants by the serfdom.

All the revolts were ruthlessly put down by the Tsar, and Razin and Pugachev were captured and executed. The two rebel leaders, however, have become heroes, forever immortalized in Russian folk songs and literature.

BELOW A secret society meeting is interrupted by Tsarist police.

It is better to abolish serfdom from above than to wait for it to abolish itself from below.

Alexander II, 1818–1881, Emperor of Russia

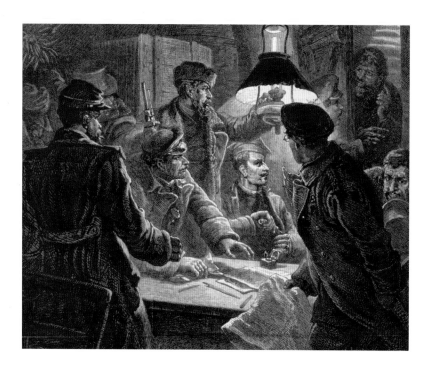

Secret Societies

As most Western European countries moved towards liberal democracy at the beginning of the nineteenth century, Russia made no attempt to change its feudal system. Discontent with social conditions led to the formation of secret societies among intellectuals, peasants, and soldiers. Decembrists were the most famous and had their origins in the Union of Salvation formed by officers of the Imperial Russian Guard in 1816. The Union of Salvation in 1820 evolved into two societies—the more moderate Northern Society and the more radical Southern Society. Concerned about them, the Tsarist regime prohibited all secret societies in 1822. The prohibition did little to stop the activities of the two societies.

Tsarist Reforms

In December 1825, soldiers belonging to the two societies staged a revolt against the Tsar and demanded liberal reforms. The Tsarist regime crushed the revolt, but it drew the Tsar's attention to the need for social reforms. In 1861, Tsar Alexander II issued the Edit of Emancipation, which freed all serfs and abolished the serfdom. The serfs, however, were disappointed by the cumbersome and unjust land distribution system and the heavy taxes they were required to pay. Many secret groups were organized throughout the country. Some of these groups resorted to violence and assassination as a tactic to promote political reforms.

Marxists

In the late nineteenth century, revolutionary groups developed.

ABOVE Rivets are hammered into the heavy chain used to constrain a prisoner on the Siberian prison island of Sakhalin.

In 1895, Lenin united all Marxist groups in St Petersburg, which later developed into the Russian Communist Party. The revolutionary groups operated clandestinely, and engaged in assassination, murder, stealing, and damaging government or private property in their struggle against the Tsarist regime. They turned armed robberies, termed as *expropriations* of private property, into a standard way of fund-raising for the cause of revolution. To the Tsarist regime, the revolutionaries were a new breed of bandits in Russia's long tradition of banditry.

Criminal Gangs

Admittedly, not all secret organizations or societies had political agendas. For many centuries, in Tsarist Russia, there were societies of smugglers, highwaymen, and thieves on the margins of ordinary life.

As early as the time of Peter the Great (1695–1725), there existed an army of thieves. On the outskirts of Moscow alone, there were more than 30,000 thieves. The thieves, however, were unorganized. They lived apart and plied their trade in isolated small gangs. They appeared to have no political agenda at all.

In the late nineteenth century and early twentieth century, Russia's industrialization brought about an increase in criminality in urban centers. Criminal gangs roamed the slums of St Petersburg and other growing cities. There was a proliferation of small gangs of pickpockets, swindlers, robbers, and forgers. The level of organization increased in the criminal gangs, and led to their own laws, traditions, and slang.

In the late Tsarist era, some outlaw bands became allies of the communist revolutionaries working in collaboration with the criminal underworld and recruiting the bandits to carry out bank robberies, kidnappings, and murders. The relationship between the two groups helped further the causes of both.

In the pre-Revolution years, there was thus no clear distinction between the revolutionaries and professional criminals, and after the establishment of the Soviet regime, Joseph Stalin recruited criminal underworld figures into his secret police.

1670 Stenka Razin leads a bloody assault on Astrakhan and turned it into a Cossack republic. He was tortured and killed for his actions in 1671.

1773-1774 Emelyan Pugachev heads a series of revolts against the government, consolidating the peasants.

1879 The revolutionary organization, Land and Liberty, splits into two groups—moderate Black Repartition and radical People's Will.

1882 Alexander III introduces laws that expel Russian Jews from rural areas and restricts their education.

1898 The Marxist Russian Social Democratic Labor Party holds its first congress.

2 INTO THE TWENTIETH CENTURY

Into the Twentieth Century
Global Foundations

During the first half of the twentieth century, crime groups around the world were laying the foundation for future world domination of almost any enterprise that paid well.

ABOVE A smiling and smartly dressed Al Capone, as he is escorted to federal prison for tax evasion.

Sicily

In Sicily, *Cosa Nostra*—Mafia—had been born from the old secret brotherhoods, and was establishing an unbreakable system of clan law within the small rural villages of the island. During World War II, dictator Benito Mussolini had sent Cesare Mori to rid Sicily of *Cosa Nostra* using all means possible. Scores of *Mafiosi* were arrested, while others managed to travel to North America where they joined the large group of Italians that had already settled in the United States and started the American version of *Cosa Nostra*.

United States

The modern-day American Mafia would come into full bloom after the violent wars in which crime families took on each other in order to control the American underworld. During this period, in the early 1920s, the American Mafia involved itself in every racket available. Bootlegging, union corruption, gambling, prostitution, loan sharking, extortion, racketeering, and anything else that gave them a nice payday.

Asia

Meanwhile in Asia, two criminal brotherhoods stood out. In Japan, the Yakuza was an important ally of right-wing Japanese politicians. Protected by the government, Yakuza established a booming business that consisted of gambling, loan sharking, extortion, and prostitution.

The second Asian brotherhood that rose to prominence was the Chinese Triads. Just like the Yakuza, the Triads, too, had great political power. So much so that during the early twentieth century they had one of their own as the first president of the Republic of China.

Russia

Where Mussolini had managed to severely weaken the Sicilian Mafia, in communist Russia a group called "thieves-in-law" managed to establish an iron grip within Russian prisons. These men were bonded by their hate of the Communist Party and anyone who supported this system. As they re-entered society, they quickly established a leadership role in the criminal world of several major Russian cities.

Narcotics

In Latin America and Europe, the drug trade was becoming a popular commodity. Several powerful groups began building their criminal empire through the spectacular popularity of heroin and cocaine—bringing much wealth and also much bloodshed.

BELOW The bound and trussed body of Walter Sage was found by state troopers in the Catskills. It's believed that he was killed for skimming from the Mafia's slot machine operations in Sullivan County, New York State.

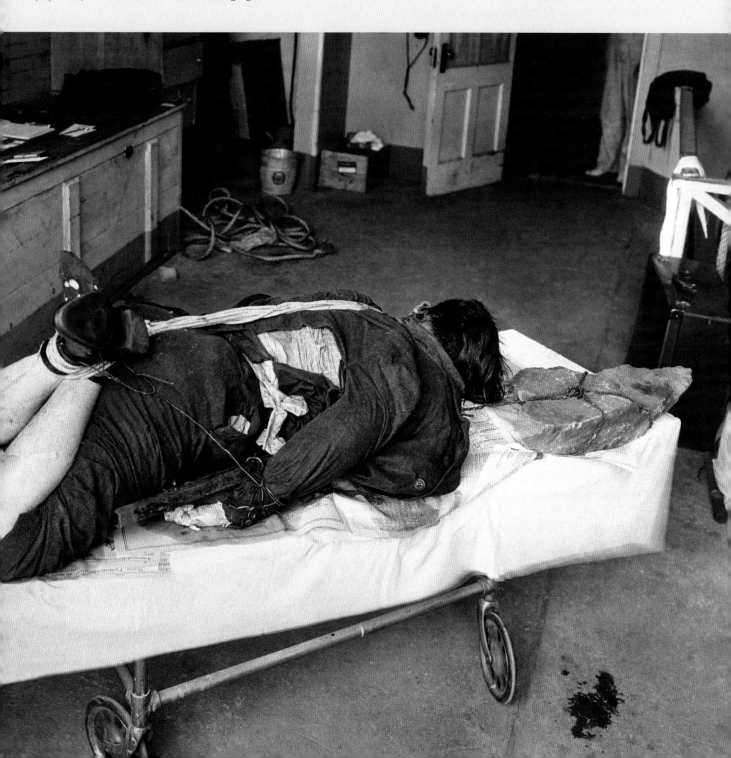

Sicilian Mafia
Fascism and Power

The twentieth century brought the advent of fascism to Italy and for Sicilian Mafia the situation changed dramatically.

Mussolini

Mussolini became Prime Minister in 1922 following the March on Rome, and in May 1924 he paid a state visit to Sicily. During his visit, he was received by the mayor of a small town near Palermo where the security services did not appear to be sufficient. When Mussolini asked the mayor to explain his laxity, the reply was that "there was nothing to fear when he was with him." For Mussolini the episode merely confirmed his suspicion that in Sicily the state did not hold any power. He returned to Rome a few days later, but did not forget the slight to his position.

He was to recall it in 1925, after the *coup d'état* that led to him becoming *Il Duce* (leader), when he decided that Sicily must be brought under control. Sicily must become fascist; the authority of the state must finally be imposed. Knowing that a clash with the Mafia could not be avoided, Mussolini appointed his most competent police officer, Cesare Mori, Prefect of Palermo, granting him full powers. Under a dictatorship it is not difficult to imagine their extent.

ABOVE Primo Cesare Mori (1871–1942) was appointed Prefect of Palermo by Mussolini in 1925. *Il Duce* told him to eradicate the Mafia, saying: "If the laws hinder you, we will draw up new laws."

The best blood will at some time get into a fool or a mosquito.

Benito Mussolini (1883–1945), Italian dictator

"The Iron Prefect"

The task assigned to Mori was not to so much to defeat the Mafia as to bring the island under state control—or rather, under the control of the regime—and in October 1925 he began the most thorough police operation ever conducted against the Mafia.

The vigorous military methods used by "The Iron Prefect," as he came to be known, were intended to demonstrate that things had changed—that authority would henceforth be vested in the state, not in the Mafia. Mori decreed that protection money—the *pizzo*—would no longer be paid to local bullies, and that the police would from now on be responsible for dealing with all problems of public order, thus removing power from the *padrini*—the Mafia bosses.

Mori had the foresight to seek the support and goodwill of the population, but in attempting "to annul the system of intermediation under which citizens could not approach the authorities except through middlemen, receiving as a favor that which is due them as their right," he was unafraid to use brutal means. In order to force *mafiosi* to surrender to the *Carabinieri* and the army, he sometimes abducted their female or elderly relatives, and even laid siege to whole towns.

Two Factions

The Mafia had never openly supported the fascist regime but had been inclined to view it favorably given their common enemy, socialism. Now, in the face of the fascist assault, they split into two factions. On one side were those who opposed fascism: They were hunted down implacably by Mori, then sent to prison or interned while awaiting a mass trial and the maximum sentences that followed. On the other side were those who realized that, instead of working against the state, it would be better to try to carry on, perpetuating their business through it: The latter decided to collaborate with Mori, helping him in every way possible to guarantee public order, even ensuring that bandits were captured in exchange for a guarantee of immunity. Their language changed, too—from being proud Sicilians they soon became the most faithful patriots of Italy. Before long, 500 members of the Mafia had fled to America.

Mori's Mission

As it was, fascism struck a hefty blow to the Mafia, but since Mori dealt with the matter purely as one of public order, he accepted the collaboration and "conversion" of any-one who was prepared to switch to the side of the state, and he did not attack the power of the landowners. Fascism never initiated a program of agricultural reform that, by redistributing the land, would almost certainly have brought an end to the power of the Mafia. Instead, the policy of the regime made it possible for the armed Mafia to bide its time and regenerate later.

Despite these limitations, the attempt to reassert the authority of the state, to seek the support of the population, and especially to eliminate impunity were all extremely important results of Mori's mission. In 1929, despite his success, Mori was relieved of his post and nominated senator. Not long before this, he had been investigating the activities of the political head of fascism in Palermo, Vincenzo Cucco.

ABOVE Orange vendor, Palermo, 1920. Land management, including control of agriculture, was one key to Mafia power that the fascists failed to grasp.

Mussolini's Fall

Italy entered World War II a year after the outbreak of hostilities. Convinced that the war would last only a few months and that Germany would win, Mussolini made a decision as foolhardy as the means and equipment of his army were inadequate. "I need a few thousand dead soldiers so that I can sit at the table of peace", stated *Il Duce* to justify his decision to join forces with Hitler.

The war dramatically exposed the weakness and the precarious state of the Italian army. The Russian campaign during the winter of 1942–1943 inflicted dreadful hardship on the army, which found itself fighting in extreme conditions made more complicated by the climate, the terrain, their allies the Germans, and their enemies the Russians, all factors that were decidedly hostile. Considering the abject failure of the Russian campaign and the hopeless state of military operations, the King began to bitterly regret Italy's involvement in the war. Nor was he the only one who began to have doubts: So did many in the fascist regime. In July 1943, following the Allied invasion of Sicily—which led to the strengthening of Mafia power on the island—Mussolini was called before the Fascist Grand Council, the governing body of fascism, and dismissed.

The King went even further: He had Mussolini arrested. He then nominated Badoglio, Chief of Staff of the Army, as Prime Minister, with responsibility to negotiate an armistice with the Allies. On September 3, the new head of government signed an armistice that was announced to the Italians on September 8, 1943.

RIGHT May 5, 1943: The first American Army vehicles roll through the mountain town of Pollina, Sicily, after it fell to the Allies. The Mafia, all but destroyed by Mussolini's regime, would be reborn under the Allied Military Government.

ASSISTING THE ALLIES

Various members of the Mafia were on the island of Sicily during the summer of 1943, including the head of the American Mafia, Lucky Luciano—who was in Palermo under a false name as personal interpreter to the head of the Allied administration in Sicily—and Albert Anastasia, Joe Adonis, Frank Costello, Vito Genovese, Nick Gentile, and Joe Profaci. All held various offices as "liberators" under the direction of the American Secret Service. The alliance between the Sicilian *Cosa Nostra* and the Americans was later reinforced through the management of illegal businesses such as drugs trafficking, while the tacit agreement with the American Secret Service later served to check the potential development of the Communist Party in Italy.

The Party of the Americans

In the summer of 1943, the Allies initiated Operation Husky and landed in Sicily. Members of the Mafia, many of whom were in the prisons of the fascist regime or in places of internment, were given their liberty, returning home as though anti-fascists who had been persecuted by the regime. It was easy for these criminals to present themselves as "the party of the Americans," suddenly becoming the new crusaders for democracy. On the one hand the Americans understood the important political role of the Mafia on the island, and on the other, the Sicilian Mafia was not slow to see the possibilities of the situation and was quick to exploit them to the fullest.

The American Office of Naval Intelligence (ONI) had previously collaborated with the American *Cosa Nostra* to protect the New York waterfront from sabotage by Axis powers following US entry into the war. A leading role in what was known as Operation Underworld was played by mobsters such as Lucky Luciano and Meyer Lansky, a Jew. Contacts with the Mafia were also exploited by the Office of Strategic Services (OSS)—a predecessor of the CIA—during the invasion of Sicily.

ABOVE Albert Anastasia, reputedly lord high executioner for Murder Inc., was one of many Sicilians who went on to make it big in America after the war.

BELOW September, 1943: The US Army cloaks Palermo in a protective smoke screen, signaling what its approach will be to the *Mafiosi* and their bosses.

Mafia Appointments

The Sicilian Mafia facilitated the advance of the American troops across the difficult and harsh Sicilian countryside, protecting the route from German snipers and organizing an enthusiastic welcome in every village to celebrate the arrival of the liberators. This show of affection was matched by that of the American "cousins" who filled the ranks of the two armies of General Eisenhower and General Patton.

The heads of the Allied Military Government for Occupied Territories (AMGOT)—the allied administration in Sicily—appointed many Mafia members, or individuals close to the Mafia, to important administrative posts. Some Mafia bosses, such as Calogero Vizzini, became the mayors of their towns.

DON CALOGERO VIZZINI

On the death of "Don Calò," as he was known, a funeral fit for a head of state was held in his hometown of Villalba. Those at the funeral recall the words nailed to the church door, "His Mafia was not delinquent, but respected the law, defended all rights, was generous in spirit. It was love."

This epitaph can still be read on his gravestone today. Little does it matter, then, that he was accused of 39 murders, 6 attempted murders, 36 armed robberies, 37 thefts, and 63 acts of extortion.

Don Calogero Vizzini was the uncontested head of the Sicilian Mafia until the years following World War II. He was an important *gabelloto*—a tenant and manager of property belonging to wealthy landowners. He also became head of the "mining Mafia" specializing in the rent of sulphur mines, where miners of all ages were forced to work in conditions close to slavery.

As the regime continued to attack the Mafia and crime in general, Don Calò too began to have troubles. In 1927 he was declared bankrupt. Arrested and accused of being the head of the "mining Mafia," he avoided going to prison thanks to the numerous depositions in his favor, but was not completely acquitted. He claimed to have been interned anyway, though there are no historical records to prove it.

Immediately after the Allied landing on Sicily in World War II, Vizzini was appointed mayor of Villalba by the Americans, and was one of the most enthusiastic supporters of the Sicilian independence movement. He saw, however, that the movement could have no future in the face of national and international events and became one of the first of the Mafia to give his support to the Catholic Christian Democrat party. Aged, increasingly shabby in appearance and with few contacts or associates left, he died quite peacefully on July 10, 1954.

TOP LEFT Calogero *Don Calò* Vizzini (1877–1954) was portrayed as "boss of bosses" by the media, accused of cattle rustling by police, and treated as a prince by his community.

LEFT Don Calò's nephew stands beside the flower-smothered casket. The nephew's name was not recorded, nor was Vizzini's successor made known, and none of the hundreds of floral wreaths bore names of any kind.

Puppet Government

While developments in the south provided the perfect opportunity for a revival of the Mafia, developments in the north of Italy, where the war was still being fought, were of some concern to the Mafia landowners. Liberated by a squad of German paratroopers on September 12, 1943, Mussolini was taken to Germany, where he was ordered by Hitler to return to Italy and establish a new republican government under the protection of the Germans. Thus, on September 23, 1943 the Republic of Salò came into being—a puppet government in the hands of the Germans.

Mafia hot spots
- ⊕ Hometown of Don Calogero Vizzini (head of the Sicilian Mafia)
- ⊕ Site of May Day Massacre, 1947
- Direction of Allied invasion

Following the signing of the armistice, the Italian army, lacking instructions of any kind from the government, had dispersed. Some soldiers had been taken prisoner by the Germans, while others had escaped and joined anti-fascist groups as Resistance fighters. Extremely ill-equipped, they continued to struggle against the Germans and against fascists who had remained loyal to Mussolini, joining him in the north of Italy. Meanwhile, shortly after Mussolini's liberation, the Badoglio government declared war on Germany on October 13, 1943.

War of Liberation

The fact that the partisans of the Resistance fought alongside the Allies was clearly a worry for the ranks of the landowners and Mafia who had re-grouped following the Allied landing in Sicily. The units engaged in the war of liberation were organized politically into Committees of National Liberation, comprising several anti-fascist parties. Given the prevalence of the working class, the communist and socialist parties were those most strongly represented. The possibility that, on emerging victorious from the conflict, these parties could take part in government and apply their political programs was a threat to both the land-based power of the Mafia and to the Americans, despite the fact that they were fighting on the same side.

Separatism

Having no valid political alternative, and unable to join forces with either the fascists or the communist-socialist block, the landowning and land-managing Mafia ranks gave their support to the Movement for Sicilian Independence (MIS), which had come into being shortly before the Allied landing and rapidly gained support throughout the island. The movement had a number of heterogeneous political strands and included barons, princes, monarchists, lawyers, and socialist revolutionaries. In its early days at least, it enjoyed the support of the Allied forces.

Although it had prohibited all political activity, AMGOT tolerated the development of this separatist movement. Some leaders of the MIS even suggested that Sicily should become the 49th star on the American flag.

ABOVE Armed jeeps accompany US Major General Keyes to the royal palace in Palermo, Sicily, for the unconditional surrender of Italian forces. The fascist war against the Mafia had ended.

Guerilla Warfare

With a small but extremely tough volunteer army, the movement for independence in Sicily—which represented a variation on the old and unattainable Mafia dream of becoming a state—began its armed struggle in the autumn of 1944, partly as a reaction to the continual and arbitrary attacks carried out by the police forces against its offices and supporters. Their attempt to bring about a separatist insurrection gave rise to vehement resistance, leading to guerilla warfare. The Italian government was forced to send the army to Sicily to support the police and *Carabinieri* and to put down the revolt. On June 17, 1945, the commander and founder of the separatist army, Antonio Canepa, was killed in a gunfight with the *Carabinieri*. His death provoked many well-founded suspicions that the Mafia was directly responsible. Given their antipathy to words such as "socialism" and "revolution," they were no doubt keen to rid themselves of such a subversive combatant.

A Sicilian Bandit

Concetto Gallo became the new head of the separatist army and then entered into an alliance with the bandits hoping to achieve victory for the revolt. He proposed that the most famous and wanted bandit in all of Sicily, Salvatore Giuliano, should join the volunteer army for the movement for Sicilian independence.

Giuliano accepted, and he and his band carried out a series of attacks on the police and *Carabinieri* as well as on the troops sent by Rome to halt the progress of the rebellion. In May 1946, a statute aimed at providing a political solution to the military crisis was authorized, guaranteeing administrative autonomy for the region of Sicily and thus effectively neutralizing the separatist cause. The Italian government granted an amnesty for political crimes, but this excluded crimes related to the use of firearms. Giuliano, who had until then been protected by the Mafia, now found himself both isolated and betrayed. Finding himself exposed, Giuliano played the anti-communism card, thus regaining the protection and favor of the Mafia.

FAMILY BETRAYAL

Following the massacre at Portella delle Ginestre, Giuliano began to lose the support of the Mafia and, one by one, members of his band were arrested by the police. This was standard practice, with the Mafia happy to use the bandits for their own ends and then get rid of them once they had served their purpose. Betrayed by his cousin Gaspare Pisciotta, a member of his own band involved with him in various shootings including Portella, Giuliano was found dead on July 4, 1950. This was two years after the victory of the Christian Democrats in the 1948 national elections which effectively halted any immediate danger of increased communist influence in Italy. Probably killed by Luciano Liggio, a member of the Corleone Mafia, his body was thrown into the courtyard of an old country farm-house, his murder tacitly sanctioned by the Mafia landowners and the governing party.

RIGHT By the time of his death in a hail of bullets, Salvatore Giuliano is said to have killed over 100 people, and to have been hunted by 5,000 police.

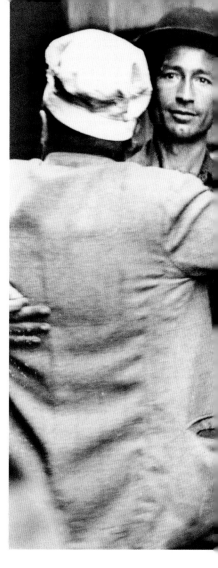

May Day Massacre

In the Sicilian local elections of 1947, partly as a result of the introduction of universal suffrage, the left—the communist and socialist parties—gained victory. Just a few days later Giuliano committed his most brutal crime. On the morning of May 1, 1947, in Portella delle Ginestre, a village near Palermo, during festivities to celebrate both the election victory and the annual workers' holiday, he fired on farm laborers, trade unionists, and anyone who happened to be in the way of his bullets, killing 11 people, including two children, and injuring 38 more.

The Mafia, to whom Giuliano was indebted for the considerable protection he had received, had ordered the massacre, but it was also rumored to have the approval of circles—both Italian and international—keen to avoid the prospect of communism gaining a foothold of any kind on Italian soil.

Terrorism

Terrorism was repeated in Italy over the following decades whenever the communists appeared to be making progress, with tragic consequences for the country and much shedding of innocent blood. Recent research and the opening of the archives of the British Secret Service relating to these events have confirmed that it was not only Giuliano who opened fire during the massacre in Portella delle Ginestre, but also a group of neo-fascists lead by the fascist commander, Prince Junio Valerio Borghese,

who had fought alongside Mussolini until the end of the war. The various gun cartridges found at different points near the site of the massacre reveal that there were several lines of fire. Behind the slaughter was the hand of the Mafia, but also the complicity of national and international anti-communist forces.

ABOVE Street musicians, Sicily, 1947. They had much to celebrate. Sicily was given limited autonomy under the Italian constitution that year.

Father, Son and Holy Spirit

At the trial for perpetrators of the Portella massacre, Gaspare Pisciotta, who had been promised an amnesty if he collaborated in the capture of his cousin Giuliano, was condemned nonetheless to life imprisonment. Feeling betrayed, he reacted by promising to provide the names of the true instigators of the slaughter. The day the sentence was read out, he made a pronouncement that became famous and explains much of the history of the Mafia and the history of Italy: "We are one body: bandits, police, and Mafia. Like the Father, the Son, and the Holy Spirit".

Before the trial could begin he was poisoned in prison by a dose of strychnine poured into the medicine he took every morning for the tuberculosis he had contracted. The secrets he knew were buried with him.

All that remains is the memory of a massacre whose innocent victims were caught in a political system formally open to all political tendencies, but which in practice excluded the forces of the left from power. The roots of the Italian Republic are sadly stained with their blood.

American Mafia
The Golden Age

In the middle of the nineteenth century, American political party bosses consciously decided to court immigrants as an ever-growing power base, setting the scene for a twentieth-century *Mafiosi*.

ABOVE A group of Italian men and boys wait for processing at Ellis Island. Italian immigrants were sponsored by party politicians in major American cities to shore up votes in future elections.

Machine Politics

Among the first party leaders to adopt the strategy was John Slidell, a leader of the New Orleans Democratic political machine known as the Ring. Slidell's move paid off immediately through election victories and the numerous patronage jobs that went with them. Using those jobs to reward party loyalty further strengthened the Ring and extended its influence into statewide political contests.

Democratic organizations in other major cities, like Kansas City, Chicago, and New York, followed suit. As waves of German, Irish, and Italian immigrants entered the big cities, the party welcomed them, espoused their interests and capitalized on their voting strength. While Democratic political machines were more effective at forging these alliances with immigrants, Republicans engaged in the practice in some communities like Buffalo, Philadelphia, and Atlantic City.

In the 1880s, with Italians arriving in the United States in great numbers, politicians saw huge advantage to linking up with immigrant *Mafiosi* and with the leaders of street gangs that sprang up in Little Italy neighborhoods. Gangsters were effective in turning out the vote for the "right" candidates and in discouraging opposition. Political bosses provided patronage jobs and protection from prosecution. As a result of the alliance, organized politics in major cities became indistinguishable from organized crime.

In New Orleans, the late nineteenth century Ring worked with both Matranga and Provenzano underworld factions. The partnerships proved extremely valuable. In some obviously questionable elections, Ring-backed candidates won voting majorities that exceeded the total number of registered voters. Ring support is thought to be a possible reason why Matranga was unharmed in the 1891 anti-Mafia lynchings in New Orleans.

New York

Tammany Hall, the Democratic organization based in New York City, formed working relationships with various underworld characters, including Five Points gangsters like Paolo "Paul Kelly" Vaccarelli, *Mafiosi* Frank Costello, and Ciro Terranova. Beginning in the early 1900s, Vaccarelli, who had command over Manhattan street gangs and great influence in dockworkers unions, provided Tammany Hall with votes and muscle on the Lower East Side. Costello formed close and mutually beneficial relationships with Tammany politicians, Jimmy Hines and Albert Marinelli.

Chicago

Chicago Democratic leaders like Mike McDonald, Michael "Hinky Dink" Kenna, and "Bathhouse John" Coughlin aligned themselves with Mafia bosses Antonio D'Andrea and Mike Merlo, as well as with the brothel and nightclub owner Jim Colosimo. At the 1920 funeral of Colosimo, Kenna and Coughlin were among the 10 city aldermen to function as honorary pallbearers. Also lined alongside the casket were Congressmen John Rainey and Thomas Gallagher, several judges, state and federal prosecutors, and a number of ward politicians.

Kansas City

The Kansas City Democratic organization, known as the Pendergast Machine, included a number of prominent Italian gamblers and gang bosses. Johnny Lazia and Charles Binaggio were the most important. Lazia organized and controlled Kansas City gambling rackets, as well as bootlegging operations during the 1920s and early 1930s, while a lieutenant and close friend of Machine boss Tom Pendergast. Lazia was shot to death on June 10, 1934. Binaggio partnered with the next generation Pendergast Machine, assuming Lazia's former duties. He and trusted aide Charlie "Mad Dog" Gargotta were murdered within the First District Democratic Club on April 5, 1950.

ABOVE The Mafia was often the butt of newspaper cartoonists. Here an habitual reformer is brought before a judge by a Tammany Hall police officer.

BELOW Democrat John Coughlin, an alderman in Chicago and friend of Jim Colosimo, was continually re-elected as his opponents dropped out of the race.

THE ARTICHOKE KING

Ciro Terranova, half-brother of Mafia boss of bosses Giuseppe Morello, created a unique racket for himself. Terranova contracted for the purchase of all artichokes shipped into New York City and became the exclusive supplier of the thorny vegetable to the city's produce markets. A hefty markup and the artichoke's popularity in Little Italy neighborhoods assured Terranova of significant income.

This hand-drawn chart shows the links between gangsters in the early days and the territory they controlled in New York City. Navy Street in Brooklyn was the breeding ground of future Mafia greats.

WE ONLY KILL EACH OTHER

According to legend, Benjamin "Bugsy" Siegel, longtime associate of Mafia boss Charlie Luciano, once reassured an acquaintance with the remark, "We only kill each other." The remark wasn't close to the truth.

The assassination in 1890 of New Orleans Chief of Police David Hennessy and the 1909 assassination of New York Police Lieutenant Joseph Petrosino during his assignment in Sicily, are among the earliest cases of *Mafiosi* targeting law enforcement.

In the 1929 St. Valentine's Day Massacre, Capone gunmen took the lives of two people who were not members of the targeted Moran gang. John May was a mechanic working on cars. Reinhart Schwimmer was an optometrist paying a visit.

In 1922, after an unsuccessful assassination attempt against "Joe the Boss" Masseria, gunmen found their escape route blocked by picketing workers and opened fire. Six people were shot, one fatally. Two others were injured when trampled by the startled crowd.

Crowds gather as police remove the bodies of victims of the St Valentine's Day Massacre. The execution style murders took place at 2122 North Clark Street, Chicago, as a result of an ongoing Mafia feud.

ABOVE Police examine the body of "Joe the Boss" Masseria, which has been flung from a car around East River Drive and 10th Street, NYC.

Early Mafia Rackets

Inner city street gangs around the turn of the twentieth century regularly sponsored rowdy dances, known as rackets. The first underworld racketeers were likely the gang members who coerced merchants into purchasing rolls of dance tickets. Refusal to purchase the tickets could be punished by gang-inflicted damage to a store or by some other reprisal. "Racket" gradually evolved into a more general term. By the middle of the 1920s, organized criminals were widely known as racketeers.

Padroni

The Padroni System was an early form of human trafficking. In this semi-legal racket, established immigrants set themselves up as labor agents in the United States. Each agent, known as a *padrone*, then offered cash payments to poor families in Sicily in exchange for the services of one or more children. Families agreed, expecting that children would have better lives in America. The children were transported to the United States and forced to work in whatever line earned their *padrone* the best return on their investments. Objections to the *padroni* date back to the 1870s. In late 1905, Italian and American officials begin taking effective steps to eliminate the system through the establishment of a labor bureau for Italian immigrants.

Black Hand

A common racket practiced in Little Italy communities was the Black Hand letter where racketeers would mail written demands to businessmen promising property damage or worse if demands were not met. The letters bore threatening symbols and some were signed with a black-ink handprint. While some recipients ignored the demands without consequence, others became the victims of bombings, kidnappings, and murders.

The fledgling Mafia organization in New Orleans is believed to have practiced this form of extortion. Around 1890, the Provenzano family came forward with extortion letters they said came from the rival Matranga clan. "Big Jim" Colosimo, politically connected vice lord of Chicago, is believed to have received repeated Black Hand threats.

Lottery

One of the most lucrative and jealously guarded Mafia moneymaking schemes was the lottery, also known as the policy racket. Underworld organizations across the country engaged in this form of gambling. Participants wagered small amounts on numbers several digits long. Large cash prizes were awarded to those whose numbers came up.

Giosue Gallucci, a politically connected entrepreneur and sponsor of Sicilian and Italian street gangs in East Harlem, New York, successfully protected his underworld lottery enterprise for years. On May 17, 1915, he and his son were cornered by gangland rivals on East 109th Street and shot to death.

ABOVE Cranberry pickers in New Jersey are watched over by a *padrone*—an agent who offers monetary reward for the services of poor Italian families. They were in effect slaves to their *padrone*.

Dock Labor

By infiltrating the labor movement on the busy wharves and docks, *Mafiosi* came to control the immigrant workforce and could demand extortion payments from shipping companies and kickbacks from workers. The Provenzano clan of New Orleans engaged in this racket. Produce shipping pioneer Santo Oteri was an 1881 victim. With a cargo of bananas ripening in his ship, Oteri found that Provenzano-controlled longshoremen refused to unload it. Oteri was compelled to turn over a large portion of his cargo to Provenzano-affiliated fruit peddlers in order for the longshoremen to return to work.

Leading Families

Suspected of murdering police official Giovanni Vella, and of counterfeiting Italian currency, Giuseppe Morello fled his native Corleone, Sicily, for the United States in the 1890s. He and his extended family lived and worked for a time in Louisiana and nearby Texas before deciding to settle in New York City. There, Morello used his influence over Mafia organizations in New Orleans, Chicago, and Buffalo, New York, to rise to the position of boss of bosses over the fledgling American Mafia.

Morello established his headquarters in a densely populated Sicilian neighborhood at the intersection of Elizabeth and Prince Streets on Manhattan's Lower East Side. He was also able to project his power uptown into East Harlem. In that community, his half brothers, Vincent, Ciro, and Nicholas Terranova, ran a ruthless Mafia-affiliated street gang from the legendary "murder stable." Within the stable, dozens of gang killings reportedly occurred. Morello acquired additional support from more distant relatives, the Catanias, the Limas, and the Lomontes, and from his brother-in-law, Ignazio "the Wolf" Lupo.

Also an immigrant from Corleone, Lupo escaped Italian justice after slaying a merchant. He crossed the Atlantic in the late 1890s. In New York, he collaborated with Morello in Black Hand racketeering and other forms of extortion. The two men became related when Lupo married Morello's half-sister in December 1903.

BELOW Ignazio "the Wolf" Lupo took up his prior career of racketeering and murder after arriving in the United States.

Sacks and Barrels

Underworld discipline was an obstacle to investigators. Gang members knew that revealing any part of the Morello operation would result in their deaths. The "sack murder" of 1902 was an example of the penalty for talking too much. A group of Bay Ridge, Brooklyn, teenagers going for a July 23 swim in New York Bay noticed a large potato sack in an area of tall grass near the shore. Within the sack, they found the remains of a murdered man. The body was identified as that of Giuseppe "Joe the Grocer" Catania, missing for two days. Catania had been nearly beheaded by a knife slash across his throat. Authorities decided that was the result of Catania's tendency to discuss his underworld connections while drinking with friends. Ignazio Lupo was known to have met with Catania on the day he disappeared. However, there was no other evidence linking Lupo with the killing. No one was prosecuted.

A year later, Morello suspected that imprisoned underling Giuseppe DePrima had provided information to the Secret Service. With DePrima locked away out of the gang's reach, Morello made an example of DePrima's nearest male relative, Buffalo resident Benedetto Madonia. Madonia's corpse was found in a barrel on a Manhattan sidewalk. The police were unable to build a case against the gang leaders. Over time, several men believed to hold information related to the Barrel Murder also were killed.

I am like any other man. All I do is supply a demand.

Al Capone (1899–1947), Chicago Mafia boss.

Business Failures

Under the guise of land developers, Morello and Lupo formed a corporation called the Ignatz Florio Cooperative Association Among Corleonesi. They sold shares, purchased properties in New York City and contracted builders. They also borrowed thousands of dollars, ostensibly to finance the construction of apartments. Morello suddenly stepped down as president of the Cooperative in 1907. A short time later, the company failed, leaving large debts. In rapid succession, two grocery businesses linked with Lupo also failed. Lupo's importing business on Mott Street closed its doors owing an estimated $100,000 USD. The Elizabeth Street grocery of Salvatore Manzella also went bankrupt, and he initially charged that extortion by Lupo had caused the problems. Investigators learned that thousands of dollars of merchandise disappeared just before the failures.

IDENTIFYING THE BARREL MURDER VICTIM

The 1903 Barrel Murder victim remained unidentified for some time. At the urging of Secret Service Agent William Flynn, Detective Petrosino took a photograph of the victim to Sing Sing Prison and showed it to jailed members of the Morello counterfeiting gang. Prisoner Giuseppe DePrima nearly fainted upon recognizing the face as his brother-in-law Benedetto Madonia of Buffalo, New York.

Always a thorn in the Mafia's side, Secret Service Agent William Flynn was Director of the Bureau of Investigation, after having reorganized the New York Dectective Force.

THE ITALIAN SQUAD
New York Police Department

ABOVE This arrest by police on Mulberry Street in NYC has attracted the interest of all ages of the Italian community.

Following a series of bombings in Italian neighborhoods early in 1905, New York Police Commissioner William McAdoo assembled a five-man squad of Italian-speaking detectives.

Command of the new Italian Squad was given to Detective Joseph Petrosino. A police officer since 1883, Petrosino had become the New York Police Department's first Italian detective sergeant in 1895.

The Italian Squad was tireless in its efforts against Black Hand racketeers and other criminals in the city's Little Italy. After a year, new Police Commissioner Theodore Bingham saw the worth of the squad and increased its membership. Petrosino's new Italian Legion included 25 men under his direct command and another 10 men in a Brooklyn branch led by Detective Sergeant Antonio Vachris.

Petrosino and his group put together a string of successes in high profile cases. In 1907, the legion arrested Enrico Alfano, leader of New York's Neapolitan "Camorra" underworld. Alfano was deported back to Italy where he was wanted for the murders of Camorra rivals, Gennaro and Maria Cuocolo. In 1908, Petrosino succeeded in convincing visiting Sicilian Mafia leader Raffaele Palizzolo, reputed killer of Italian politician and banker Emanuele Notarbartolo, to cut short a visit to New York and return across the Atlantic.

Law Enforcement Martyr

In an effort to gather information on Italian criminals who had relocated to the United States, Bingham sent Petrosino to Italy in February of 1909. The assignment was supposed to be secret, and Petrosino sailed under the assumed name of Guglielmo DeSimone. However, Commissioner Bingham let New York media know about the mission before Petrosino even landed in Italy.

On March 12, 1909, after interviewing officials and reaching out to underworld informants, Petrosino had a late meal at the Caffé Oreto in Palermo, Sicily. Afterward, he walked to the Garibaldi Garden in the city's Piazza Marina. As he stood at a garden fence, the 48-year-old unarmed detective was struck by three bullets, killing him instantly.

Though numerous windows looked out onto Piazza Marina, police could find no one who had seen the assassination. They suspected the involvement of Sicilian Mafia boss Vito Cascioferro, but Cascioferro was protected by government collaborators and an airtight alibi. No one was ever prosecuted for the killing of Petrosino.

Dismantling the Squad

Antonio Vachris was generally regarded as Petrosino's successor in the NYPD's Italian unit. Immediately following Petrosino's assassination, Vachris arrested a number of Brooklyn underworld figures and had them charged with "having knowledge of the recent assassination of a detective of worldwide repute." The men soon were released.

Vachris traveled to Italy to gather Petrosino's paperwork and investigate the Petrosino killing. His visit was cut short due to political problems at home. Theodore Bingham had been ousted as police commissioner and his replacement, William Baker, had little interest in the missions of Petrosino and Vachris. He recalled Vachris and subsequently ignored the 742 certificates of criminal activity Vachris brought back from Italy. The Italian Squad was dismantled, its detectives spread out among the various police precincts in New York City. Vachris retired from the police force in 1919 to open a private detective agency.

Resurgence

A former Petrosino protégé, Detective Sergeant Michael Fiaschetti, led a brief resurgence of the Italian Squad between 1918 and 1922. Once again, the squad was assembled in response to a sudden increase in Black Hand outrages. Fiaschetti was placed in command of 150 men. However, the venture was troubled from the start, as many in the city questioned why the police department singled out Italian crime for special attention.

Fiaschetti had the same toughness as his mentor and also had an impressive physique. He described himself as "husky enough to make a reputation as a piano mover." Compared with Petrosino, he suffered in one important characteristic: He did not have Petrosino's selfless dedication to superiors. Fiaschetti was arrogant.

Despite a number of high-profile successes in the fight against the Italian underworld in New York, Fiaschetti rubbed his bosses the wrong way. In 1922, concluding a shouting match with an influential city politician, Fiaschetti physically kicked the politician out of the Italian Squad office. Almost immediately, the Italian Squad was broken up and Fiaschetti was busted down to patrolman.

ABOVE Magistrate William McAdoo and other officials examine a bullet proof vest that has been tested at close range.

BELOW Italian police officer stands guard outside a suspended bank, watched on by citizens of Little Italy.

CAGED WOLF

Sentenced to 30 years in prison for counterfeiting, Ignazio "the Wolf" Lupo entered Atlanta Federal Penitentiary in February 1910. Paroled in June 1920, he obtained a commutation of sentence from President Harding. Lupo found underworld rivals gunning for him. He managed to outlive his foes, but in 1936, President Roosevelt decided Lupo violated his commutation terms. Lupo went back to prison until 1946. He died the following year.

Ignazio Saietta, aka Ignazio "the Wolf" Lupo, managed to avoid prison for 16 years before he was recommitted to an Atlanta prison in 1946.

BELOW The US Postal Service was used to uncover one of the largest counterfeit rings in the USA. Here workers in 1920 hand sort incoming mail into slots.

Counterfeiting

The US Secret Service was aware for some time that the Morello-Lupo organization was involved in counterfeiting. While agents were able to assemble convincing cases against the lower-ranking gang members who passed counterfeit bills on the streets, acquiring evidence against the leaders proved difficult.

William Flynn, agent in charge of the New York regional office of the Secret Service, noted the May 1909 appearance of counterfeit two-dollar and five-dollar bills in New York, Boston, Philadelphia, Pittsburgh, Buffalo, Chicago, and New Orleans. All the bills looked to have been produced by the same source. Their simultaneous appearance in major cities suggested a large-scale distribution network.

Flynn was convinced that the Morello-Lupo gang was behind the phony bills. He and his men secretly had been watching the gang leaders since before the Barrel Murder. Flynn knew of Giuseppe Morello's background in counterfeiting and his numerous trips across the country, all to cities where bogus money had turned up. He had a good idea of the mechanisms used by Morello and Ignazio Lupo to insulate themselves from physical contact with counterfeit currency. Because earlier efforts to jail the gang bosses had been unsuccessful, Flynn carefully assembled his case before making a move against the men.

Informant

The Secret Service managed to obtain the cooperation of a Pittston, Pennsylvania, resident named Sam Locino. Locino had business dealings with a Morello underling named Giuseppe Boscarino. Flynn used Locino to make mailed requests for samples of the latest Morello counterfeit printings. He also had Locino meet Boscarino and negotiate the purchase of counterfeit notes.

With the cooperation of the US Postal Service, Flynn had a number of incriminating letters—some containing purchase orders for counterfeit notes—sent to Morello and his associates by registered mail. The mail carriers, cooperating with Flynn, had the recipients sign documents to acknowledge receipt of the letters and then had others present sign as witnesses to the recipients' identities. In this way, Flynn amassed a paper trail of counterfeit currency transactions.

Turncoats

On June 4, 1909, Flynn personally led a raid against suspected counterfeiters in rooms above an employment agency on East 13th Street in New York. Seven men were arrested. One of them, Vincenzo Battaglia, confessed his involvement in spreading counterfeit notes. He said that Morello associates Boscarino and Antonio Cecala forced him to buy the phony bills at 25 percent of face value.

The Secret Service's big break in the case occurred when Antonio Comito, a printer who was reportedly terrorized into working for the

Morello counterfeiting operation, agreed to provide evidence against the gang leaders. Comito told of gang meetings at which Morello and Lupo were present. He also recalled that the gang had foreknowledge of the assassination of New York Police Lieutenant Joseph Petrosino and celebrated the killing afterward.

ABOVE This 1935 counterfeiting machine was used to produce millions of dollars of bogus one- and five-dollar bills.

Bosses Behind Bars

In November 1909, Flynn's agents arrested 14 men associated with the counterfeiting. The defendants were separated into groups. Morello, Lupo, Cecala, and five others went to trial on January 26, 1910. Flynn's mountain of evidence won a conviction with the jury needing just over an hour to deliberate. On February 19, Judge George W. Ray sentenced the group to a total of 150 years in Atlanta Federal Penitentiary. Judge Ray sentenced Mafia boss of bosses, Giuseppe Morello, to 25 years and a $1000 USD fine, effectively removing him from command of the Sicilian underworld in the United States. After hearing Lupo's criminal history, Ray sentenced "the Wolf" to 30 years and a $1000 USD fine. None of their co-defendants received less than 12 years in prison.

Time in prison was tough on Morello. After about a year, rumors indicated he hoped to reduce his sentence by providing information on the Petrosino assassination. Newspapers reported that Morello met with officials and dictated a statement outlining the plot against the Italian Squad leader. The statement was never revealed, however. Some newspapers said Morello reconsidered and refused to sign it.

Morello suffered numerous health problems, including indigestion, chest pains, and poor circulation. Letters from home provided little comfort. In spring 1912, the former boss of bosses received staggering news. His son Calogero had been killed in an East Harlem gunfight. Four years later, Morello's half-brother Nicholas Terranova was shot to death at a supposed peace conference with Brooklyn gangsters. With the help of influential friends, Morello secured a Presidential commutation reducing his sentence to 15 years. After good behavior, he was released in March 1920.

ABOVE James Colosimo and his second wife, Dale Winter. He proposed before his divorce decree was finalized.

Chicago's Vice Lord

"Big Jim" Colosimo, an immigrant from the Calabria region on the southern Italian mainland, married Chicago brothel manager Victoria Moresco in 1902. The union launched Colosimo's career in vice and planted the seeds for a vast criminal empire. Colosimo eventually took over his wife's business, the New Brighton bordello at Armour Avenue and Archer Street. He added to his vice operations over time, creating brothels and buying his way into others. Soon he branched out into gambling joints, nightclubs, and drug dens.

While Mafia tradition opposed any involvement in prostitution, non-Sicilian Colosimo existed outside of that tradition. Never a *Mafioso*, he did establish working relationships with the local Mafia, commanded by Antonio D'Andrea and his lieutenant Mike Merlo.

Politics and Crime

At the same time, Colosimo cultivated contacts within the Democratic machine. His control of vice operations in Chicago's Levee District provided him with the money and the influence to become a key intermediary between the vice district and political bosses Michael "Hinky Dink" Kenna and "Bathhouse John" Coughlin. He served as collector of "licensing fees"—protection payments—from gaming houses and brothels in the First Ward. In addition, Colosimo functioned as a sort of *padrone* to new arrivals in Italian neighborhoods. He found them jobs and demanded kickbacks from them.

FAMILY REVENGE

At the dawn of the Prohibition Era, as trade in illegal alcohol became a terrific moneymaker, Colosimo became the constant companion of a cabaret singer in his employ, Dale Winter. On March 31, 1920, Colosimo divorced his wife of 18 years. He and Dale Winter were engaged before Colosimo's divorce decree was issued. They were married April 16, 1920.

In the afternoon of May 11, Colosimo was called to his café. He was needed to meet a shipment of bootleg whiskey. He arrived after 4 p.m., spoke to some of his employees and went to the front foyer. Workers heard two gunshots and rushed to find Colosimo dead on the tile floor.

Police focused much of their suspicion on the brothers of his first wife, Victoria Moresco, feeling that the men might have killed Colosimo for humiliating their sister. The brothers were taken in for questioning and then released. However, there seemed no end to the list of possible suspects in the Colosimo murder. Many, including business, political, and underworld rivals, had reason to want the vice lord dead. Some suggested that a Chicago gang lord had contracted with Frankie Yale and another New Yorker to come west and eliminate Colosimo.

Though no one ever was convicted of Colosimo's killing, history has pointed an accusing finger at the man who benefited most from it—Johnny Torrio. With Capone's help, Torrio took complete control over Big Jim's vice empire, invested heavily in bootlegging operations and built up enough underworld muscle to rival Chicago's established Irish-Jewish and Sicilian gangs.

James Colosimo made so many enemies that the list of suspects in his murder included people from all walks of life. It's believed that Al Capone had a hand in his demise.

Johnny Torrio and Al Capone

James Colosimo's wealth and status did not escape the notice of the other Chicago criminals. According to legend, the vice lord was a target of unknown Black Handers.

Around 1909, becoming fearful of reprisals, Colosimo sought help from tough New York gangster Johnny Torrio. An associate of racketeer Paul Kelly, Torrio like Colosimo was born on the southern Italian mainland. After his arrival in the "Windy City," Johnny Torrio became manager of one of Colosimo's businesses and assembled a small army to look after Colosimo's many illicit enterprises.

In 1912, Colosimo opened a new business at 2126 South Wabash Avenue. He named the restaurant and saloon for himself, Colosimo's Café. The longtime brothel owner's move into the café business possibly represented a reach for legitimacy.

Soon after joining Colosimo, Torrio sent for Brooklynite, Alphonse Capone, an American-born thug who earned a reputation for brutality while working in a Coney Island nightspot run by gangster Frankie Yale. Colosimo, Torrio, and Capone presided over a growing non-Sicilian underworld organization in Chicago. As Colosimo moved more and more toward legitimate business, Johnny Torrio controlled a greater share of the criminal empire in Chicago. He established vice operations throughout the Chicago region and then opened his own saloon, the Four Deuces, a short distance from Colosimo's Café.

Johnny Torrio took over Colosimo's enterprises following his murder in 1920 and it is suspected he was responsible for Colosimo's death with the help of Al Capone.

OPPOSITE Al Capone, center, looking relaxed and arrogant with his lawyers, during his hearing for tax evasion before a federal Grand Jury.

ABOVE Ingenious methods were used to hide alcohol. This supposed truckload of lumber was filled with good quality scotch.

The Noble Experiment

A "noble experiment" to outlaw the manufacture, sale, and transport of intoxicating beverages was proposed in 1917 as the United States entered World War I in Europe. Alcohol bans had been tried in the United States from time to time as far back as 1826. However, the 1917 proposal was fueled by two widespread concerns. Temperance groups suggested that the manufacture of alcoholic beverages used up grain resources more appropriately needed for the making of bread for wartime consumption, and social reformers saw restrictions on alcohol as a means of controlling the saloon-frequenting immigrants and of opposing the political machines that catered to them.

Rum-runners and Moonshiners

Much of the support for the 18th Amendment had been lost by the time Prohibition became the law of the land. Many who believed in wartime restrictions on alcohol consumption saw little reason for nationwide abstinence to begin in 1920. The failure of Prohibition appeared preordained. Organized criminals in the United States, who had previously engaged in gambling, narcotics smuggling, protection, and prostitution rackets, quickly found that the public's resentment of Prohibition made vast fortunes possible. Gangsters in border and coastal cities engaged in rum running, and the illegal import of name-brand whiskeys and rums from Canada, Europe, and the Caribbean. Mafia organizations in cities like Buffalo, Chicago, Detroit, and New York became pipelines for illegal liquor. For a time, many of the outlaws who openly defied the government and worked to quench the public's thirst were looked upon as folk heroes.

Inland Mafia organizations, including those in Cleveland and Kansas City, found there was profit in supplying the materials and equipment for moonshine operations.

Consolidation

Criminal organizations around the country found it very beneficial to cooperate on bootlegging and rum-running enterprises. The Torrio-Capone gang in Chicago used its old relationships with New York gangsters to great advantage and formed new alliances with organizations in Detroit, St. Louis, and Philadelphia. The Mafia in Pittsburgh established connections with Chicago and East Coast mobsters who had better access to imported alcohol. In New York, a criminal network organized by Arnold Rothstein included German, Jewish, Irish, and Italian gangsters. New York cooperation reached a point where rivals assembled at a curbside "Liquor Exchange" to swap their surpluses. This operated under the protection of *Mafiosi* and a police force that was on the Mafia payroll.

Competition

The quest for bootlegging dollars caused conflict between a number of underworld organizations. In New York, the Dutch Schultz gang feuded with the Rothstein gang, and later dealt with a rebel faction led by the Coll brothers. In Detroit, a number of high profile assassinations occurred as Mafia groups competed for dominance. In Chicago, the Torrio-Capone mob found itself in a life-and-death competition against Irish-Jewish and Sicilian organizations. As the violence spread and innocent bystanders became victims, the public's attitude toward gangsters began to change.

ABOVE When illegal liquor was confiscated, it was destroyed. These barrels of beer are being emptied into the sewer.

18TH AMENDMENT

Congress approved a proposed 18th Amendment to the US Constitution at the end of 1917 and sent it to the state legislatures for their consideration. By January 16, 1919, the measure had been ratified by more than enough states for adoption. Though the amendment was only to become effective a year after ratification, Congress approved an interim measure—the inaccurately named Wartime Prohibition Act—on November 21, 1918. That measure, which did not become law until after the war ended in an armistice, was supported as a measure to control returning troops during demobilization.

One further piece of legislation was required for the start of the Prohibition experiment. That was the Volstead Act, which defined prohibited beverages and empowered the Department of the Treasury to enforce alcohol-related restrictions. Congress overrode a veto by President Woodrow Wilson to pass the Volstead Act on October 28, 1919.

BELOW Small-time moonshiners popped up all over the country. These sisters in Minnesota stand armed guard over the family's moonshine operations.

Banner-holding demonstrators march in New York in Fourth of July parade to oppose Prohibition.

War in the New York Mafia

Early in the Prohibition Era, New York City's Mafia was dominated by the Brooklyn organization of Salvatore "Toto" D'Aquila. D'Aquila became boss of bosses of the American Mafia following the 1910 counterfeiting conviction of Giuseppe Morello.

About 1920, after Morello was released from Atlanta Federal Penitentiary, D'Aquila felt that his position was threatened. He responded by pronouncing a death sentence against Morello and a number of his supporters. A gang war resulted.

Joe the Boss

Within New York City, the anti-D'Aquila cause was championed by Giuseppe "Joe the Boss" Masseria, an immigrant from the Sicilian town of Marsala who led a combination of Sicilian, Calabrian, and Neapolitan gangsters. Among those who supported Masseria were Ciro Terranova of East Harlem, Tommy Penocchio of Manhattan, and Frankie Yale of Brooklyn.

In May 1922, gang fighting took the life of Vincent Terranova, Morello's half-brother. Later the same day, a Valenti associate, Silvio Tagliagambe, was mortally wounded in an explosion of gang violence near the lower Manhattan Liquor Exchange. Six bystanders were struck in the exchange of gunfire. Police captured Masseria fleeing from the scene, but they were unable to hold him on murder charges.

Masseria nearly lost the war and his life in August 1922, when two assassins cornered him near his Manhattan apartment building. However, he managed to dodge the bullets. Masseria's men caught up with Valenti just a short time later as he stepped out of an East 12th Street spaghetti restaurant. Shot through the chest, Valenti collapsed on the street and died.

New Boss of Bosses

Deprived of his most threatening weapon and facing an enemy who seemed able to dodge bullets, D'Aquila seemed to lose much of his influence. In 1926, he withdrew from his old Bath Beach, Brooklyn, headquarters to a more secluded Bronx home.

With the aid of old-timers like Morello and up-and-comers like Charlie Luciano and Vito Genovese, Giuseppe Masseria replaced D'Aquila as Mafia boss of bosses. On October 10, 1928, Joe the Boss's victory was completed with D'Aquila's assassination at the corner of Avenue A and 13th Street on Manhattan's East Side.

Masseria did not learn from the mistakes of his predecessor. He, too, began meddling in the affairs of other Mafia families by endorsing Al Capone's efforts against old-line *Mafiosi* in Chicago and making Capone his personal vassal. He supported the violent overthrow of bosses in the Bronx, in Cleveland and in Detroit. He installed allies into leadership roles over Bronx and Brooklyn crime families, and he subjugated a Brooklyn-based organization of *Mafiosi* that originally came from the Castellammare del Golfo, Sicily.

ABOVE "Joe the Boss" Masseria was head of the Union gang and a major participant in the Castellammarese War.

THE ST. VALENTINE'S DAY MASSACRE

Legend says that the gang of Chicago boss Bugs Moran gathered at a North Clark Street garage on February 14, 1929, to greet a hijacked whiskey truck, but there is evidence the group assembled for an underworld peace conference. Top Moran gunmen wearing fine clothes would not have unloaded a truck. Capone killers, disguised as policemen, burst into the garage and murdered seven Moran men.

The bodies of victims of the St. Valentine's Day Massacre lie where they fell, against a wall, blasted by Capone's men with sawn-off shotguns.

The Castellammarese War

Masseria's meddling and his inclusion of non-Sicilians into the American Mafia sparked resentment within the ranks of conservative *Mafiosi*, particularly those who emigrated from the western Sicilian town of Castellammare del Golfo. Tightly knit Castellammarese *Mafiosi* were powerful in Brooklyn, Buffalo, and Detroit, and they were closely allied with the Mafia leadership in Chicago. Masseria loyalists went to war against the Castellammarese network between 1929 and 1931. The conflict became known as the Castellammarese War.

Chicago and Detroit

In 1929, Joe the Boss was called upon to settle things between Mafia boss Joe Aiello and Al Capone. Masseria met with Aiello in Chicago. Gaspar Milazzo, a leading figure in the Detroit underworld and a native of Castellammare, also attended. Masseria took a hard line against Aiello.

Frustrated by Milazzo's unwillingness to deal, Masseria supported the overthrow of the Detroit boss. Masseria ally Chester LaMare set up an ambush at a fish market in May 1930. Gaspar Milazzo and his bodyguard were killed by shotgun blasts. The conservative faction countered by having LaMare killed early in 1931.

Meanwhile, Aiello went scrambling for allies, and entered into an anti-Capone pact with an Irish and Jewish Chicago gang led by George "Bugs" Moran. Capone ended the Moran threat through the brutal St. Valentine's Day Massacre of February 14, 1929. Gunmen then ambushed and killed Aiello in September of 1930, leaving Capone the unrivaled leader of Chicago's underworld.

ABOVE Gangster Frankie Yale reached celebrity status at his funeral. Thousands lined the streets to see the cortege pass on its way to Holy Cross Cemetery in Brooklyn, NYC.

BELOW The shirt worn by Joe Aiello, when he was slain, shows 37 holes from Tommy-gun bullets. His body was struck 50–100 times and was almost cut in two.

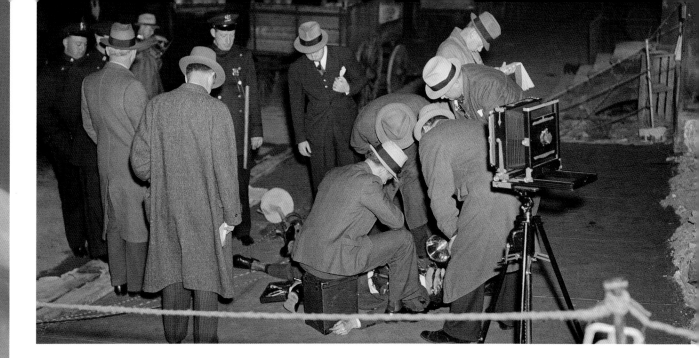

New York

Masseria attempted to subjugate the Brooklyn Castellammarese by humiliating and removing their boss Cola Schiro. Masseria supported Joseph Parrino as leader of Schiro's old family, but the membership quietly backed a new champion, Salvatore Maranzano. After Joe the Boss learned that Bronx Mafia leader, Gaetano Reina, was cooperating with the conservative faction, he had Reina killed in February 1930. Masseria backed Joe Pinzolo as boss of the Reina organization.

Tide Turns

With funding and manpower assistance from Buffalo, Philadelphia, and other areas, the Castellammarese faction led by Salvatore Maranzano proved itself able to counter-punch. The Bronx and Brooklyn families quickly threw off the leaders imposed by Masseria. In the second half of 1930, they managed to turn the tide against Joe the Boss. In August, Maranzano gunmen murdered senior Masseria advisor Giuseppe Morello in his East Harlem office. Three months later, a Castellammarese ambush at a Bronx apartment building eliminated Masseria allies Manfredi "Al" Mineo and Steve Ferrigno. Mineo had risen to the command of Salvatore D'Aquila's Brooklyn organization. With his death, that Mafia family went over to the Castellammarese side.

Masseria attempted to negotiate peace early in 1931. Maranzano, certain he held advantage, continued the war. The Castellammarese boss knew by then that a number of Masseria's top lieutenants were preparing to defect. On April 15, Masseria was shot to death as he had lunch with his group leaders. Charlie Luciano took command of the Masseria organization and called a halt to the war.

Underworld Caesar

Maranzano appointed himself the boss of bosses and held coronation-like ceremonies in Brooklyn's Coney Island, and Chicago. Viewing himself as a Mafia emperor, he announced his intention to separate from the day-to-day operations of a single crime family and rule instead over all American Mafia families. Secretly, Maranzano compiled a list of *Mafiosi* who did not fit the new order. Luciano's name was on it. Maranzano realized too late that Luciano had his own list. The new boss of bosses was stabbed and shot to death in his Park Avenue offices on September 10, 1931.

CHARLIE "LUCKY" LUCIANO

Between autumn 1931 and summer 1936, Charlie "Lucky" Luciano was the most influential Mafia boss in the United States.

Born Salvatore Lucania in the village of Lercara Friddi, Sicily, on November 24, 1897, young Luciano entered the United States with his family in 1907. The family settled on the Lower East Side of Manhattan, where Luciano became involved with Jewish and Italian street gangsters.

During Prohibition, he ran gambling and bootlegging enterprises and became associated with the Mafia empire of "Joe the Boss" Masseria. Luciano gathered about him a group of powerful friends. But there were also enemies. Near the start of the Castellammarese War, police discovered Luciano stabbed and beaten on Staten Island. He refused to identify his assailants.

A conspiracy of Luciano and underworld allies led to the April 1931 assassination of Masseria and allowed Masseria's rival, Salvatore Maranzano, to become supreme boss of the American Mafia. Luciano and Maranzano mistrusted each other. Additional bloodshed was inevitable. Luciano acted first, having Maranzano killed in his Park Avenue offices in September 1931.

Rather than attempt to succeed Maranzano as boss of bosses, Luciano claimed authority only over the old Masseria Crime Family. He endorsed the creation of a representative body—the Commission—to substitute for the supreme boss in resolving differences between various Mafia units.

Luciano was removed from power in 1936, when he was linked to a ring of gangsters organizing New York prostitutes. He was convicted of compulsory prostitution and sentenced to a long prison term. Assistance rendered to the US military during World War II earned Luciano an early release in 1946 after which he was deported to Italy.

From Italy, Luciano organized narcotics smuggling operations between Europe and the United States. He was working on an autobiography when he died of a heart attack on January 26, 1962.

TOP Lucky Luciano sits in the prison van after the first day of his trial, before he had a chance to cover his face with his handkerchief.

BOTTOM At Naples airport to meet a friend, Lucky Luciano drops dead of a heart attack at age 65. Here they hoist him into a casket.

ABOVE Out and about at a baseball game between the White Sox and the Cubs, Al Capone chats with Gabby Hartnett of the Cubs as he signs a ball for Al (Sonny) Jr.

Al Capone and The Tax Man

Prohibition agents of the Treasury Department had little luck in their long battle against bootleggers like Chicago's Al Capone. However, Internal Revenue Service agents fared much better, managing to prosecute a number of leading Mafia criminals.

Al Capone, himself, went to trial in October of 1931 on charges of tax evasion. There had been little time for him to enjoy his position as undisputed Tsar of the Chicago underworld. Capone already was clearly living the high life. He had an elaborate residence in Florida, in addition to his home, rackets, and businesses in Illinois. The IRS charged that his luxurious living was derived from untaxed income. Capone was specifically accused of evading taxes for the years 1924 through 1929.

On October 17, 1931, a federal jury found Capone guilty. A week later, he was sentenced to 11 years in prison and a fine of $50,000 USD. He avoided prison while his appeals were heard, but he was finally locked up in Atlanta Federal Penitentiary in May 1932. He later was transferred to Alcatraz Island.

His mental and physical health deteriorated during his imprisonment. After parole late in 1939, he moved to Palm Island, Florida, in the care of his family, where he died after a heart attack in January 1947.

The Capone tax investigation also uncovered evidence that led to tax evasion cases against other members of Capone's underworld "Outfit." Jake "Greasy Thumb" Guzik, T.J. Druggan, and Frank Nitti were among those who were convicted of tax crimes.

Waxey Gordon

At the conclusion of the Capone case, IRS investigators turned their attentions to the finances of Waxey Gordon (real name Irving Wexler), a bootlegger in the New York-New Jersey area. The IRS estimated that, at the height of Prohibition, Gordon was earning more than $1 million USD a year through the alcohol trade. Gordon claimed he made a small fraction of that amount and paid next to nothing in taxes. Thomas Dewey, then a US Attorney, prosecuted Gordon for tax evasion in 1933. The case was open-and-shut. The jury needed less than an hour to convict. Gordon was sentenced to 10 years in a federal penitentiary.

Thomas Dewey and Dutch Schultz

While successfully prosecuting Waxey Gordon, US Attorney Thomas Dewey also set his sights on New York gang boss "Dutch Schultz". But Schultz was harder to catch and found ways to avoid conviction.

At first, Schultz simply took a vacation. After nearly two years of dodging the authorities, and after Dewey had left the US Attorney's Office, Schultz resurfaced to deal with the tax evasion indictment. His trial ended in a hung jury. A second trial for tax evasion was scheduled in Malone, New York, a small upstate town. Schultz and his entourage arrived in advance of the trial and threw their money around. The gang boss became an instant celebrity. At the conclusion of the trial, a jury of local citizens found him not guilty. But Dewey and not forgotten Schultz.

Dewey returned to public office as a special prosecutor. He won another indictment against Schultz on a lesser tax charge and started an investigation into some of Schultz's rackets. Schultz did not live long enough to stand trial a third time. He was shot to death in October 1935 while free on bail.

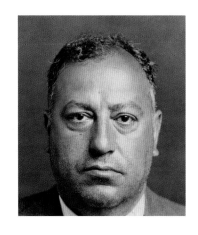

ABOVE Irving Wexler, aka Waxey Gordon, was one of the most successful bootleggers in New York. The IRS arrested him at his White Lake hideaway.

"DUTCH SCHULTZ"

Born August 6, 1902, to a German-Jewish family on the Lower East Side of Manhattan, "Dutch Schultz" (real name Arthur Flegenheimer) already had a burglary conviction and a prison term in 1920. He then became associated with Jack "Legs" Diamond, Charlie "Lucky" Luciano, and legendary underworld financier Arnold Rothstein.

The "Dutchman" staked out a territory in the Bronx and Harlem and partnered with Joey Noe in a speakeasy. Schultz moved aggressively into other Harlem area rackets, sparking a feud with Legs Diamond. Diamond fled the city after a 1929 ambush nearly took his life. As the Prohibition Era closed, Schultz engaged in restaurant extortion and racketeering and also took over a lucrative Harlem policy racket, sharing proceeds with the Mafia organization of Ciro Terranova.

Schultz was targeted by special prosecutor Thomas Dewey. Dewey brought the gang boss to trial twice without winning a conviction. As Dewey prepared for a third trial, Schultz let his Mafia friends know that he'd had enough and that he intended to murder the prosecutor.

Fearing the fallout of a Dewey assassination, the Mafia Commission ordered Schultz killed. Mob gunmen entered the Dutchman's hangout, the Palace Chophouse in Newark, New Jersey, on October 23, 1935. When they left, Schultz and his three top men all were mortally wounded. Schultz died at Newark City Hospital the next evening.

Beer baron and racketeer Dutch Schultz surrounded by admirers as he calmly smokes a cigarette outside the New York Federal Court in 1935.

CELLULOID MAFIA

The Untouchables

Two TV series (1959, 1993), a video game (1991), and a movie (1987) bear the name *The Untouchables*, such is the popular fascination with US Treasury agent Eliot Ness in 1920s Chicago, as he grappled with the legendary Al Capone.

ABOVE Robert Stack as Eliot Ness in the original TV series,1959–1963. The violent drive-by shootings gave the series the hard edge the public was looking for.

The Original

The 1959 series was the longest running and most popular of the two television series, with Robert Stack as Eliot Ness leading his incorruptible agents for 118 episodes. At the time, this series was regarded as groundbreaking television for its gritty portrayal of crime and criminals.

The Movie

The 1987 movie was written by acclaimed writer David Mamet, inspired by the Ness book, and directed by Brian De Palma. The film paints the prohibition era in Chicago as totally corrupt, so Ness (Kevin Costner) handpicks the most trustworthy colleagues as his associates for the task of bringing down infamous Al Capone (Robert De Niro). The hard-as-nails old school cop, Jim Malone (Sean Connery), Police Academy graduate sharpshooter, Agent George Stone (Andy Garcia), and accountant-with-a-gun, Oscar Wallace, (Charles Martin Smith) form the team. Sean Connery won the Best Supporting Actor Oscar for this performance, and Morricone's score was nominated—winning the award in the same category in Britain's Academy Awards.

In Costner's portrayal, Elliot Ness is basically a naïve nice guy, given the job of catching Chicago's Public Enemy Number One. Malone nudges Ness towards a more aggressive approach than Ness is used to. He tells Ness, "He pulls a knife, you pull a gun. He sends one of yours to the hospital, you send one of his to the morgue. That's the Chicago way, and that's how you get Capone."

As is now well known, it wasn't the macho muscle that put Al Capone away. It was his tax returns, which simply didn't match his lifestyle, as Oscar Wallace noted.

Action Sequences

In his signature style, Brian De Palma's movie contains a number of spectacular action sequences. The most notable and acclaimed of these is a scene at Union Station, where Ness and Stone are chasing Walter Payne (Jack Kehoe) one of Capone's bookkeepers, who is trying to flee the city, guarded by Capone thugs.

If you're afraid of getting a rotten apple, don't go to the barrel. Get it off the tree.

Malone (Sean Connery)

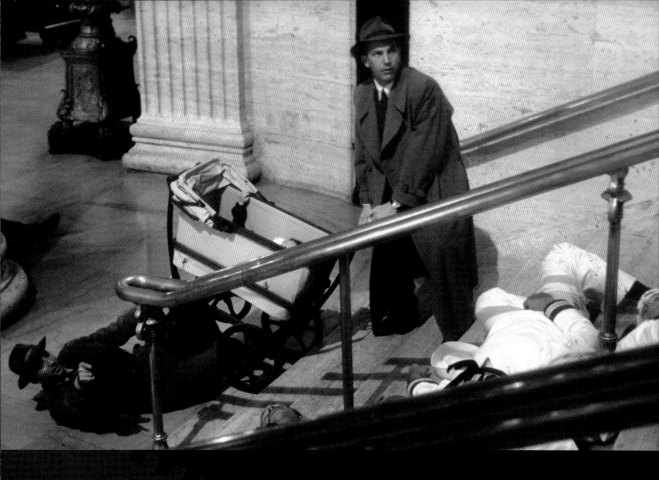

The extensive shootout has its climax on the grand wide staircase, where amidst the chaos, a fleeing mother's baby carriage—with baby inside—goes bouncing down the stairs surrounded by gunfire, heading for certain disaster at the bottom.

Another Capone bookkeeper, George (Brad Sullivan) is captured by Malone, who gives him a beating as part of his attempt to get George to provide evidence that might incriminate Capone. When George refuses, Malone shoots another thug in the mouth to frighten George. George didn't know that the thug was already dead.

At the end of the film, a reporter approaches Ness and asks what is he going to do next, now that Prohibition is about to be repealed. "I think I'll have a drink," replies Ness dryly.

ABOVE The staircase scene has often been cited as an homage to a similar scene in the silent, black and white movie, *The Battleship Potemkin* (1925), by the legendary Russian filmmaker Sergei M. Eisenstein.

REAL TO REEL

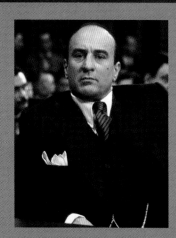

During casting, Brian De Palma met English actor Bob Hoskins over a drink in Los Angeles to discuss playing Al Capone if Robert De Niro were to pass on the role. Hoskins told De Palma he would do it if he were available. When De Niro finally took the role, De Palma sent Hoskins a thankyou note, and the studio paid Hoskins, who had a "pay or play" contract, $200,000 USD. Hoskins called De Palma and asked if there were any more movies the director didn't want him to be in.

Robert De Niro tracked down Al Capone's original tailors and had them make him some identical clothing for the movie. He also insisted on wearing the same style of silk underwear that Capone wore, even though it would not be seen on camera.

Robert De Niro in a remarkable portrayal of the tax man's favorite gangster, Al Capone

ABOVE Glamorous Virginia Hill, wrapped in mink, tells the Senate Committee that her income comes from friends. Bugsy Siegel was shot at their home in 1947.

BELOW Meyer Lansky, one of the most clever accountants and gangsters in the Mafia, is questioned about the death of Albert Anastasia in 1958.

Mafia's Golden Age

As Charlie Luciano consolidated his control of the former Masseria organization in 1932, the old position of boss of bosses was abolished. A Commission comprised of representatives of the more powerful Mafia families was established to resolve inter-family squabbles and coordinate multi-family enterprises.

With the potential for inter-family warfare greatly reduced, Mafia organizations flourished. They also cooperated like never before with each other and with non-Italian criminal organizations. Jewish gangsters like Meyer Lansky, Louis "Lepke" Buchalter, Benjamin "Bugsy" Siegel and Mickey Cohen established mutually beneficial relationships with the American Mafia, opening up new territories and racket opportunities.

The new order was tested almost immediately. A mostly Jewish gang based in Brooklyn became the Mafia's enforcement arm. Its members were on retainer as mob killers, their activities coordinated by Buchalter and Albert Anastasia. The gang became known as Murder, Inc.

Prostitution and Gambling

The 18th Amendment was repealed near the end of 1933. Bootlegging was no longer the great moneymaker it had been and crime families sought new forms of income.

A number of gangsters affiliated with Luciano's crime family decided to organize prostitution in and around New York City. Special prosecutor Thomas Dewey led a legal assault on the growing prostitution ring. With witnesses testifying that Luciano was the man behind the ring, he was convicted of compulsory prostitution and sentenced to 30–50 years in prison. The imprisonment and deportation of its most powerful boss did little to check the growth of the American Mafia. Luciano's longtime associate Frank Costello stepped to the leadership of New York's largest crime family and led the underworld move into gambling.

BENJAMIN "BUGSY" SIEGEL

Benjamin "Bugsy" Siegel was born in Brooklyn early in 1906. He grew up with fellow gangster Meyer Lansky, and during childhood he came to know Charlie Luciano. Siegel's violent temper in street confrontations earned him the nickname "Bugsy" (crazy). He was believed to have killed at least 30 people.

At the dawn of the Prohibition Era, Siegel, Meyer Lansky, and a few associates formed a gang known as the Bug and Meyer Mob and contracted bootleggers to provide security for alcohol shipments. In 1937, Siegel was sent west. In southern California, Jack Dragna's Mafia organization was warring against racketeer Mickey Cohen. Siegel halted the fighting and organized gambling operations in the Los Angeles area. He then became involved in various enterprises including race tracks, the race wire service, casinos, and narcotics trafficking.

In the mid-1940s, Siegel's attention was drawn to Las Vegas, Nevada, where gambling was legal. He funneled huge Mafia investments into the construction of the Flamingo hotel and casino. Millions in cost overruns, long building delays and a poorly attended December 26, 1946, opening of the Flamingo combined to infuriate Siegel's business partners.

In early June 1947, as checks for the Flamingo construction began to bounce, Siegel confided to a friend that he needed to raise at least $1.5 million USD immediately. On the evening of June 20, Siegel and his associate Allen Smiley chatted in the Beverly Hills mansion Siegel and his girlfriend, Virginia Hill, shared. An assassin armed with a military M1 carbine, fired nine times through a window, striking Siegel twice in the head. He died on the spot.

Bugsy Siegel met a gruesome end when he was shot dead on the sofa in the Beverly Hills home he shared with Virginia Hill. She was in Switzerland at the time.

Racing Wire

The Chicago Outfit came to dominate a lucrative racing wire operation, which circulated horse race results by telegraph. Disguised as a nationwide news service, the operation became the chief supplier of race results in the country.

Havana and Las Vegas

New York-based gang leader Meyer Lansky and Tampa Mafia boss Santo Trafficante Jr. established a foothold in gambling rackets on the island of Cuba. Just 90 miles from the Florida coast, Cuba was within reach of American vacationers and big-money gamblers while beyond the jurisdiction of American law enforcement. It seemed the ideal place to set up a major gamgling operation.

Meanwhile, Lansky's boyhood chum, Benjamin "Bugsy" Siegel, went out to the West Coast and worked with Mickey Cohen on the management of gambling enterprises in southern California for a while before noting the potential of Las Vegas, Nevada, where gambling was legal. With financial backing from his friends in the underworld, Siegel undertook the construction of an up market hotel and casino in Las Vegas named the Flamingo. Both enterprises proved unsuccessful.

With the end of World War II, came an increased interest in ending Mafia control of gambling and other enterprises, resulting in the Kefauver Committee Hearings.

Yakuza Elite Class

Although Yakuza can be traced back to gamblers and street peddlers, the Yakuza were not only street gangsters. In the late nineteenth century and the early twentieth century, there emerged an elite class of Yakuza.

ABOVE This painting, *Tattoos*, by artist Utagawa Kunisada, depicts the intricacy and story-telling of traditional tattooing that was common among early bandits.

Infiltration

In the period spanning the late nineteenth century and the early twentieth century, Japan transformed from a feudal society into a modern industrial state and the Yakuza expanded in step with the growing economy. Apart from gambling and extortion, the Yakuza found new ways to prosper. The Yakuza gained substantive control in organizing casual workers for construction projects in big cities and recruiting dockworkers for shipping companies. The Yakuza also gained control over the newly emerging business of rickshaw services in big cities.

Flexing Muscles

The increasingly militant labor movement in the early twentieth century provided the Yakuza yet another opportunity to flex their muscles and make profits. They became hired strikebreakers. Big companies, especially mining and manufacturing companies, were more than willing to pay the Yakuza to help them contain the labor unrests.

This clannish and clandestine combination of bosses, hoodlums, and racketeers is the greatest threat to American democratic aims in Japan.

Colonel Charles Kades (1906–1996), architect of the post-war Japanese Constitution.

The most significant development of the Yakuza at this time, however, was their engagement in politics and their increasing ability to swing government policy.

In the early twentieth century, Japan witnessed the maturation of parliamentary politics. The first parliament was established in 1889 and universal suffrage was introduced in the 1920s. The Yakuza, powerful and highly organized, were ready to profit.

Playing Politics

When the Meiji Government implemented the anti-gang law in the mid-nineteenth century, the Yakuza secured a comfortable environment to operate by bribing police. With the advent of parliamentary politics, the Yakuza saw a new way to ensure their survival. They began to play politics. They used their money, and the block of votes they could deliver, to support certain politicians. In return, the Yakuza bosses developed close ties to important officials, which ensured some measure of government sanction and freedom from police harassment.

As the nation began to experience democracy, there arose an ominous new force of ultranationalism. And, as the country swung to the extreme right, the Yakuza found a suitable environment to grow and increase their influence in politics. Allied with ultranationalists, the elite class Yakuza became an important political force. They played a significant role in the rise of militarism and Japan's overseas military expansion including World War II. After the war, riding on the fear of leftists and communists, the Yakuza continued to play a notable role in Japanese politics and social life.

OPPOSITE Young Japanese women traveling by rickshaw in the early twentieth century. The Yakuza quickly took control of the rickshaw business in major cities.

1947 Kinosuke Ozu, the tekiya boss of Tokyo is named as "Tokyo's own Al Capone" by the *Saturday Evening Standard*

1948 Kodama is released from prison and becomes linked to the Prime Minister Ichiro Hatoyama

1959 A public rally is held by Matsubakai, a leading Yakuza gang

1964 The *Mainichi*, the national newspaper in Japan, publishes a series of articles on underground gangs and their influence in Japan

LEFT This outdoor bathhouse is popular with members of the Yakuza. Here the tattoos, usually covered by clothing, can be seen easily.

THE OLD GANGSTER

OPPOSITE Strikers from the Jomo Muslin Company leave the police station after asking for mediation. Yakuza gangs were heavily involved in corporate disruption, extorting money for peace.

No one played such an essential role as Mitsuru Toyama (1855–1944) in joining organized crime with Japanese politics.

Dark Ocean Society

Toyama's hometown, Fukuoka City in southern Japan, was a mining region and home to a large community of discontent ex-*samurai*. Toyama organized the disgruntled soldiers and enlisted the listless city toughs. He transformed them into a disciplined workforce and a force of strikebreakers. Following the Yakuza tradition, Toyama built himself a reputation as a local Robin Hood. He handed out money to his followers on the street and was called "Emperor of the Slums." His ruthlessness in crushing miners' riots and strikes also earned him the name "the Emperor of the Mines."

His role in founding the Dark Ocean Society in 1881 brought Toyama to national power. The society's goal was none other than placing Japan on the path of military expansion abroad and authoritarian rule at home.

Toyama and his Dark Ocean followers launched a fierce campaign to accomplish their ambitious agenda. They used money gained from rackets to promote or shatter the careers of politicians depending on their ideology.

Toyama made the society a terrorist organization. Through a campaign of terror, blackmail, extortion, and assassination, Toyama wielded his influence in parliamentary politics and in government bureaucracy.

During the 1920s, Toyama and his thugs killed so many prominent politicians that the political environment was described as "politics by assassination." Toward the end of the 1920s, the liberal and left-wing politicians were effectively silenced, for no one dared to speak freely. During this period, Toyama formed a power base through his political dealings that enabled him to become a major influence in Japan.

BELOW Mitsuru Toyama (left), and other party leaders, meet with R. B. Ramos (second left) of the Philippines in support of their demand for freedom.

Black Dragon Society

In 1901, the Dark Ocean Society was succeeded by the Black Dragon Society, founded by a Toyama right hand man. Under the patronage and guidance of Toyama, the Black Dragon Society carried on its predecessor's agenda. The Black Dragon gangs operated with the strong support of the government and the police. Part of Toyama's legacy was that he joined the forces of organized crime and politics in such a way that, even today, there is no clear distinction between gangsters and rightists in the minds of Japanese.

Boss of Bosses

Toyama remained an extremely private citizen throughout his life, but he was

referred to as "the boss of the bosses." In the 1930s, Toyama continued to rise in stature. He became such an influential figure that he was invited to dinner at the Imperial Palace with high-ranking government officials, and with so many of his allies in power, Japan was now on an irreversible course of military expansion. The dream of Toyama and his fellow ultranationalists came true. Many believe that Toyama played an instrumental role in Japan's road to militarism and its eventual involvement in the World War II.

The eruption of the war in the Pacific, however, marked the end of the love affair between the militarist government and the Yakuza. The militant government, secure in power, no long needed the service of the Yakuza. As a result, most Yakuza members either joined the army or were sent to jail. The Yakuza's rank-and-file membership shrank considerably during the war.

Inspiration

Toyama died in 1944 at the age of eighty-nine. He witnessed Japan conquer much of Asia and Pacific but also saw the empire he helped build begin to crumble. His influence in the underworld lived on. His Dark Ocean Society became a model for Japan's modern secret societies. Even today, the old gangster remains a source of inspiration for the Yakuza and the rightists alike.

ABOVE A senior tattoo artist shows his Yakuza client a range of designs to choose from.

ABOVE Heavily tattooed men display their body art while a man points out the intricacies to his son. Many US service-men were tattooed while on duty in Japan, despite the criminal inference.

Yakuza gang leaders
⊕ Hometown of Mitsuru Toyama
⊕ Birthplace of Yoshio Kodama, 1911

CHINA

Honshū

Nihonmatsu
(Nihommatsu)

J A P A N

Fukuoka ○Kobe
Shikoku ○ Tokyo

Kyūshū

N

0   250   500 kilometers
0   125   250 miles

Gangbusters

During the period of US occupation (1945–1952), the US authority, aware of the role played by the Yakuza in the rise of militarism, made abolishing secret societies a top priority in its plan to rebuild Japan. The Yakuza nonetheless staged a quick comeback after the war.

Japan lay in ruins by the end of the war. The shortage of food and daily necessities quickly spawned a black market underworld. Veterans in such operations, the Yakuza wasted no time taking control of the black market economy. These markets dealt with not only food and essentials but also drugs. The authority, however, was in no position to crack down on the markets, for it found itself reliant on many of the goods and services provided by the Yakuza.

Black Curtain

Because of the deep involvement of the Yakuza in Japanese politics, a term, the *kuromaku,* was coined to describe those who serve as a bridge between Yakuza and mainstream politics. The word—literally "black curtain"—is taken from classic Kabuki theater, in which an unseen person controls the stage by pulling a black curtain. Today it connotes a behind-the-scenes powerbroker. Mitsuru Toyama, the founder of the Dark Ocean Society, was the most famous of the early manipulators. In the post-war era, the role was claimed by Yoshio Kodama (1911–1984), another towering figure of the criminal underworld in the twentieth century.

CLASS A WAR CRIMINAL

Yoshio Kodama used a mix of crime and political dealing to grow his power base and further his fortune.

Origins

Born in 1911 in Nihonmatsu, Japan, Yoshio Kodama turned first to socialism then ultra-nationalism as a teeenager. He became an admirer of Mitsuru Toyama and organized his own ultranationalist group in his early twenties. He made a fortune during World War II by dealing with war materials and drugs. At the end of the war, he was arrested and classified as a Class A war criminal. But he was never tried. After striking a deal with the US intelligence agency to aid fighting communism in Asia, he was released. Using his fortune and underworld connections, he helped quell labor disputes and root out communist sympathizers.

ABOVE The political ally come criminal, Yoshio Kodama, was contracted by the Japanese government to help with the war effort.

Political Sponsor

His most crucial move was sponsorship to the founding of the Liberal Party that merged in 1955 with the Democratic Party to form the Liberty and Democratic Party (LDP). The LDP became the longest ruling party in the post-war era and Kodama's close ties with the LDP and the Yakuza made him the single most important person in Japan, wielding influence in both the government and the criminal underworld.

Gang Mediator

The proliferation of gangs in the post-war era brought about bitter and bloody gang wars. Attesting to his authority in the underworld, Kodama managed to unite various gangs and brokered a truce between two major Yakuza clans—the Yamaguchi-gumi and the Inagawa-kai.

In the early 1960s, seeing the strength of a united gang force against the communism, he envisioned an all-Japan gangster coalition. Although the federation did not come to fruition, he succeeded in forming an all-Tokyo coalition, comprising seven major gangs. The coalition was short-lived, but Kodama's efforts earned him renewed respect. He was looked upon as the underworld's visionary godfather.

BELOW The Executive Director of the Marubeni Corporation listens to questions regarding the Lockheed pay-off scandal that rocked Japan.

Scandals

Kodama was involved in a number of scandals. The most notable one was the Lockheed scandal in the 1970s. He received more than $2 million USD from the US aircraft giant to influence the Japanese market toward Lockheed and away from its US competitors. Kodama made payoffs to politicians and toppled the president of All Nippon Airways by sending the Yakuza racketeers to storm the company's shareholders meeting. He shifted the deal in Lockheed's way but the scandal brought about his downfall. Kodama and a score of high-ranking government and LPD officials, including Prime Minister Kakuei Tanaka, were indicted. Kodama never stood trial because of his poor health. He died in 1984 at the age of seventy-three.

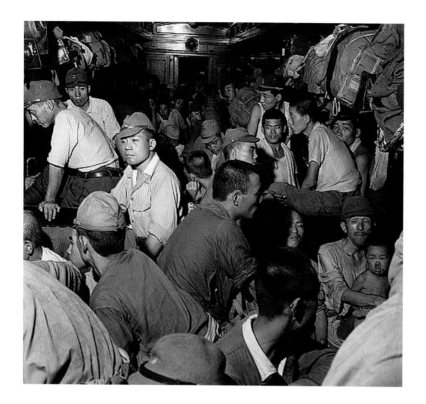

The Luxury End

In the 1950s, as Japan's economy started to pick up, the black market was no longer needed. But the Yakuza's financial basis did not wither away with its disappearance. They quickly moved to the more lucrative business of providing luxuries. They dealt with drugs and made profits in prostitution and entertainment. In the early 1950s, with the end of Occupation, the Yakuza also saw a revival of their fortune in politics.

Hoodlums

The post-war era saw the rise of another Yakuza group, the *gurentai,* or the hoodlums. The ranks of *gurentai* were swelled with unemployed youths and demoralized repatriates. Racial tension was running high after the war. The rage of the racial minorities, mainly Koreans, Taiwanese, and Chinese who were brought to the country as forced labor, exploded after Japan's surrender. There were numerous incidents of Japanese citizens being attacked by racial minority gangs. The police, disarmed and discredited, were unable to protect citizens from gang violence.

ABOVE Discharged soldiers crowd the trains as they travel home free after the war. It is from these ranks that the Yakuza group, *gurentai*, was born.

The void was filled by the *gurentai* gangs who battled the minority gangs not only for citizen protection but also for other lucrative enterprises. The new gangs fought with modern firearms, including machine guns. Because of the reasons behind the formation of the the new gangs, the *gurentai* was a more violent form of Yakuza.

EXCEPTION TO THE RULE

The Yakuza is an all male society. Women are not trusted because they are not born to be street fighters. The place of women in the Yakuza has long involved their roles as prostitutes, wives, and girlfriends. Wives, mistresses, and girlfriends of prominent gang bosses often undergo extensive tattooing to demonstrate their affiliation with the gang lifestyle or their loyalty and devotion to their husbands or lovers.

In a Yakuza clan, the only visible woman is the boss's wife. She commands the same respect from gang members as her husband but she is not involved in gang business, for she is not a member of the gang. Occasionally, women do rise to the top and there are women bosses, but they usually do not openly show their faces. Fumiko Taoka was an exception. After the death of Yamaguchi-gumi's godfather Kazuo Taoka in 1981, the police and the Yakuza underworld were equally shocked to see Taoka's widow, Fumiko, emerge as the syndicate's new boss. Under Fumiko's rule, the gang expanded in both membership and racket territory. But she was destined to be a temporary leader. Within three years, she handed the power to a council composed of men.

ABOVE The female partners of Yakuza members are often tattooed in order to show their devotion and loyalty to the gang.

Close Ties

The conservative government, gripped by the fear of leftists marching to power, resumed its pre-war tactic of using the Yakuza as a force to combat the leftists, the communists, and the labor unions. Throughout the 1950s and in the early 1960s, government officials, including the Prime Minister and the Minister of Justice, maintained close ties with the Yakuza. The criminal underworld provided various government requested services. Apart from sabotaging labor unions and harassing left wing politicians, the government enlisted the Yakuza to help counter anti-government demonstrations and to rally support for unpopular government policies.

In 1960, the government even hatched a plan to use the Yakuza as a supplementary security force for a planned visit by the United States President Eisenhower. Ironically, the government had to cancel the visit from the US President after a student was killed in a violent confrontation between anti-US demonstrators and the Yakuza.

Setbacks

In the 1970s, the Lockheed scandals, which involved Kodama's bribing high-ranking government officials, brought about his downfall. His disappearance from the political scene marked a setback for the Yakuza influence in politics but not its complete disappearance. Mob connections still stretched far and wide among elected officials, but corruption went deeper underground.

Gangsters changed tactics and transformed themselves and their gangs into modern industrialists, ready to take on the bigger corporations forming in the post-war period. And all the while maintaining their special place in Japanese life.

ABOVE Former Prime Minister, Kakuei Tanaka, waves to reporters after being found guilty of taking $2 million USD in bribes from the Lockheed Corporation.

Triads Their Finest Hour

ABOVE Two members of the Boxer Society kneel before the Chinese High Court waiting for punishment.

One of the most important reasons for the existence of many Triad societies was to overthrow the Qing emperor. But by the early 1900s the Qing Dynasty was still in power and no Triad had succeeded in bringing an end to the reign of their ancient nemesis.

Secret Society

Things were about to change in their favor, however. The Triads had members from all walks of life including many successful businessmen, doctors, and other very highly educated men. One of these was Dr Sun Yat-sen who had risen to power within the Three Harmonies Society. In order to overthrow an imperial army Sun Yat-sen needed man-power, money, and a political movement he could present to would-be followers. A great way to achieve all three was to start another secret society. In late November 1894, he founded Hsing Chung Hui—Revitalize China Society. The timing was perfect as earlier that year a Japanese-Korean politician had been murdered in Shanghai causing Japan officially to declare war against Qing authorities at the beginning of August.

SUN YAT-SEN

Dr Sun Yat-sen was born as Sun Wen in Guangdong in 1866. At age 12, Sun Wen joined his older brother in Hawaii and began studying Christianity, angering his older brother, who sent him back to China. Back in China Sun Wen joined the San-ho Hui—Three Harmonies Society.

As is a custom among Triad members, Sun Wen started training in kung fu and eventually moved to Hong Kong. There, at age 18, he was baptized a Christian and given a Mandarin name—Yat-sen. Sun Wen, now known as Sun Yat-sen, had now caused his family even more embarrassment and his older brother ordered him back to Hawaii.

Sun was a difficult young man and in Honolulu he joined the Kwok On Wui Triad, borrowed money, and fled back to China.

Back in China, surprisingly, Sun enrolled in the Po-Chi Hospital Medical School in Guangzhou where his brother decided to pay Sun's school fees. Sun went on to study at the College of Medicine at the University of Hong Kong. In Hong Kong Sun also got in touch with his Triad brothers of the Three Harmonies Society. His new Triad friends were all very active opponents of the Qing dynasty and persuaded Sun to join them in their plans to overthrow the emperor.

After a failed coup in 1895, Sun Yat-sen went into exile and spent almost 16 years drumming up support around the world. While still in exile, the military uprising in 1911 that brought about the revolution, also brought Sun Yat-sen to power. He was elected provisional President of the Republic of China and is considered the father of modern China. He died in 1925, aged 58, from liver cancer.

Dr Sun Yat-sen was an early member of the Three Harmonies Society, a Triad group. He moved through the ranks of politics and is now revered in China.

Uprising

With the Qing forces busy fighting the Japanese, and suffering heavy losses, Sun decided it was time to go for the kill. He and his fellow revolutionaries decided to start the uprising on October 26, 1895, a national holiday in China when everyone pays respects to their ancestors. To Sun and his followers the day had special meaning because their actions on that day would show an ultimate sign of respect to their Ming ancestors. Despite the deeper meaning of the day, it would end in disaster. The invasion forces missed their boat from Hong Kong to China while arguing over who had the best guns. Qing authorities were also tipped off about the plot and arrested almost 50 Triad members the next day.

Gaining Triad Support

Sun went on the run, first to Japan and then to Hawaii where he joined the Che Kung Tong—Achieve Justice Society, quickly climbing the ranks. As a Triad member, he traveled through the United States trying to stir up support for a new uprising.

The Chinese-American Triads were not as interested in supporting his cause as he had hoped. Most donated money, but hardly any would provide physical support. He traveled to Britain, Japan, and French Indo-China. While he was drumming up support, his fellow Triads in Hong Kong and China were also making progress. In October 1911, in Wuchang, Sun's men started an uprising that would spread through China and cause the downfall of the Qing Empire. On January 1, 1912 the Republic of China was officially born and Sun Yat-sen became its first president. After two centuries the Triads had finally defeated their Qing enemies and avenged their ancestors.

ABOVE Staff and partial forces of the South China government headed by Dr Sun Yat-sen gather in Guangzhou (Canton) shortly before General Qiung Ming was made military leader in 1922.

1921 Communist Party of China is formed

1928 Chiang Kai-shek sets up government in Nanjing, China

1949 The Green Gang removes gold reserves from the Bank of China in Shanghai

1955 The 14K gang in Hong Kong has a total membership near 80,000

1956 Unrest throughout Hong Kong involves 14K Triad gang members, who were incited to riot

Pay Back

As Chinese president, Sun hardly acknowledged the important part his fellow Triad members played in the uprising, but behind the scenes he treated them with utmost respect. Triad members were given important positions within the government and army as reward for their role in defeating the Qing Empire. And although the role of Triads was barely acknowledged, after the birth of the Republic of China all Triad societies rapidly increased their membership. By now the Triads had so much power they became an integral part of the system. It was no surprise then that Sun's successor Chiang Kai-shek was also a Triad member.

Red Gang

Despite the increase in high-level Triad members, there was still a large portion that came from the streets and were very content making money through crime. One of those was Du Yeah-sheng who went by the nickname "Big-eared Du" and was one of the most important crime bosses in Shanghai during the 1900s. Born at the end of the 1880s, Du quickly made his presence known. As a teen he became a member of the Red Gang and befriended its leader, Huang Chih-jung, also known as "Pock-marked Huang," arguably the most powerful crime boss in Shanghai and heavily involved in the opium trade.

After Du helped get back a stolen package of raw opium, Huang appointed Du as his main opium runner. Still only in his late teens, Du had made a fierce reputation on the streets of Shanghai. Besides his ties to Huang, he also had a reputation for violence

BELOW This pictures shows the victims of the 1927 Shanghai massacre by Chiang Kai-shek and the Green Gang to purge the country of communists.

Chiang Kai-shek (left), President Roosevelt, and Madame Chiang Kai-shek (right) meet in the hope of finding a solution to the Southeast Asian problems, 1944.

FRIENDS IN HIGH PLACES

Du Yeah-sheng's most important associate was Chiang Kai-shek. Chiang met Du as a young man and, with the backing of Du's enormous wealth and military strength, became President of the Republic of China. As president, Chiang returned the favor by appointing Du as government adviser and later even putting him in charge of the National Opium Suppression Committee, which essentially meant Du was policing himself. During World War II, Du fled to Hong Kong. He continued running his criminal empire, but the years of opium use, combined with old age, were beginning to weaken his grip. He stayed in Hong Kong and died on August 16, 1951.

Life doesn't have take two.

Slogan used by Hong Kong government to remove the glorification of Triads in popular media.

and contract killings. At age 21, Du controlled a large chunk of the opium dens around Shanghai, and operated a loan company with a clientele consisting of local shopkeepers and rich foreign businessmen. Enjoying so much success, Du was soon promoted to the position of Red Pole.

BELOW This hand-colored cartoon depicts an Englishman, protected by armed men, selling opium to a Chinese man.

Opium Cartel

As a Red Pole, Du had the total trust of his boss Huang, and he started using this to his advantage by proposing a plan to combine the opium operations of the three main Shanghai gangs. Those three gangs were Huang's Red Gang, the Green Gang, and the Blue Gang. Huang saw advantages of the gangs operating as one and gave Du permission to go ahead with his plan. When the Green Gang leader was wary of the idea and refused to take part, Du simply murdered him and took over as Green Gang leader. Negotiations with the leader of the Blue Gang went a lot smoother and an opium cartel was formed.

Triad Incorporation

With Huang as his Shan Chu, or boss, Du continued expanding their criminal empire by incorporating more and more Triad societies and criminal gangs into the Green Gang. As Huang's deputy, or Fu Shan Chu, Du accumulated enormous wealth and by the age of 30, his personal fortune was around $40 million USD. He was connected to criminals, important politicians, and businessmen. Du befriended or threatened those he could use to further his business empire.

ABOVE China showed great brutality when it came to executions. Here a man (probably a Triad) is beheaded in the street in front of spectators.

Hong Kong

By the end of the nineteenth century, several Triad societies had established many branches outside mainland China. When Chinese workers and their families began migrating to Europe, the United States, and Southeast Asia in search of a better life, the Triads moved with them. At the beginning of the twentieth century, one of the places with the highest concentration of Triad societies was Hong Kong.

Banning of Triad Membership

In 1842, the British established the Crown Colony of Hong Kong, and immediately they had to deal with existing Triad societies, as well as new ones, that were founded as opposition to the British rulers. Within three years of taking over the island, the British implemented laws that made it illegal to be a Triad member, or even to impersonate one. If you were convicted of Triad membership you received a prison sentence of three months and 100 lashes with a bamboo cane.

China, however, was a lot more brutal—convicted Triad members were killed by decapitation, strangulation, or worse. This caused a lot of Triad members to set up shop in Hong Kong.

Second Wave

By the 1930s, there were several powerful groups of Triads in Hong Kong. These were the Wo group, the Chuen, the Tung, the Shing, the Fuk Yee Hing, the Yee On, and the Luen. Though these Triads were in firm control of Hong Kong's underworld, they tried to maintain a legitimate front.

Many registered themselves as charitable organizations, while most chose to present themselves as martial arts clubs. The martial arts clubs promoted health and respect, but also were a great training center for young recruits and foot soldiers. And despite their fronts, their income was still derived from a wide variety of criminal activities such as drug dealing, gambling, prostitution, and extortion. And because membership within Triads was so diverse, they had no trouble investing in legitimate businesses.

As their power and membership grew, so did disputes between and inside the Triads. During the 1930s, several of these disputes resulted in numerous killings and slashings. One of the favorite weapons used by Triad members was the meat cleaver, though other weapons such as knives and swords were popular as well.

Japanese Invasion

In December 1941, Japan invaded Hong Kong and occupied the island. The Hong Kong Triads all had different feelings regarding this new foreign invasion force. Some were against the Japanese army, while others were working with the Japanese forces. Most of these pro-Japanese Triads had been recruited by Japanese spies and had been preparing the occupation for over a decade.

Pro-Japanese Triads

Among the cooperating Triads were the Wo Shing Wo and Yee On. After the Japanese had imprisoned or killed most of the anti-Japanese Triads, the Japanese army started organizing the loyal pro-Japanese Triads into one combined society they named the Hing Ah Kee Kwan—Asian Flourishing Organization. This society saw to it that all remaining anti-Japanese elements were eradicated. Besides arresting Chinese officials, soldiers, and spies, they also took out their competition.

Japan allowed the combined society to continue with its illegal activities and took a percentage of the illegal income. The Triads set up special brothels that catered exclusively to Japanese soldiers. Money was pouring in from everywhere. The black market was booming during the war, just like in so many other countries, and the opium dens were doing spectacular business selling opium to thousands of people who wanted to forget the hardship of war. When the war came to an end the Triads were even richer than ever before. They were ready for the rebound in the world's economy.

Triad Hierarchy

In a Triad society each rank has its own specific number. The leader, or Shan Chu, is a 489—sometimes known as a 21 (4+8+9). He is followed by a 438—the incense master or Heung Chu—who is responsible for the ceremonial duties. Then there is the advisor (under 415), the Red Pole (under 426) who is a master in kung fu and is part of the military wing, the messenger (under 432) who meets with members of other Triads, and a 49 who holds the lowest rank. The 49 stands for the 36 (4 x 9) oaths sworn during the initiation.

ABOVE Kung fu students at the Wushu Training Center at Shaolin, China. Kung fu is practiced by most Triads.

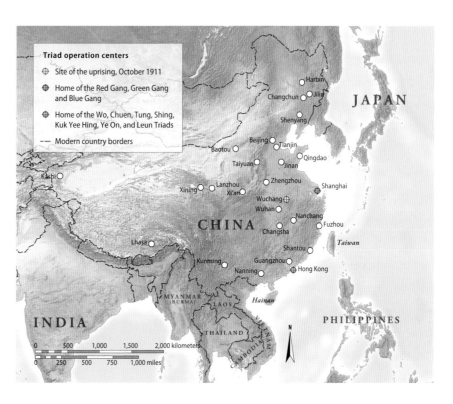

Triad operation centers

⊕ Site of the uprising, October 1911

⊕ Home of the Red Gang, Green Gang and Blue Gang

⊕ Home of the Wo, Chuen, Tung, Shing, Kuk Yee Hing, Ye On, and Leun Triads

-- Modern country borders

Russian Mafia
Vory v Zakone

In the turbulent years after the Russian Revolution of 1917, instability, chaos, panic, and a shortage of food and daily necessities created the suitable environment for the rise of criminal gangs.

Thieves in Law

Pickpockets, swindlers, robbers, and forgers plied their trades almost undisturbed. The armed gangs that profiteered during the disorder of the Revolution, proliferated and became known as the "*vorovskoy mir*" or "thieves' world." From this "thieves' world" there later emerged its elite class—the *vory v zakone* or "thieves in law."

Gulag

Under Stalin's rule, while there were undoubtedly crimes, the dictator's iron-fist rule made it impossible for organized crime to develop in Soviet society. By 1930, as the country was brought back to order, thieves and gangsters were sent to labor camps in great numbers. A vast prison camp system, known as *gulag,* was constructed across the country. The prison camps were not constructed only for street criminals. The majority of the incarcerated were political prisoners. Among them were political dissidents, intellectuals, party officials, and common workers and peasants who stood up against Stalin's policies of coerced industrialization and collectivization.

BELOW The remains of a former gulag at Pevek, in the rugged and harsh area of east Siberia, Russia.

By the end of 1930s, the incarcerated population in the Soviet Union reached 15 million. The vast prison camp empire became the primary spawning ground for the *vory v zakone*—secret fraternities that were comparable to the Sicilian Mafia and the Japanese Yakuza.

Elite Criminals

The *vory v zakone* (translated not only as "thieves in law" but also as "thieves professing the code") were an elite class and the inner circle of a wider criminal milieu. The thieves in this context—*vory*—were not ordinary pickpockets and robbers but honored members of an underground crime institution.

Not all thieves were admitted to the fraternity. To be admitted, one must have been recommended by a *vor* and elected at the *vory* meeting. A criminal's leadership skills, personal power, toughness, intellect, and charisma were all factors to be considered for admission. To be accepted into the *vory* was the highest possible honor for professional criminals who aspired to the fraternity.

THIEVES' CODE

The *vory* are governed by their own distinct laws.

- The *vor* must forsake his birth family and have no family of his own. He should have only one family—the fraternity.
- The *vor* is prohibited to work and he must live only by criminal activity.
- The *vor* has the obligation to recruit the young and teach the trade of theft to beginners.
- The *vor* must limit his drinking and gambling. He should not become drunk or gamble without being able to cover the debt.
- The *vor* has the obligation to give moral and material support to other thieves.
- The *vor* has the obligation to abide by, and carry out, the punishment determined by the thieves' meeting.
- The *vor* is prohibited from involvement with the authorities in any form, including participating in social activities, joining social organizations, taking up weapons on their behalf, serving in the military, or working in labor camps.

The *vory* also have their distinctive initiation ritual, complex systems of tattoos, an extensive jargon, and customs of nicknames, songs, and gestures.

Harsh conditions are evident as a Russian prisoner receives his food bowl through a crude opening in the steel door.

1927 Article 58 of the Russian Penal Code is passed allowing the arrest of almost anyone who acts in a counter-revolutionary way. The reasons for arrest are vague.

1930 The name *vory v zakone* is well known across Russia.

1933 The numbers in Gulags increase to over three million.

1949 Over 10 percent of the nation's production is carried out by prisoners across the country.

Origins

Thieves, in this unique culture, did not mind long prison terms. They regarded prison as their native home and the length of time spent in prison a source of prestige and a badge of honor. The long imprisonment provided an ideal environment for the secret fraternity to evolve and for a criminal subculture to develop. Many political dissidents who encountered the *vory* in prison camps described the *vory*'s behavior, dress code, tattoos, language, and even "court." They also found the encounter with the *vory* to be the most unpleasant experience that they had in prison camps.

Fraternity

When a novice was accepted into the fraternity, a ceremony known as "crowning" was held. At the ceremony, the new *vor* would take an acceptance oath, swearing his loyalty to the fraternity. The new *vor* would be warned by his mentors of the punishment if he failed to abide by his oath. At the initiation, the new *vor* would also be given a nickname. The *vory* had their own customs of nicknames. Giving and receiving a nickname was not just ceremonial. It marked the new life the *vor* was about to enter. The adoption of the nickname, like the taking of monastic vows, signified the new *vor*'s commitment to complete submission to the laws of criminal life.

Work of any form, if enforced by the authorities, was seen as collaboration with the authorities. To honor the thieves' law, the *vory* consistently refused to work in prison camps. Refusal to work was a punishable offense under Soviet law. The *vory* would rather endure the punishment, ranging from beating and starvation, or even confinement in freezing cells, than participate in any work.

The bond formed within the camps extended beyond the prison walls. If released from prison, each *vor* would join a thieves' commune known as *kodla*. The thieves banded together to make a living out of crime. The size of a *kodla* was not large, with each group comprising no more than 20 to 30 people. The group usually would be made up of thieves with different specialties, such as pickpocketing, burglary, and motor vehicle theft.

Either inside or outside prison camps, professional killers were not allowed to join the fraternity. The *vory* allegedly had a code against murder. The thieves were expected to steal or rob without bloodshed. A thief was permitted to kill only to defend his life or honor. The fraternity preached procuring economic gains without resorting to violence. Besides stealing, thieves were permitted to earn money by limited gambling. Card playing was not only a way to make money but also a way to tell a fortune. Winning a card game was a good omen, which might impel a thief to commit a daring theft, whereas losing a game was a bad omen, which might stop a thief from carrying out a planned theft.

BELOW Alexander Solzhenitsyn, the Russian novelist, wrote the novel *The Gulag Archipelago* about his time as a political prisoner in Russia. He lost his citizenship but won the Nobel Prize.

ABOVE A desperate mother holds up a photo of her missing son and a poster about him in a Moscow subway in the hope of information. Many people simply disappeared in the crime wave in Russia.

Thieves' Law on Women

The thieves' law professed complete contempt towards women. Women could not become members of the privileged clan under any circumstances. Within the society of thieves, fraternal life was a source of fierce pride, which would leave no room for a *vor* to develop attachment to anyone else. As a result, permanent families or wives were not allowed. The thieves' law nonetheless contained no prohibition against marriage. A *vor* could marry but was not permitted to develop real attachment to his wife. A wife's status was not very different from that of a prostitute, there to satisfy the needs of others; it differed only in that she had an "owner." The thieves' wives, or any women involved with the fraternity, were forbidden to have a sexual relationship with any men who were not members of the thieves' family. A woman would kill a non-thief attempting to have sexual relationship with her.

Mother Cult

Despite the prohibition against family ties, there existed in the thieves' subculture an outward cult of motherhood. The mother, romanticized by the criminal underworld, was the subject of numerous thieves' songs. The mother that was so lovingly praised in the songs, however, might not be a thief's real mother. The thieves' professed cult of motherhood contrasted sharply to their indifference to their own mothers. It is quite likely that the mother cult was developed under the influence of the traditional Russian mother-cult. It is also possible that the mother so warmly praised in the thieves' songs was nothing more than a metaphor for the thieves' fraternity. The thieves may have been celebrating their rebirth in the family of the thieves.

TATTOOS
Russian Gangster Style

The Russian criminal underworld has a complex system of tattoos that form a secret language understandable only to the members of the secret fraternity.

BELOW A Russian prisoner displaying his tattoos. Each tattoo indicates the rank and status of the *vor*.

Symbols

The *vory* understandably try to maintain exclusive use of their tattoo symbols and designs. Wearing *vory* tattoos by non-*vory* is an offense punishable by death. Sporting false or unearned tattoos is also punishable by death.

Within the *vory*, the complex system of symbols serves to give detailed information about the wearer—his rank, status, and affiliation. Until the 1950s, the most typical *vory* tattoo was a heart pierced by a dagger. Early researchers of the *vory* also described a *vory* tattoo featuring inside a cross the four aces from a deck of playing cards. This symbolized membership in the fraternity. Today, the *vory* usually have an eight-pointed star tattooed on their chests symbolizing their status as professional criminals. The same design may also be tattooed on the knee-cap, signifying that they do not bow to anyone or anything.

Status

Tattoos can be applied voluntarily to show one's ranks and status or forcibly to stigmatize those criminals despised by the *vory*. A *vor* may be forcibly tattooed if he fails to pay his gambling debts, or otherwise fails to obey the thieves' code. Tattoos of punishment are usually placed on the forehead and are designed to humiliate the bearer or warn others about him.

The tattoos may contain blatant sexual images to embarrass the wearer. They could also consist of slurs about the bearer's ethnicity, sexual orientation, or his status as an informer. The *vory* may forcibly apply derogatory tattoos on criminals con-victed of a crime they do not approve of—for instance, child rape or molestation.

The four suits of playing cards all form part of the tattoo system. Spades are the suit of thieves. Clubs, representing a sword, are a suit for ex-warriors. Diamonds and hearts are suits reserved for criminals of inferior status. Diamonds, usually forcibly applied, signify the wearer's collaboration with the authorities. Hearts are a sexual symbol. This suit, also forcibly applied, marks the wearer out as a passive homosexual or a sex toy within the prison.

Prison Power

Before the "Great Patriotic War" of 1941–1945, the prison authorities began to tolerate the existence of the *vory v zakone*, making shrewd use of the criminal underworld in their dealings with the regime's real enemies—political prisoners.

Within the prison camps, the prison authorities gave the thieves a free rein with political and ordinary prisoners. The horror stories about the life in the prison camps served the purpose of increasing people's fear of prison life, which in turn helped keep the regime's political foes at bay. The *vory*, with the tolerance of the authorities, enjoyed a privileged position in the prison camps.

Soldier Prisoners

The tide turned against the *vory* with the outbreak of World War II. Desperate for manpower in the front, the authorities made a deal with prisoners by offering them freedom if they agreed to join the army. An estimated one million prisoners, including thieves, were released and sent to the front. Taking up arms for the state, however, violated the thieves' law. At the completion of the war, many thieves were sent back to prison camps to face a horde of angry and revengeful thieves who had been faithful to the thieves' code and refused to serve the state.

BELOW A Soviet soldier stands guard next to a freight train surrounded by bodies of people killed in a battle.

Have not prisons—which kill all will and force of character in man, which enclose within their walls more vices than are met with on any other spot of the globe—always been universities of crime?

Peter Korpotkin (1842–1921), Russian anarchist

Collaborators

Those who collaborated with the authorities were called "bitches"—*suki*. For their act of betrayal, they deserved to be expelled from the brotherhood. The bitches, however, did not wait to be judged by their former brothers. They formed their own groups with a revised code, which allowed certain collaboration with the authorities. A conflict between the two groups, termed the "bitches' war," ensued.

The prison camp authorities viciously sided with the bitches, hoping to use them to exterminate the *vory*. Having served in the military and been trained in weaponry, the bitches were not shy in using violence. The prison camp authorities assisted the bitches in many ways, deliberately placing the warring groups in the same facility, and allowing only the bitches to carry weapons in the clashes. They also helped identify any *vory* who were trying to hide by forcing prisoners to strip to reveal their tattoos. The bitches easily gained an upper hand in the war with the *vory*.

OPPOSITE Soviet soldiers during World War II gather around to listen to their commander's message.

Prisoners in a gulag near Norlisk in northern Siberia, in 1991, enjoy a hot lunch in the mess. By this time, the number of *vory* had been greatly reduced as a result of the bitches' war.

SURVIVAL INSTINCT

The thieves in the old fraternity faced the choice of either converting to the new group or be killed. Many of the thieves stood their ground, choosing to face death rather than betray their ideals. The murderous vengeance of the bitches, with the backing of the authorities, greatly reduced the ranks of the *vory*. By the late 1950s the reign of the traditional *vory v zakone* was all but over. The *vory* were defeated but not destroyed.

The survival instinct made them adapt to the new environment. The *vory* lived through their worst ordeal and survived to play yet another role in the future of Russian organized crime.

Drug Cartels
The Business of Illegal Drug Trafficking

The global drug trade is a multilayered and complex enterprise that involves a wide diversity of players from peasant farmers to organized crime syndicates.

OPPOSITE Spectators watch as government authorities destroy a large quantity of seized drugs in Paraguay in 1989.

Global Influence

The global drug problem is multidimensional in that it impacts the integrity of the state, politically, economically, and socially. The profits derived from this enterprise are huge. Consequently, the people at the top of the "food chain" have enormous political influence and input into national politics. Drug wealth, which often represents billions of dollars, can have a corrupting influence on the recipient state's economy and political institutions.

Drug Trafficking

Drug trafficking is the illegal transport of an internationally banned or controlled substance, such as opium, morphine, heroin, and cocaine. Controlled substances include plant-based as well as synthetic substances, and may also include certain precursor agents such as acetic anhydride, a chemical agent that is used in the production of heroin.

The Process

Drug trafficking involves the producing agent who cultivates or produces the product such as coca or raw opium; the middleman or trader who purchases the product from the farmer or producer—this person may also further refine or chemically alter the original substance; and the organizations such as traffickers, smugglers, or other criminal elements responsible for transporting the product into designated consumer countries or regions.

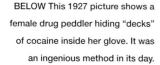

BELOW This 1927 picture shows a female drug peddler hiding "decks" of cocaine inside her glove. It was an ingenious method in its day.

Growing Profits

Drug trafficking is one of the most profitable activities engaged in by national and international criminal groups. Due to the growing and persistent demand for illegal drugs and the huge profits that are derived from their sale, eliminating the illegal trade in these controlled substances is a war that will not easily be won. Billions of dollars have been spent on efforts to legislate and arrest the problem. However, due to the multi-dimensional facet of the drug problem, such efforts, up until now, have not brought much success. In some of the major producing countries like Colombia and Afghanistan, where drug eradication and crop substitution efforts have been successful in certain areas or regions, the problem surfaces or expands in another area—the balloon effect.

Measures to curtail and regulate the production and sale of illicit narcotics have given rise to criminal organizations, which today are transnational in scope and threaten global political and financial institutions.

ABOVE Process workers measure and load cocaine paste—"pasta"—into bags in a laboratory in Peru.

ABOVE This popular drug dealing street in Southern California is loaded with signs warning of the punishment if caught purchasing drugs.

OPPOSITE Chewing coca leaves—used to produce cocaine—is a cultural tradition dating back to the Incas. This Peruvian miner's teeth have turned black as a result.

Early Uses

The coca leaf was used by the indigenous Andean populations of principally Bolivia, Brazil, Colombia, Ecuador, and Peru to treat a variety of physical ailments including altitude sickness, headaches, stomach pain, and fatigue. Its stimulant properties also provided a sense of wellbeing and allowed the user to perform tasks requiring a lot of energy on very little food intake. Coca leaves also provided some important vitamins such as A, B, C, and other nutrients including proteins, carbohydrates, and iron. The indigenous people of the Andes considered coca vital for their survival—a sacred plant that had mystical properties. Indeed, coca was part of their social fabric and was an important component of their culture and daily existence extending into all areas of their lives and daily rituals. It was also used for religious and other ceremonial purposes such as marriages and burials.

EARLY LEGAL BANS

Mass criminalization of drugs was spawned when the Opium Exclusion Act was passed by US Congress in 1909. This law in effect banned the smoking of opium that, at the time, was mainly engaged in by Chinese immigrants to the United States. This law stemmed from the Shanghai Convention in 1908 that convened to implement international control of illicit drugs.

This prohibition against illegal opium drove the trade underground and into the hands of drug traffickers. In an effort to circumvent enforcement of the newly enacted law, opium users began using morphine, an opium derivative. This was followed by a second international convention, The Hague Commission of 1912, and the US Harrison Narcotic Act of 1914, that made the non-medical use of opium, morphine, and cocaine a criminal offense.

The 1936 Geneva Convention for the Suppression of the Illicit Traffic in Dangerous Drugs was the first time that an international body sought to stem the flow of illicit substances by drug traffickers and propose punitive measures on those who engaged in this activity. For a number of reasons including the outbreak of World War II, this Convention, which came into force in 1939, was another unsuccessful attempt to address this growing global problem.

Additionally, international treaties signed in 1961, 1971, and the late 1980s, sought to further place controls on the production and distribution of a wide range of illegal narcotics and psycho-tropic substances.

The United Nations recognized that problems caused by the illicit manufacturing, production, and distribution of illegal narcotics were a global concern that impacted public health and the security of producer as well as consumer states. Despite international attempts to address this global issue, the drug problem continued to expand and proliferate.

In 1938, this roundup of alleged narcotics dealers was the most important bust in New Orleans to date. Detectives Martinez and Gerlinger stand watch at the rear.

The Drug War cannot stand the light of day. It will collapse as quickly as the Vietnam War, as soon as people find out what's really going on.

Joseph McNamara, former Police Chief, Kansas City and San Jose, and Fellow, Hoover Institution, 1976

Inca Tradition

It could be said that the coca plant was instrumental in the development of the Inca Empire. The traditional method of usage is chewing—a process called *acullico*. This practice, which is deeply embedded in Andean culture and traces its roots to the Incas, is still carried out today. Use by the indigenous population was widespread and usually had its genesis in the adolescent years. From that time, a pattern of steady use began that continued throughout their lives.

Attempts at Ban

Following the Spanish conquest of the Incas in the mid-sixteenth century, the colonial powers eventually viewed coca as having commercial value due to its physical benefits. This spawned an increase in cultivation in Peru as more and more Spaniards took over coca plantations and became involved in the trade, selling the leaves to Indian laborers and mine workers for a handsome profit. This practice continued despite the fact that the Catholic Church, that held tremendous influence over the colonists, believed that the plant was inherently evil and attempted to have it eradicated. After many attempts to ban coca, the Church ultimately benefitted financially from the trade by imposing a 10 percent tax. In fact, the colonial government taxed coca at a higher rate than normal produce thus providing a steady stream of revenue that it badly needed.

Crop Substitution

Attempts at crop substitution—declaring a universal ban on the crop—and eradication efforts failed. The Spaniards built their economy on the coca plant and the backs of the indigenous people of the Andes. Coca was used to subdue the Indian population as leaves were given to Indian workers who toiled long hours in the silver mines. Coca

BELOW A group of villagers in Kero, Peru, chew coca leaves as they sort through the day's crop.

seemed to increase productivity and hence more revenue. For the Spanish colonists, coca was indeed a very profitable enterprise. Moreover, the native population refused to work the arduous hours in the mines without an adequate supply of coca. Hundreds of thousands of Indians would ultimately perish in service to their Spanish conquerors.

Evolution of Cocaine

Prior to the discovery of cocaine, trading in coca leaves was minimal. In 1860, cocaine was isolated by Albert Niemann, a Gottingen University student, in his PhD dissertation. Over the next two decades cocaine production and sales were relatively modest with the majority of sales going to medical researchers. By the early–mid 1880s cocaine was touted as a wonder drug by many members of the medical community, most noteworthy, Sigmund Freud who wrote a treatise—*On Coca*—on the subject in 1884. In this treatise Freud espoused the positive physical and psychological effects that cocaine had on the user.

However, it was the analgesic properties of cocaine, discovered by the Austrian ophthalmologist, Karl Koller, that drew the attention of the medical community to possible medicinal applications. It became a medical breakthrough in pain relief.

1901 US Senate adopts a resolution to forbid the sale of opium and alcohol to "aboriginal tribes and uncivilized races."

1938 Since the Harrison Act of 1914, 25,000 physicians have been arraigned on narcotics charges.

1956 The US Narcotics Control Act provides the sentence of death for anyone over the age of 18 selling heroin to anyone under the age of eighteen.

1960 A UN Commission states that there are almost 45,000 US drug addicts.

THE COCA PLANT

There are over 250 species of coca but few contain enough of the psychoactive alkaloid cocaine to warrant mass production by legal or illegal suppliers. The coca plant—*Erythroxylum coca*—is native to the Andes mountains, located on the western coast of South America, encompassing Argentina, Bolivia, Chile, Peru, Colombia, Ecuador, and Venezuela.

Erythroxylum coca is a perennial plant that can be harvested up to six times per year and prior to the mid-1980s provided most of the world's cocaine. Another species, *Erythroxylum novogranatense* is found in Colombia and now accounts for the majority of the world's cocaine.

Coca leaves typically yield approximately .05–1 percent cocaine during the chemical processing of the leaves. The processing of coca leaves into cocaine hydrochloride became a major activity among Colombian traffickers as United States and European demand for the drug increased during the 1970s.

TOP Colombian farmer inspects new coca leaves in La Quarenta, Caqueta Province.

BOTTOM Close-up of the leaves and berries of a coca plant. The leaves are processed in a local lab to produce the paste that is turned into cocaine.

World Demand

As world demand increased, new sources of supply were sought. Coca cultivation in non-traditional areas such as Africa, Southeast Asia, and Australia was initiated for the sole purpose of cocaine production. In fact, by the early 1900s, cultivation in Indonesia, which produced a higher quality plant yielding on average 1.5 percent cocaine per leaf, threatened the South American supply and eventually surpassed Peruvian coca exports.

Public Consumption

It was the analgesic property of the drug that made it popular throughout Europe and the United States. As the drug became available for public consumption, and people began snorting and taking the drug intravenously. The addict population began to rise as cocaine was prescribed as a remedy for morphine dependence and alcoholism. Consequently, morphine addicts transferred their dependence to cocaine or became addicted to both substances.

OPPOSITE A woman harvests coca leaves on the hillside near Quillabamba, in the Peruvian Andes.

In the latter years of the nineteenth century the price of cocaine—about $2 USD per ounce—made it affordable to the average street user, middle-class citizen, and criminals. Cocaine was also used to increase labor productivity. Similar to the Indians of the Andes, cocaine was given to migrant agricultural workers, laborers, and others performing jobs requiring long hours and much physical exertion and stamina.

US Epidemic

At the dawn of the twentieth century, the United States became the largest consumer of coca/cocaine with imports exceeding 600 tons per annum. Cocaine had become an epidemic and was taken more for its euphoric effects than as an analgesic or other medicinal purposes. Global cocaine production peaked at around 1,500 tons in the early 1900s. At the time, most coca came from Peru and to minimize production costs and the degradation of the leaf during transport processing, labs were established in the source country.

It didn't take long for this once-thought-to-be-harmless drug to become a major public health concern as hospital admissions and cocaine-related deaths began to be routine in the first decade of the twentieth century. As the number of addicts grew, organized crime saw the profits and cocaine became a law enforcement problem in the 1920s and beyond.

VIN DE PAYS

In 1863, Angelo Mariani (1838–1914), a French chemist mixed wine with an extract from the coca leaf and produced "Vin Mariani," which had international appeal and brought him great wealth and celebrity, including a medal from Pope Leo XIII who derived much satisfaction from using the product. Other notables who were impressed with the elixir included Queen Victoria, Thomas Edison, Jules Verne, and US President William McKinley.

Colorful label from the coca-based wine made in the nineteenth century. It was based on Bordeaux wine which leached the cocaine from the leaves.

ABOVE Despite the constant police presence, this back alley in Bolivia is the meeting place of dealers and users, in amongst family living.

Perceptions

Cocaine use was attributed not only to a rise in crime but also to personality changes that were thought to cause otherwise normal people to engage in criminal and often vicious behavior such as rape and murder. Whether this was true or not was not the issue. This was the perception that existed at the time and this view spawned concern and enhanced efforts to rid society of this demon.

US Legislation

In the United States, individual state legislatures enacted laws that made it a criminal offense to dispense cocaine without a license. Federal legislation was also enacted to assist states in curbing the cocaine problem. These legislative measures, rather than

eliminating the problem, drove it underground where organized criminal groups would eventually replace the pharmaceutical companies in keeping the supply of cocaine available to those who wanted to take it and were willing to pay the inflated prices the drug would ultimately bring.

Cocaine's toxic side effects virtually ended the medical community's use of it as an analgesic drug around 1920, and by the late 1920s the public's demand for cocaine had subsided. By the beginning of World War II, cocaine usage had ceased to be a major problem.

The Illicit Cocaine Industry

Modern-day Latin American cocaine cartels began their ascendancy in the late 1960s and started to attract the attention of state and federal law enforcement the following decade. The drug trade operates on the basic economic principles of supply and demand. Demand for cocaine had increased in the late 1960s and by the mid-1970s the demand led to a dramatic rise in coca output in Bolivia and Peru.

Due to its geographical topography and location, perpetual violence promulgated by various armed non-state actors, a weak political regime, and a general permissiveness regarding illicit activity, Colombia became the capital of the illegal cocaine industry. Additionally, Colombia had access to a large diaspora population in the United States that facilitated the establishment of drug distribution conduits.

The cocaine epidemic of the 1970s through the mid-1990s, particularly in the United States, would be fed by two major drug cartels located in Colombia.

ABOVE Officers in the Colombian army seize the luxury island property of drug trafficker, Jose "El Mexicano" Gacha, of the Medellin Cartel.

Transnational Crime
Gang Interconnections

In all countries early in the twentieth century, wherever organized crime groups or gangs were involved in illegal activities, they shaped their wealth through an ability to efficiently manage markets—both classical and specific—that had evolved over the years.

Classical Markets

Classical markets of the early twentieth century included such "violence" industries as bootlegging, prostitution, extortion, robberies, and racketeering, along with more lucrative black market industries such as loan sharking and gambling.

Specific Markets

Specific markets are generated mainly by political events, culture, and local regulation. For example, the black market that grew up during the Prohibition Era in the United States (1920–1933) made the fortunes of large Italian families in Chicago, New York, and many other cities in that country. It also allowed these families and their associates to take over from Irish and Jewish organized crime groups, sometimes through violent incidents such as the "St Valentine's Day Massacre."

Gang Interconnections

Italian clans also made useful and fruitful contacts with the West Coast Asian Tongs, thus gaining access to the Asian market and the new opportunities it offered, such as the opium trade in China, led by British companies, and the gambling industry in both Portuguese Macau and the East Indies held by the Dutch. Reciprocally, the doors of the world opened to Chinese Triads through Portugal and the Netherlands.

The Industrial Revolution

Organized crime groups react strongly to major political events, deftly reshaping their balance of power to suit the prevailing circumstances. In the nineteenth century, the Industrial Revolution brought a new balance of power through the acquisition of money, weapons, and global trade, and saw the largest and most active groups, such as Italian clans, Yakuza, Triads, and Russian Mafia, alter their operations to suit.

The "industrialization process" of illegal activities is perfectly demonstrated through the links between Irish and Jewish organized crime groups and the so-called "Robber Barons" in the United States during the eighteenth century. Links between wealthy industrialists and organized crime groups can also be found in Britain, France, Italy, and China, where the underground power of organized crime groups helps to enforce economic strategies by mastering territories and people through violence.

The Industrial Revolution also led to massive migration worldwide, especially from Europe to the United States, and from the colonies to Great Britain. During the years 1900–1920, more than two million Italians emigrated to the United States, joining millions of Irish nationals fleeing harsh living conditions and British oppression.

Multi-national Crime Groups

Such massive migrations led to a rebalancing of power between crime groups, with the empowerment of Italian, Irish, and Polish families in the United States, and Chinese, Irish, and Indian families in the United Kingdom. Illegal markets consisted at the time of extortion, illegal labor, alcohol, prostitution, and gambling.

Jewish Organized Crime

The history of Jewish organized crime is interwoven with that of the migration, during the sixteenth and seventeenth centuries, of Jewish people fleeing Europe to avoid persecution and rampant anti-semitism. In Russia, under the tsars, Jews were confined to Russia's western territories—Pale of Settlement—and the *shtetls*, which included Poland, Ukraine, Latvia, Lithuania, and Belarus. They lived in reserved ghettos in all major cities; many professions and occupations were closed to them. The poverty and misery they endured caused millions of Jews to flee to the United States, particularly to areas already occupied by criminals, many of them Irish. As in every diaspora, some new criminal elements were introduced that evolved into organized Mafia-like gangs in various places of settlement. Two of these places of settlement were the United States and Latin America, especially Argentina.

1900 Monk Eastman and his gang take over the east side of New York.

1908 Raffaele Palizzolo leaves Sicily and escapes to New York, avoiding murder charges.

1923 The Thompson submachine gun—"Tommy gun"—is first used in a drive-by shooting of Frank McErlane.

1934 John Dillinger is killed in Chicago by the FBI.

1935 The Metropolitan Police Forensic Laboratory opens in the United Kingdom.

1946 The Metropolitan and City Police Company Fraud Department is formed in the United Kingdom.

Organized crime constitutes nothing less than a guerrilla war against society.

Lyndon B. Johnson (1908–1973), thirty-sixth President of the United States

ABOVE Shoppers on New York's Lower East Side stock up for Passover, 1926. Tammany Hall cultivated the loyalty of many of the city's immigrant groups.

BELOW Having killed his political rival in a duel and served as Vice-President of the United States (1801–1805), Aaron Burr was arrested for treason in 1807.

Irish and Jewish Links

In the early twentieth century, most of the preeminent gangsters on the east coast of the United States had links with Tammany Hall, a Democratic Party political machine well versed in graft and corruption. Although led mostly by the Irish, the Tammany Hall coalition also included Jewish gangs. One of the most powerful presidents of Tammany Hall during the late eighteenth century was a Jew named Aaron Burr.

Gangs of New York

Two of the most notorious gangs of that period were the famous Lower East Side Gang, one of the largest Jewish gangs in New York, which was led by Monk Eastman (born Edward Osterman in 1873), and a gang known as the Five Points, led by an Italian ex-pugilist, Paolo Vaccarelli. Vaccarelli preferred to go by the name Paul Kelly because Irish names were more respectable than Italian names at that time in New York. Allegedly both Al Capone and Lucky Luciano belonged to the Five Points Gang.

The Purple Gang

During Prohibition in the United States, the Jewish Purple Gang was entrenched in Detroit, Al Capone's gang in Chicago. Although all other Jewish organized crime groups in the United States at that time operated from an inter-ethnic base, the Purple Gang was exclusively Jewish. Based in Detroit's Lower East Side, the Purple Gang engaged in classical activities such as bootlegging, hijacking, gambling, narcotics, loan sharking, and kidnapping.

They were also involved in the widely publicized murders in Detroit known as the Miraflores and Collingwood Massacres. Others suspected that the Purple Gang was involved in the St Valentine's Day Massacre in Chicago.

Major leaders of the Purple Gang were allegedly Raymond Bernstein, and his brothers Abe, Joey, and Izzy, as well as Philip and Harry Keywell, and Sam and Harry Fleischer. Even though the gang was dismantled by arrests and convictions, Abe Bernstein continued to run his bookmaking business until he died of a stroke in 1968.

BELOW Shot and fatally wounded, noted gangster Arnold Rothstein refused to identify his killer, telling police: "You stick to your trade, I'll stick to mine."

Murder Inc.

One of the largest and probably most successful Jewish organized crime groups was called "Murder Incorporated" or "Murder Inc." This gang was at its height during the 1920s and 1930s. Its business included classical illegal activities such as bootlegging, gambling, racketeering, pimping, and, of course, murders, professionally committed. It is now known that this group killed over 1,000 people on contracts in the United States.

For decades, Murder Inc. made up the most powerful international crime syndicate in the world. Its story involves encounters and alliances between the Jew, Meyer Lansky, and the Italian, Lucky Luciano, as well as Dutch Schultz and Louis Lepke. The training and subsequent rise of Meyer Lansky, Benny "Bugsy" Siegel, and Lucky Luciano through their teacher, the famous Jewish gangster Arnold Rothstein, shows how the figures of organized crime met, organized, and did business together, one contact supporting the other and vice versa. The great contribution of Arnold Rothstein was that he didn't care about race, origin, or religion: He was recruiting people. There were Jews, Irishmen, blacks, Italians, and even women working in the organization.

CONTRACT TO KILL

The key to Murder Inc.'s success, according to several mobsters' historians, is that they scrupulously followed an eight-point process in murdering people. First, the contract was made. No contract was to be approved without the advice of the "board of directors." Second, the killer was selected from a state completely different from the one where the murder was going to occur. Third, the selected hitman must pack his bag for no more than a week's stay. Fourth, once on the spot, he would keep a close eye on his target, conducting proper surveillance in order to find the

right place and just the right moment to commit the murder. Fifth, the hitman, having chosen the spot, would secure it. Sixth, he would commit the murder, preferably using one of the time-tested methods such as shooting, strangling, or stabbing with an ice pick, in order to avoid unnecessary mess and leave as little evidence as possible. Seventh, the killer would make the body disappear, for example by burying it in a pit or dumping it in an open but discreet field. The eighth step was to get on a train and get out of the state as quickly as possible.

The "chalk fairy," according to one historian, always disappears the moment investigators start asking who contaminated the scene.

Intertwined Histories

The story of Irish organized crime in the twentieth century began with the massive immigration of Irish escaping persecution in their homeland and trying to find a safe haven overseas. Even more so than Italian organized crime in the United States, Irish organized crime would become a deeply rooted part of the nation's history.

Irish Ghettos

The first wave of Irish immigration had deposited a strong criminal base in the saloons and in the political machine. In the early 1920s, Irish organized crime groups were the most powerful in the United States. Though they did not have a homeland base to rival that of the Italians, Irish organized crime figures maintained strong links with groups in Ireland fighting the English for freedom from oppression and, later, for independence.

Irish Gangs

Gangs developed among the poor and often illiterate population of the suburban Irish ghettos in cities all over the United States. The most renowned of all Irish criminal organizations, however, developed in areas on or near the East Coast—New York and Boston, and Chicago. One of these—the North Side Gang, also known as the North Side Mob—was almost exterminated during the St Valentine's Day Massacre.

BELOW These six members of the Fred Burke Gang—wearing civilian clothes—committed roughly 20 murders and earned $10 million USD from robberies.

Forty and More Thieves

Organized crime groups in the United Kingdom underwent continuous slow development until World War II. While organized crime groups flourished in the United States during the Prohibition Era, the pre-World War II UK crime scene was dominated mainly by two organizations known as "The Sabini Brothers" and "Forty Thieves."

Scottish Italians Take Over London

From 1918 until the beginning of World War II, London was under the control of a gang ruled by the half-Scottish, half-Italian Sabini brothers. Directed by Charles Ullano "Darby" Sabini, they were active in horse racing, book-making, nightclubs, and gambling. After a war in the mid-1920s with a rival gang—the Brummagen Boys—over the control of various racetracks, an agreement on territory was reached, allowing the Sabini Brothers to develop into a major force in the London underworld. In 1940, when Italy entered the war, they were imprisoned under wartime regulations requiring persons of alien descent be interned for the duration of hostilities.

Shoplifting for the Queen

The gang named "Forty Thieves" is unusual in the history of organized crime in that it was composed exclusively of women. Established in the late nineteenth century and continuing up until the 1960s, Forty Thieves was a well-structured gang of female shoplifters based in South London. The leader was known as "the Queen." At the height of its power, the gang was led by Maggie Hill—sister of the famous gangster Billy Hill, king of the London underworld during the 1950s.

ABOVE Betting office, Dublin, 1926. The Betting Act had just made cash betting off racecourses legal in Ireland, though "undesirable practices" came with it.

MANHATTAN MADAME

Of mixed French and African descent, "Queenie" of Manhattan—also known as Stephanie St Clair, Madame St Clair, and Madame Queen—emigrated from Martinique to the United States via Marseille in 1912. Briefly affilliated with Forty Thieves—New York's oldest street gang, not to be confused with the London gang of the same name—she soon branched out into policy racketeering. During Prohibition, she found herself involved in the Jewish-Italian-Irish gang war and was forced to pay extortion to the Bronx mob's boss, Dutch Schultz. She and her chief enforcer Ellsworth "Bumpy" Johnson reluctantly made an agreement with Lucky Luciano and the Five Families of New York that saw the absorption of the St Clair gang by the Mafia Commission. When Schultz was gunned down in 1935, Madame St Clair sent a telegram to his hospital bed saying, "As ye sow, so shall ye reap."

Madame St Clair was charged by police with using her estranged husband as a target.

3 TOWARD THE TWENTY-FIRST CENTURY

Toward the Twenty-first Century
Changing Face

The golden age of organized crime lingered into the 1950s. Mafia-style organizations could be found in every corner of the globe and in every imaginable criminal enterprise. But as the new century approached, underworld societies gained influence within the legitimate governments of various nations through corruption and cooperation.

ABOVE A Yakuza showing off his body art, done by the artist Horitaka. Tattoos such as these are now becoming less popular with younger gangsters.

Embracing the Mafia

In America, the mutualistic relationship between organized crime and organized politics dated back generations and was stronger than ever. The anti-Mafia movement of Italy's Fascists was reversed through the post-World War II American occupation of Sicily. Aware that *Mafiosi* were among the more devoted anti-Fascists, US officials returned them to power on the island.

Cuba, hoping to free itself of the communist influence and its economy from the ups and downs of the sugar market, welcomed the opportunity to become the world's gambling mecca and embraced the racketeers who could make that happen.

Multinational Crime

Underworld organizations from various regions and ethnic backgrounds worked together, as criminal activity became multinational in scale. Narcotics trafficking, weapons smuggling, gambling, money laundering, and other rackets became global problems.

Yamaguchi-gumi, Sumiyoshi-kai, and Inagawa-kai became the three largest Yakuza clans in Japan, extending their reach to corporations and debt collection. In the rest of Asia, Triads controlled the major trade in the Golden Triangle, feeding the habits of addicts in the west.

Meanwhile in Russia, the fall of communism opened the gates for organized crime. Beginning with the black market, Russia saw a revival of the *Vory v Zakone*, with greed taking over from

thieves' law. Suddenly rich was good and the more gaudy the display of wealth the better. The new breed of *vory* was ready for the meteoric rise of Russian Mafia.

The drug barons of South America also saw a change in circumstances as the United States began actions to stop the importation of illegal narcotics. The invasion of Panama was only one front in the fight to keep Americans clean.

Changing the Game

As the FBI began employing effective weapons and techniques in the fight against the American Mob, much of the global organized crime was taking a simultaneous beating around the world. As the twenty-first century approached, it appeared that organized crime was on the run. Instead it was bracing for a transnational leap.

BELOW Discussing the state of play? A group of senior men gather in a street in Corleone, the traditional stronghold of Sicilian Mafia.

Sicilian Mafia
Prosperity and Arrests

1957 Joe Bonanno returns to Sicily with a red-carpet welcome from government officials. The trip results in the New York Mafia franchising the heroin-trafficking operations to their Italian cousins.

1962 Calcedonio Di Pisa is shot dead in Piazza Principe di Camporeale in Palermo. Suspicion falls on the Chicago Mafia who received a shortfall in the supply of heroin from Pisa.

1978 Lucky Luciano dies of a heart attack while waiting at Naples airport.

1978 Red Brigade kidnaps former Prime Minister Aldo Moro. His body was found 55 days later.

1986 Mafia maxi trial begins in Palermo, lasting for almost two years.

1993 Father Giuseppe Puglisi, an anti-Mafia priest, is shot at the door of his church in Palermo.

The victory of the Christian Democrats in the 1948 elections, the demise of the separatist movement, and especially the beginning of the Cold War brought a period of great prosperity for the Mafia.

Anti-communist Strategy

Throughout the 1950s, the Mafia was spoken of little or not at all in Italy. In fact, some people even denied its existence and claimed that talk of the Mafia simply perpetuated a racist image of Sicily invented by the rest of Italy. When no one talks about the Mafia, however, it always means that it is in good health and, protected by political powers, has no need to draw attention to itself.

RIGHT Communist Party billboard in Sicily, 1955. Along with the Christian Democrat party, the Mafia was a major anti-communist force on the island.

FAR RIGHT Ingrid Bergman films Federico Fellini at Taormina, Sicily, in 1957. Hollywood loved gangsters, and the compliment was often returned.

LATIN LOVER AND INFORMER

Tommaso Buscetta was born into an extremely large and extremely poor family in Agrigento, Sicily, on July 13, 1928. He was the last of 17 children. His father was a glassmaker. Buscetta was already married at 16, and to support his family during the war years he began trading on the black market. He also fought on the side of the Italian Resistance against the Germans and it was then that his skill with firearms was noticed by the Mafia. At the age of 20 he joined their ranks. His first job, legend has it, involved smuggling cigarettes.

At the end of the war, the economic situation forced him to emigrate to Argentina where he opened a glass works. The business was not a success however and in 1957, Buscetta decided to return to Sicily and to Palermo. Following violent feuds within the Mafia in the 1960s, he fled again, first to Brazil, then to Mexico, and lastly to New York. During this period, from 1962 to 1972, he dealt in drugs, creating such a large international business in trafficking that he became known as the "boss of the two worlds."

He had two more wives, the Italian Vera Girotti, and the Brazilian Cristina de Almedia Guimares, both of whom bore him children. He was expelled from *Cosa Nostra* because he had too many wives and too many lovers. Adultery was a far worse crime than murder in the eyes of his associates.

Arrested in Brazil in 1972 and sent back to Italy, Buscetta was held in the Ucciardone prison in Palermo until 1980. Gang warfare broke out again in Palermo in the late 1970s when, in a bloodthirsty series of killings, the Corleone clan took control of *Cosa Nostra* and assassinated figures of state who tried to oppose the rise of the organization. Buscetta realized the danger of the situation and fled once more to Brazil in 1980. He was arrested there in 1983, accused of international drugs trafficking, and extradited to Italy. After an unsuccessful attempt at suicide, he became the most important informer in the history of the Mafia, a decision that cost the lives of 39 of his relatives. He never revealed anything about himself and made use of his position to attack his enemies. He died in New York in 2000, surrounded by his family and under the protection of the United States government.

LEFT Tommaso Buscetta arrives in Italy, 1984, having been extradited from Brazil. He would soon start talking, but it would be nearly a decade before he acknowledged the Mafia's links to politicians.

In the international context of the Cold War, the Sicilian Mafia took on a key role as a foil to the development of a communist political left in Italy. There were two main forces in Italian politics. In the center of the political spectrum was the Christian Democrat party, and on the left was the other main block of parties, major members of which were the socialists and the communists. In addition to these two groups were other smaller parties. The Christian Democrats always obtained the most votes, but never held an absolute majority in parliament. In successive elections the communist party increased its share and if it had achieved electoral success, Italy would have entered the Soviet Union's sphere of influence.

Christian Democrats

Historically Sicilians have always tended to return a solid vote for the same traditional political party—the Christian Democrat party—and thus their vote played a key role in limiting potential electoral victories by the communists. The underlying reason for the electoral unanimity that saw the introduction of universal suffrage was the control or at least the insidious influence of the Mafia, whose power on the electoral front was such that a protective silence fell over its members and their activities.

American Influence

Within this anti-communist political scenario, the Mafia was reorganizing itself. Contact with American society, albeit indirect, followed the Allied victory in World War II and stimulated a desire among Italians, including the Mafia, for a new way of life. The appeal of modern America, mainly fueled by Hollywood films, eventually helped to transform the Mafia too. Previously its key business had been the control of property, especially in the citrus orchards of the *conca d'oro* (golden valley) around Palermo, and the control of related businesses. The chance to develop a new, much more lucrative, type of business came unexpectedly from the building sector.

Land Reform

The agrarian reform approved in 1950 did not substantially modify the ownership and distribution of land. The reform was based on the principle that the state would buy from major landowners, then sell the land on to agricultural workers and their families through a lottery system. The Sicilian parliament organized the transfer by introducing a limit of 150 hectares for each property and a special authority, the ERAS, was created to manage and oversee the reform. But it was not difficult for large landowners to find and exploit loopholes in the system. They kept the best lands for themselves, sold the worst ones to the state, receiving handsome compensation, and ceded the rest to friends or relations. On the whole, therefore, the workers received the poorest land, insufficient and inadequate for feeding their large families.

The agrarian reform had been passed by the Christian Democrat government in response to pressure from the political forces on the left, in particular the Communist Party. From a political point of view, the reform was considered a success because the vast properties of the landowners had been finally dismantled, but from a social point of view it was a failure. The intention of giving land to peasants who were exploited by the Mafia did not succeed. With centuries of hopes once more betrayed, the only alternative left to landworkers was, once more, migration.

Urban Flood

During this period Italy was experiencing an unprecedented economic boom, and internal migration offered a solution. Palermo had been badly bombed by the Allies during the war and was now in need of reconstruction. Thus, following the failure of the agricultural reform, increasing numbers of impoverished peasants flowed into the city from the countryside in search of a job.

The Pillage of Palermo

While political forces were marshaling votes to oppose the rise of communism, the Mafia sought out ways to conduct its business undisturbed. The result was an alliance between the Christian Democrats and the Mafia, and the subsequent pillaging of many Sicilian cities. The most obvious case was Palermo itself, where a joint venture came into being uniting Mafia, business, and politics.

The pillage of Palermo and other cities consisted of nothing less than the systematic violation of planning regulations in ways that enabled Mafia businesses to profit from building permits. In only a few years, the once beautiful city of Palermo was defiled and ruined. The mayor, Salvo Lima, and the councilor in charge of public works, Vito Ciancimino, both Christian Democrats and members of the Mafia, gutted the center of the city, knocking down old palaces and Art Nouveau villas, replacing them with tower blocks. Parks were cemented over and suburbs became concrete jungles. In the brief period from the late 1950s to the early 1960s, the city utterly changed character.

The Mafia became more deeply entrenched in Sicilian politics during these years, their influence based on a system of contracts and sub-contracts which included not only building permits but also public contracts for the maintenance of roads and drainage systems, as well as the contracts for garbage collection. Everything was now controlled by an emergent Mafia bourgeoisie—a new class of lawyers, businessmen, professionals, and politicians—working in collaboration with the armed Mafia. It was, in effect, the systematic plundering of an entire city.

ABOVE After a career dedicated to reform and solidarity in the post-war Italian government, Aldo Moro was kidnapped in 1978 and killed 54 days later and left in a car in Rome.

ABOVE The Regaleali Vineyards, in one of the coldest inland parts of Sicily, had been producing wines since 1830, but became much more profitable once the American market opened up.

PALERMO

GRAND HÔTEL
& DES PALMES

I.R.E.S. Palermo

ABOVE The Grand Hôtel et Des Palmes in Palermo, Sicily, was chosen as the meeting place for American Mafia bosses in October 1957.

MEETING OF THE BOSSES

During the 1950s, while a compliant political system turned a blind eye, the Mafia began to re-organize. In October 1957, the American **Mafia's** most important bosses visited Palermo, staying in the luxurious Grand Hôtel et des Palmes for a few days. They had not come to Palermo simply to meet their old friends and cousins. They were up to something, but the Italian state authorities seemed not to notice, or did not realize that the meeting in Palermo was set to launch an important new phase of expansion for the Sicilian Mafia.

Now President of the United States, Dwight D. Eisenhower had been commander of one of the two Allied armies that landed in Sicily in June, 1943. He had been present when Italian *Mafiosi* liberated from prison had proclaimed themselves anti-fascists and were duly rewarded by the Allied army with positions of power. Now, thanks to their efforts, the president had a serious

drug problem to resolve. Every year, increasing numbers of young Americans, almost all under 21 years of age, were dying from heroin addiction, and since the drug was supplied by the American **Mafia**, Italo-Americans had become the greatest enemy of the United States government. The country's youth was being cut down and the situation had to be dealt with urgently.

In 1956, to help combat the problem, the *Narcotics Control Act* was passed by the US Congress. This allowed American courts to hand out severe sentences to anyone involved in drug trafficking. It therefore became too risky for the Mafia in America to deal directly in heroin. A solution to the problem had to be found—one that would save part of the lucrative income from the heroin trade. The American **Mafia** decided to hand over exclusive rights to drug importation into the United States to their Sicilian cousins. This was formally agreed at the Grand Hôtel in 1957.

Cosa Nostra

The Sicilian Mafia consisted of a loose group of bosses, with no pyramidal structure. Their American confreres realized that such a structure had to be established so as to improve communications within the organization and enable them to negotiate with a more compact body, so they instructed their Sicilian cousins to group various neighboring families into districts. Each district would elect a member to represent it on a Commission. This Commission, which was to have an arbitrating role in any conflicts between families, at once became a key center of Mafia power. The "Honored Society" had evolved into *Cosa Nostra* following the lines of its American brothers.

Drug trafficking was not yet the most lucrative part of Mafia business. This was still represented by the building sector, which was a better source of income for the urban Mafia. The main Mafia families in the suburbs and the province of Palermo therefore formed an alliance and began a war against their urban counterparts. In 1962 and 1963, several cars were blown up, and the *lupara*—a sawn-off shotgun, the weapon traditionally used by the rural Mafia—was replaced by the more modern and lethal Kalashnikov.

In 1963, a bomb placed in a housing estate in Palermo, intended to murder the Mafia boss Salvatore Greco, exploded unexpectedly, killing seven police. The killings forced the Italian state to act. Shedding its inertia and breaking its silence to placate public opinion, large contingents of the police and army were dispatched to Sicily, mainly as a government face-saver. As always, the state only actively opposed the Mafia in an emergency.

A parliamentary commission of enquiry into the Mafia was set up, but proceeded so slowly that years passed before it reached any conclusion and, while the results it produced were commendable, they arrived much too late. By then *Cosa Nostra* had profoundly transformed its operations.

ABOVE A worker in the Beretta Factory in Italy inspects a batch of 300,000 92F Beretta guns, used across the world.

Mafia hits and mass trials
⊕ Bomb kills seven police, 1963
⊕ Sites of Mafia trials, 1969

BELOW The early Italian gun called the *lupara* remained in use until the 1960s. The intricate engraving is typical of Italian workmanship.

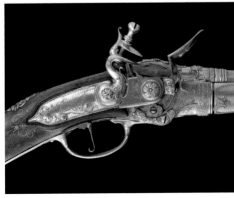

ABOVE Together with his wife and their driver, General Carlo Alberto Dalla Chiesa, Prefect of Palermo, was killed in 1982 on the orders of Mafia boss Salvatore Riina.

Internal Conflicts

The Sicilian *Cosa Nostra* had to wait until the late 1970s before drug trafficking began to produce serious monetary gains. The internal conflicts of 1962–1963 had weakened the organization considerably. Many bosses or important *Mafiosi* had fled abroad and those who remained had to reckon with constant police repression in the crackdown that followed in the wake of the bungled bombing of 1963.

In 1969, however, at two trials held in Catanzaro and Bari, most of the Mafia members responsible for a series of murders that had turned the streets of Palermo into a gangland were acquitted due to lack of evidence. At the same time, in the United States, the Nixon administration declared a "war on drugs" and succeeded in closing down the processing laboratories in Marseilles. Consequently, these laboratories were moved to Sicily, and in the early 1970s the Sicilian Mafia began to make vast profits. They now controlled nearly all stages in the business of trafficking—from the importation of opium, to its processing, and exportation to the United States. The Sicilians found themselves handling quantities of cash they had never before seen.

Murder and Mayhem

By 1981, increasing rivalries over money caused a revolt in the Commission and resulted in a series of murders within the families. In the same period, many figures involved in combating the Mafia were assassinated. Journalists, judges, prosecutors, policemen, and politicians were murdered. Those killed included much-esteemed personalities such as the Prefect of Palermo, Dalla Chiesa, the city's Chief Prosecutor Rocco Chinnici, and Pio La Torre, the politician who proposed a law—approved after his funeral—enabling the state to confiscate property in the hands of the Mafia and to pass sentence on those convicted of Mafia associations. In 1982, more than 140 years after its creation, the Italian state finally recognized Mafia membership as a crime.

Collaboration

ABOVE Luciano Liggio, former head of the Corleonesi clan, conducted his own defence during the Mass Trial of 1986.

The only means of counterattack left to the defeated *Mafiosi* was to collaborate with the law, breaking *Cosa Nostra's* fundamental rule of silence. Meanwhile, following the death of Rocco Chinnici, an anti-Mafia group had been set up in Palermo consisting

of a small group of trustworthy prosecutors who exchanged and coordinated information. The structure of *Cosa Nostra* was now opposed by that of the anti-Mafia group.

Mass Trial

As a result of the unprecedented phenomenon of collaboration, first by Buscetta then by two others, a mass trial of Mafia bosses became possible. This trial began in 1986 and ended in 1992 with the convicted receiving life sentences. During the trial however, a scandal emerged. When Caponnetto's term of service as head of the anti-Mafia pool came to an end, the Magistrates' Governing Council—officially independent of the executive administration but in fact greatly influenced by political parties—decided not to replace him with his natural successor, Giovanni Falcone. Instead, they installed another more senior magistrate who had no experience in the fight against the Mafia. The anti-Mafia group was effectively dismantled in the middle of the trial.

To rectify this serious loss of credibility, the Italian government appointed Falcone to an important position in Rome coordinating the fight against all organized crime. The sentences resulting from the mass trial were confirmed early in 1992. The Courts of Justice in Rome upheld the first sentence of the tribunal in Palermo, made in 1987, thus overturning the appeal judgment of 1991.

The legal system thereby endorsed Buscetta's evidence that *Cosa Nostra* has an oligarchic structure controlled by a Commission that directs its operations.

ABOVE In 1985, in Naples, 640 members of the urban Neapolitan *Camorra* stood trial in what used to be the soccer field of the Poggioreale prison. Three hundred lawyers and more than a thousand policemen attended this trial.

Mass Trial Aftermath

The heads of *Cosa Nostra* who were still at large attempted to interfere with the trial, but were unsuccessful. They sought help from the Sicilian politician Salvo Lima, urging him to corrupt the proceedings, but he paid with his life. He was killed in March 1992, just two weeks after the sentence was announced. A few weeks later the Mafia murdered their greatest enemy, Giovanni Falcone. Great change was taking place in Italy at the time and within a year it led to the disappearance from the political scene of the two parties that had dominated politics since the war—the Christian Democrats and the Socialists. *Cosa Nostra* in Sicily found itself without political support. Earlier in 1989, with the fall of the Berlin Wall, the Italian Communist Party had also disbanded. Defeated in the mass trial, the Mafia had also lost its role as an anti-communist force.

Bombings

After the assassination of Falcone in May 1992, the Italian state instructed Mario Mori, a colonel in the Special Operations Task Force of the *Carabinieri*, to initiate negotiations with *Cosa Nostra*. Mori asked the Mafia politician Vito Ciancimino, who was in Rome at the time under house arrest, to contact those heads of *Cosa Nostra* who were still in hiding. At the same time, the investigating magistrate Paolo Borsellino began to fear for his life, speaking to his family of the time "when they kill me." His fears were well founded: He was murdered on July 19, 1992. The gelignite that killed him came from the north of Italy, not from Sicily, and the remote control that detonated the bomb was of a type used by the secret services. Placed in front of the house where his mother lived, it also killed five members of his escort. Their relatives refused state funerals. When the five policemen of the escort were buried, the people of Palermo attacked the politicians, holding them responsible for the deaths.

Change of Leadership

In 1993, the head of *Cosa Nostra*, Salvatore (Totò) Riina, was arrested. Bernardo Provenzano took control and the bombs continued to explode, but now in the rest of Italy. The Mafia demanded that both the protection scheme for informers and hard labor for *Mafiosi*—introduced just a year before in 1992—should be annulled and urged that the mass trial be reviewed.

At the same time, with a new political era about to begin—Silvio Berlusconi announced his decision to enter politics.

During a football match between Lazio and Udine at Rome's Olympic Stadium, an attack failed when the remote control did not detonate a car bomb located near the security guards just outside the stadium. Following this failure, *Cosa Nostra* changed strategy, and since that time the Italian media has paid little attention to the Mafia with only its armed branch being discussed or referred to in news reports.

RIGHT A devoted father and husband, Salvatore Riina, head of the *Corleonesi* and later *Cosa Nostra*, lived by the philosophy that if a man's finger hurt, it was best to cut his arm off, just to make sure.

Riina's Rise

Salvatore (Totò) Riina, often referred to (though never to his face) as the "The Beast" or "The Short One," was born on November 16, 1930, in Corleone. While still a young boy, his father and brother were killed by an explosion as they tried to remove the gunpowder from an unexploded American bomb. He came into contact with the criminal Luciano Liggio, also from Corleone, and began to steal and collect protection money from farm laborers, thus beginning his life of crime. He spent six years in prison for killing a young man who, during a game of bowls, accused him of killing all his cattle. When he was released, he set up a clandestine slaughterhouse.

Working in the shadow of Liggio, Riina helped to extend the power and influence of the Corleone Mafia. However, he was again arrested for involvement in the violent events stemming from the Mafia's internal feud in 1962–1963. Released from prison in 1969, he was again indicted for murder but went into hiding, and when Liggio was imprisoned for murder in 1974, Riina became head of the Corleonesi.

The Brains Behind the Organization

During the 1970s, the most important Mafia families of Palermo concentrated on the enormous, easy earnings to be derived from the trafficking of drugs. Salvatore Riina was responsible for the idea of burying syringes, pointing upward, their needles infected with AIDS, in the sandy beach at Rimini, a famous tourist resort. Meanwhile, the Mafia of Corleone depended on kidnapping to finance itself and to prepare its takeover of *Cosa Nostra*.

Unknown to his allies, Riina organized a private army and established contacts with various Mafia families in order to isolate and destroy his rivals. In 1981, he launched his attack on the Palermo Mafia, killing two of the most important Mafia bosses within two weeks and seizing control of *Cosa Nostra* in a surprise coup. Over the next two years he hunted down and exterminated the armed gangsters of rival families. Some changed sides,

BELOW Salvatore Riina's sons have carried on the family business. In 2002, Giuseppe was imprisoned for his Mafia-related activities, but in February 2008 he was released on a technicality.

He who doesn't fear death dies only once.

Giovanni Falcone (1939–1992), Italian magistrate investigating the Mafia in Sicily

joining the victors, very few managed to escape, and many were assassinated. So great was the carnage that it led many to collaborate with the forces of justice, so that one result of Riina's rampage was that the mass trial of Mafia bosses was made possible.

The Mafia counterattacked in Sicily first, killing the investigating magistrates Falcone and Borsellino. Sadly today the Italian media have completely forgotten these murders. The brains behind this operation—a direct frontal attack on the state to force it into a deal and end its battle against *Cosa Nostra*—was Riina. Early in 1993, however, he was betrayed and arrested. Convicted of over 100 counts of murder and with assets worth over $125 million seized by the state, he is still in jail.

ABOVE This anti-Mafia demonstration in Palermo, on June 28, 1992 would have been unthinkable at other times in Sicily's history. The banner remembers some of those killed by the Mafia over the years.

American Mafia
A Nationwide Network

Following World War II, the United States began to look at its internal structure, and the Mafia and all forms of organized crime became the focus of politicians and special commissions.

Kefauver Committee Hearings

In 1950 and 1951, Senator Carey Estes Kefauver, chairman of a special committee assigned to investigate gangster activity in interstate commerce, conducted a series of hearings across the United States. Those hearings were broadcast on the new medium of television. By taking his inquiries into 14 of the nation's most populous cities via television into living rooms across the land, Kefauver both literally and figuratively brought home his point about the American underworld: "The tentacles of organized crime reach into virtually every community throughout the country."

The Kefauver Committee revealed connections among the nation's organized crime groups at a time when the nation's top law enforcement officer, FBI Director J. Edgar Hoover, insisted there was no such thing as a nationwide network of criminals.

Gambling

The Kefauver Committee discovered that known racketeers from New York, Detroit, Philadelphia, Chicago, and other major cities frequently gathered together in Florida. Through subpoenaed business records, it learned that gangsters such as Joe Adonis and Meyer Lansky of New York held interests in Florida gambling houses. Adonis, Frank Costello, and racketeers from other cities also were seen working together on gambling ventures in Saratoga, New York. Similar cooperation was seen in Louisiana, where Costello, Phil Kastel, and Meyer Lansky's brother Jake worked with New Orleans crime boss Carlos Marcello in the Beverly Club casino. The committee found many of the same underworld figures lurked behind front men who ran casinos in Las Vegas.

Within New York City, the underworld held major interests in slot machines, bookmaking, and numbers, protected by corrupt authorities. Gambling was also a major underworld enterprise in Kansas City, where an Italian-Jewish combination supervised various rackets.

In Philadelphia and Detroit, organized crime and its political allies ran efficient numbers operations. With cooperation from local authorities, Tampa's Mafia ran a variation on the numbers racket known as Bolita. In Cleveland, another alliance of Italian-Jewish gangs

SENATOR KEFAUVER

Senator Carey Kefauver was born July 26, 1903, on a farm in rural Tennessee. Few locations were more distant from the growing Mafia clans of America's large cities. Carey Kefauver earned his bachelor's degree from the University of Tennessee at Knoxville and then headed east. He graduated in 1927 from Yale University Law School in New Haven, before returning to Tennessee to practice law.

On September 13, 1939, he was selected to fill a Congressional vacancy caused by the death of Democrat Sam McReynolds. Kefauver was reelected to the House of Representatives four times. He ran for the US Senate in 1948, and won the election as a reformer. He was lauded for his even-handed and thorough committee investigation of racketeering. He ran unsuccessfully for US President in 1952 and in 1956. He was reelected to the Senate twice. Kefauver died in 1963 after suffering a heart attack on the Senate floor.

administered widespread casino-style gambling and also invested in Nevada gaming establishments. Chicago gangsters oversaw betting parlors, slot machines, numbers, horse and dog-racing tracks as well as the wire service racket across the country.

BELOW New Jersey racketeer Willie Moretti lies in his own blood after being shot. He was a longtime friend of rackets kingpin Joe Adonis and his brother, Sal.

Narcotics

The Kefauver Committee uncovered evidence of a highly organized network of narcotics smugglers. Testimony pointed to exiled American Mafia boss, Charlie Luciano, as the overlord of heroin traffickers. Evidence suggested that Tommy Penocchio, an aide to Luciano in New York, had a role in the import of marijuana through Mexico.

Corruption

Most significantly, the committee found that organized criminals tended to corrupt law enforcement agencies, using bribery and political pressure to keep their illicit enterprises free of police interference. The wire service racket alone made political contributions totaling hundreds of thousands of dollars each year, giving it great influence among elected officials.

Corruption reached beyond local police forces. The committee learned that state and federal governments were involved. In one case, officials of the Internal Revenue Service had been bribed.

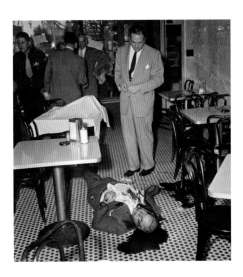

ABOVE Joseph "Socks" Lanza was convicted of extortion at New York's Fulton Fish Market. It was one of many offences revealed in Senate hearings.

The Mob's Worst Year

The American Mafia's Golden Age came to an abrupt end in 1957. The Mafia had grown virtually unchecked from the end of Prohibition, as J. Edgar Hoover and the FBI denied its existence. However, the criminal network and its allies were exposed in 1957 as never before, and Hoover was compelled to recognize it and to join the fight against it.

Socks Lanza

Early in February 1957, a career racketeer named Joseph "Socks" Lanza was picked up on a parole violation in Eastchester, New York. There seemed no question that Lanza had broken parole restrictions by associating with known gangsters from waste hauling, newspaper delivery, and waterfront rackets. However, New York state legislators had plenty of questions when Lanza was not immediately sent back to prison. An investigation revealed that Lanza had strong connections to political bosses in the city. It was just the first of many Mafia-related revelations to reach the American public in 1957.

Teamsters

A committee led by Senator John McClellan of Arkansas and aided by legal counsel Robert Kennedy, explored racketeering within the leadership of the Teamsters union. The committee found that Teamsters President, Dave Beck, had profited from his position. In the summer of 1957, Beck was charged with grand larceny, tax evasion, and falsifying union documents. But Beck's wrongdoing proved to be the tip of the iceberg.

The McClellan Committee established that Teamsters Vice President, James Hoffa of Detroit, had extensive ties to organized crime figures across the country and had worked with New York mobsters to create phony locals in an effort to seize control of the union's top office. In July, Hoffa went on trial for attempting to purchase the McClellan Committee's secret files. A jury acquitted Hoffa, but his reputation was damaged. McClellan and Kennedy publicly outlined his links to Lucchese Crime Family members. Despite their efforts, he was elected successor to Beck in October.

High-Profile Hits

Frank Costello, leader of the powerful New York Crime Family, was nearly killed by an assassin's bullet on May 2, 1957. The attempted murder was big news, as authorities believed Costello underboss Vito Genovese had decided he should be boss.

Another attack, also reportedly initiated by Genovese, occurred when Frank Scalise, underboss to Genovese arch-rival Albert Anastasia, was selecting some fruit

> *The FBI didn't know anything, really, about these people who were the major gangsters in the United States. That was rather a shock to me.*
>
> Robert Kennedy after asking for information on Apalachin convention gangsters from the FBI.

from a Bronx market and two men shot him dead. In October, Albert Anastasia was murdered in a Manhattan barbershop. Authorities learned of his rivalry with Genovese and his efforts to establish a casino in Havana, Cuba. They heard that Anastasia had argued with Santo Trafficante, boss in Tampa and Havana, and his aide Joseph Silesi.

Apalachin Convention

New York State Police crashed a party at the Apalachin residence of former bootlegger Joseph Barbara on November 14, 1957. Dozens of *Mafiosi* from all over the country poured out of the home. The police gathered and identified them, encountering such gangland big shots as Vito Genovese, Carlo Gambino, and Joseph Profaci of New York; John LaRocca and Michael Genovese of Pittsburgh; Santo Trafficante Jr. and Joseph Silesi of Havana; Nicholas Civella of Kansas City; and John Scalish of Cleveland. Nearly all indicated that they had traveled there to visit Barbara, who had been ailing. Though the police knew that was false, they had no reason to hold them and all were released. The underworld convention became a media sensation and a huge embarrassment for Hoover as it established that a nationwide network of *Mafiosi* did exist.

BELOW From left, Pat McNamara, Barry Goldwater, John McClellan and counsel Robert Kennedy, members of the Labor Rackets Committee, listen to testimony.

1971 Joe Colombo is shot and killed in New York at the end of Italian-American Unity Day parade.

1984 The FBI brings charges against 11 members of the Colombo Crime Family.

1985 Paul Castellano is killed on orders from John Gotti, who then takes control of the Mafia.

1997 Global Stragegies Group, a brokerage firm in San Francisco, establishes loans with the Gambino Crime Family to stay afloat. It is closed down in 1998 by the FBI.

1999 John Gotti Jr. pleads guilty to racketeering and extortion. He gets a six-year sentence.

FBI Joins the Fight

The Apalachin revelations of 1957 forced FBI Director J. Edgar Hoover to admit to the existence of a nationwide criminal network and to allocate resources to fight it. Hoover, who was personally more interested in fighting the spread of communism, had long dismissed the idea that crime was organized on anything more than a local or regional scale.

Hoover suddenly found himself in the uncomfortable position of having to play catch-up. Larger state and municipal police forces, the Federal Bureau of Narcotics, the US Postal Inspection Service, and the US Secret Service had already recognized interstate links among Mafia criminals.

Narcotics Bureau Commissioner Harry Anslinger, a rival bureaucrat to Hoover, had been particularly outspoken on the subject. In the wake of the underworld's Apalachin conference, US Senate inquiries found that the FBI had files on only a few of the attendees. And most of those files were no more than collected newspaper clippings. Anslinger's agency, however, had extensive information on all of the attendees.

Top Hoodlum Program

Within two weeks of the Apalachin conference, Hoover instituted the Top Hoodlum Program. Under that program, FBI field offices across the country were instructed to list the more powerful racketeers in their regions and to allocate manpower and other resources to acquire information on those racketeers.

Most field offices responded eagerly to the new marching orders. Chicago's FBI had been used to acquire a good deal of information on Al Capone and other leaders of organized crime in the "Windy City." The Top Hoodlum Program energized that office. However, some FBI offices continued to deny the Mafia's existence. The field office in New Orleans, home of the earliest Mafia presence in the United States, insisted that there were no known racketeers to place on its Top Hoodlum list.

J. EDGAR HOOVER

J. Edgar Hoover began his association with the FBI in 1919, when the Justice Department agency was known simply as the Bureau of Investigation. The 24-year-old Hoover was appointed to lead a new Anti-Radical Division within the Bureau. He was also given the title of Special Assistant to the Attorney General. While William Flynn was Bureau chief, by virtue of a dual role in the Justice Department, Hoover answered directly to Attorney General Alexander Palmer.

Young Hoover took an active role in the deportation of alien communists rounded up in the Palmer Raids. At the same time, he revolutionized the Bureau's filing system, allowing for the easy tracking of suspected criminals and anti-American individuals and groups.

In 1921, the new administration of Warren Harding cleaned house at the Justice Department, removing all of Palmer's men except Hoover, who was appointed Assistant Chief of the Bureau. Hoover's promotion to Bureau Chief followed in 1924. He continued to serve in that role within eight Presidential administrations, for just over 48 years, until his death in 1972.

J. Edgar Hoover gives testimony before a Senate Internal Security Subcommittee probe in 1953. Because of his lengthy and controversial tenure in the role as Director of the FBI, current incumbents are limited to a 10-year term of office.

Mafia Monograph

In 1957, Hoover also ordered his Bureau to assemble all available knowledge related to the Mafia into a single document. The resulting two-volume *Mafia Monograph* explored the criminal network's evolution from its legendary beginnings in Sicily, through trans-Atlantic immigration, to the crime families known to exist in the 1950s.

Among the document's conclusions was a clear statement on the existence of the Mafia criminal network: "Available evidence shows that beyond a shadow of a doubt, the Mafia does exist today in the United States, as well as in Sicily and Italy, as a vicious, evil, and tyrannical form of organized criminality."

Backpedaling

The FBI director was not entirely happy with his hasty responses to the Apalachin conference. In 1958, he temporarily cut back the Top Hoodlum Program. He also suppressed the *Mafia Monograph* document, which directly contradicted many of his former assertions regarding organized crime.

Weapons of the FBI

With Hoover's commitment to the fight against organized crime, American racketeers suddenly had to deal with an impressive array of FBI tools and techniques. Those included wiretapping, electronic surveillance, the development of informants, and infiltration of target groups. All had been honed over decades of FBI use in the war against communism. The new tools permitted law enforcement a greater understanding of organized crime and allowed for the words and actions of the racketeers to be used as evidence against them.

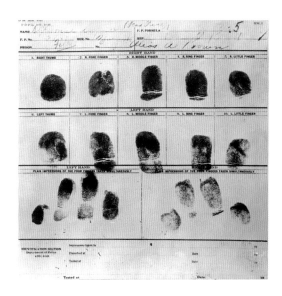

ABOVE Philadelphia police records show Al Capone's fingerprints, taken when he was arrested, with his bodyguard, for carrying a concealed weapon.

The Move into Cuba

The American Mafia invested heavily in Cuban gambling operations in the 1940s and 1950s. Using Meyer Lansky and Santo Trafficante Jr. as middlemen, the mob channeled millions of dollars into casino projects, racetracks, and nightclubs in and around the Cuban capital of Havana. The intensely corrupt administration of Cuba's Fulgencio Batista welcomed mob investments and under-the-table payments that went with them.

Mafia Influence

Batista's control of the island became evident in 1933, when he led a successful coup. Batista manipulated a series of puppet rulers until 1940, when he won election as president. He immediately was embraced by both American gangsters and American anti-communists. Batista was voted out of office in 1945, as former President Ramon Grau briefly returned to power.

The American Mafia remained influential during Grau's term. New York Mafia boss Charlie Luciano, deported from the United States to Italy in February 1946, showed up in Havana in October. By the end of December, it was clear that Luciano intended to remain involved in Mafia affairs from a Cuban base just 90 miles (145 km) from Florida. The United States pressured Cuba to send Luciano back across the Atlantic. Only after the United States cut off medicine exports did Cuba accede to the demand. In March 1947, Luciano was put on a steamship bound for Europe.

Batista returned to island politics in 1948, winning a seat in the Cuban Senate. When his candidacy in the 1952 presidential election appeared doomed, he staged another coup. Through the suspension of personal and press liberties and strong opposition to the labor movement, Batista acted as a dictator.

ABOVE Actor George Raft (right) had many gangster acquaintances. He even testified on behalf of friend "Bugsy" Siegel, charged with bookmaking.

BELOW Entering court to testify before a grand jury, Santo Trafficante Jr., crime boss, raises his hands in innocence. He controlled crime in Florida and Cuba.

Casinos

In 1952, upon regaining governmental power, Batista announced tax incentives for casino construction and passed legislation easing casino requirements. He sought to make Havana a tourist mecca and to free Cuba of its economic reliance on sugar exports. Meyer Lansky promptly set to work building the 21-story Riviera hotel and casino in Havana. The facility was opened in 1956.

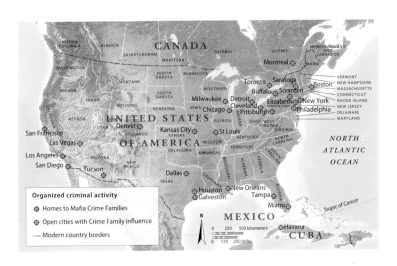

The following year, Santo Trafficante Jr.—already partnered with Pittsburgh *Mafiosi* in the ownership of the Sans Souci nightclub—opened his own Hotel Capri. Actor George Raft, old chum of racketeer Benjamin Siegel, held a share of the Capri. Trafficante also owned the Comodoro hotel and controlled the Deauville. Lansky and Trafficante associate Joe Silesi became a major figure in the Havana Hilton. Hotel and casino investments were jealously guarded. Shortly after New York big shot Albert Anastasia attempted to circumvent Lansky-Trafficante control to open his own casino, Anastasia was shot to death inside a Manhattan barber shop.

Havana became the playground of the Western Hemisphere, catering to an upper-class clientele. However, the glitz and glamor of Havana's nightlife masked the poverty of many Cuban nationals.

Revolution

Cuban revolutionaries including Fidel Castro were jailed in 1953 after storming the military barracks in Santiago, Cuba. Two years later, Batista released Castro, who fled to Mexico to reorganize his forces. Batista's despotic reign fueled opposition. A failed coup attempt prompted Batista to imprison many of his best military leaders just as Castro was leading a new revolutionary force onto the southern portion of the island.

Uncertain of the future, the American Mafia hedged its bets and began supplying funds and arms to both sides of the conflict. At the end of 1958, Batista's depleted military was on the verge of collapse. The dictator formally resigned his position on New Year's Day 1959 and went into exile in the Dominican Republic.

Gangsters Left Behind

Meyer Lansky also departed from Cuba, leaving his brother Jake, along with Trafficante, to look after the casinos. As Castro forces took the capital a week later, the casinos, hotels, and nightclubs all were closed down. However, Castro made no immediate move against racketeers in Havana.

In May, Cuban police arrested Riviera manager Jake Lansky, Tropicana casino boss Giuseppe DiGiorgio, and several other men, charging them all with being part of a large drug trafficking conspiracy. In June, Trafficante was arrested, also for suspected involvement with narcotics. Eventually, the imprisoned racketeers were all forced to leave the island.

Lost investment

In 1959 and 1960, Castro's government seized the casinos and luxury resorts. The Mafia's investment was lost. On the Riviera project alone, the US underworld is believed to have sacrificed $8 million USD.

BELOW The Riviera Hotel in Havana, Cuba, was built by Meyer Lansky, turning Havana into a gambling mecca. Castro seized all assets on assuming power.

CELLULOID MAFIA

The Godfather Trilogy

ABOVE The famous wedding scene from *The Godfather* shows the close-knit ties of a Mafia family. Marlon Brando, with red rose, stands next to the bride's mother.

This trilogy of movies, based on the imaginary Corleone family, has become the iconic celluloid representation of the Mafia. Spanning decades of interconnected family and crime, they form the basis of what most people think of as Mafia.

From Novel to Film

Mario Puzo's iconic 1969 novel, *The Godfather*, about the Italian Mafia in New York during the early twentieth century, jumped onto the New York Times Best Seller List and stayed there for months. Before long, the book was turned into a film directed by Francis Ford Coppola, who won Academy Awards for *The Godfather*, Parts 1 and II and nominations for Part III.

Never hate your enemies. It clouds your judgment.

Michael Corleone, The Godfather (1972)

The Godfather (1972)

The Godfather is the first in the trilogy about an Italian family led by the migrant Don Vito Corleone (Marlon Brando). The story traces the family's inner turmoils and tragedies, and its relationships with the mob in a young America. In this first part of the story, the so-far innocent young Michael Corleone (Al Pacino) is dragged into the bloody family business when his father is critically wounded by rival gangsters who want to start selling drugs in New York— against Corleone policy.

The Godfather Part II (1974)

This is both a sequel to the original and a prologue. The two storylines are told in parallel and follow the life of Michael Corleone (Al Pacino) as the now firmly established head of the Corleone Crime Family. As he struggles with an attempt on his life and trying to legitimize the family business, the film details the early years of his father Vito Corleone—here played by Robert De Niro—as he flees Italy after the murder of his parents by a local mob boss.

The Godfather Part III (1990)

In this final chapter, the Corleone family is at the height of its power. It is 1979 and the family trust, headed by Michael Corleone (Al Pacino) and daughter Mary (Sofia Coppola, daughter of the director), enters into negotiations with the Catholic Church to take controlling interest in their real estate holdings company, The Immobiliare. Unfortunately for Michael, other families want in on the deal. Once again fearing for his family, Michael turns to his nephew, Vincent Mancini (Andy Garcia) to help him deal with the situation, at the same time dealing with Vincent's forbidden love for his daughter Mary.

ABOVE Jack Woltz (John Marley), movie mogul, wakes to find the severed head of his beloved stallion in his bed, retribution for defying Mafia demands.

OSCAR QUIRKS

Marlon Brando and Robert De Niro played Don Vito Corleone in *The Godfather* and *The Godfather Part II* respectively, both winning an Academy Award for playing the same character—unique in the history of the Oscars.

Nino Rota's score for *The Godfather* was first nominated but then removed from 1973 Academy Award nominees when it was discovered that he had previously used the same theme in Eduardo De Filippo's 1958 comedy, *Fortunella*. Although in the earlier film the theme was played in a brisk, staccato, and comedic style, the melody was the same. Despite this, Nino Rota, with Carmine Coppola, won the 1974 Oscar for the Best Music, Original Dramatic Score, with their work on *The Godfather Part II*, although it featured the same theme that made the 1972 score ineligible.

Marlon Brando (left) and Robert De Niro in a scene from the movie, *The Score* (2001). Both known for their acting excellence, they played the same role of Don Vito Corleone in *The Godfather* trilogy.

TRAITOR TO THE MOB

Raised in East Harlem, Joseph Valachi fell under the influence of Ciro Terranova. After his 1928 release from prison, Valachi established relationships with mobsters including Tom Gagliano, a group leader in the Bronx crime family of Gaetano Reina who quietly opposed Terranova and Mafia boss of bosses Giuseppe Masseria.

At the conclusion of the Castellammarese War in 1931, Valachi moved to a crime family controlled by Charlie Luciano and his underboss Vito Genovese. Genovese assumed control of the old Luciano organization in 1957.

In 1960, Genovese was sentenced to 15 years in prison. Valachi joined his boss in Atlanta Federal Penitentiary in February 1962, sentenced to 20 years for drug trafficking. Narcotics agents advised Valachi that Genovese was preparing to have him killed and, sure of the inmate assigned to end his life, Valachi beat the man to death. Valachi was now facing murder charges as well and the threat of being slain in prison. He decided to talk to authorities in a quest for leniency and protection. He spoke with narcotics agents and later with the FBI, using the term *"cosa nostra"* to refer to the Mafia. While the term—translated "our thing"—represented an effort to refer to the Mafia in Italian without naming it, in FBI hands, the term became a proper noun, *"La Cosa Nostra."* Valachi testified before Senator John McClellan's committee in 1963 revealing three decades of bloody Mafia history.

Mafia rat, Joseph Valachi, was the first person to openly use the words *"cosa nostra"* to describe the Mafia. He turned state's evidence after his prison term turned sour and he was faced with additional murder charges. His 30 years as part of the family made him an excellent informer.

ABOVE Joe Colombo and his son taking part in the 1970 pickets outside FBI headquarters against Italian bias.

Commission Wars

Aside from the imprisonment and deportation of boss Charlie Luciano, the Mafia Commission membership remained stable from the early 1930s until the 1950s. After that, changes came quickly, particularly to the five major New York families. Vincent Mangano disappeared in 1951 and was succeeded by Albert Anastasia. In 1953, Tom Gagliano, who took over the old Reina Family, was succeeded by Tommy Lucchese. Frank Costello, who had been looking after Luciano Family interests during Luciano's exile, was forced to surrender control to Vito Genovese in 1957. Upon Anastasia's assassination in the same year, Carlo Gambino took control.

Gallo-Profaci War

About 1960, "Crazy Joe" Gallo and his allies started to pull away from the crime family led by Joseph Profaci, an original Mafia Commission member. Their rebellion was encouraged by Carlo Gambino's and Tommy Lucchese's organizations. Profaci's death of natural causes in 1962 brought his brother-in-law Joseph Magliocco to power.

Colombo's Ascension

With assistance from Joseph "Joe Bananas" Bonanno— the last of the original Mafia Commission members—Magliocco began plotting against Gambino and Lucchese. A trusted Magliocco aide, Joseph Colombo, turned coat and informed the Commission of his boss's plans. Magliocco withdrew from the leadership and died of a heart attack in 1963. The Mafia Commission placed Colombo in command of the Profaci Family.

The Banana Wars

Implicated in Magliocco's plotting, Bonanno separated himself from the Mafia Commission and other crime families and confided in his cousin, Buffalo boss Stefano Magaddino, that he was considering retirement. Seizing on this, Bonanno opponents encouraged one of his underlings, Gaspar DeGregorio, to take over as the crime family's new leader.

On October 20, 1964, Bonanno was to appear before a grand jury but he never showed up. According to his autobiography, he was kidnapped by Magaddino, who attempted to convince him to abdicate. Magaddino eventually let Bonanno go. Now fearing an underworld conspiracy, as well as the wrath of prosecutors, Bonanno hid himself in Tucson, Arizona. During Bonanno's short absence from New York, his crime family broke into warring factions. The press dubbed the resulting conflict, "The Banana Wars." In a series of skirmishes, Bonanno's son, Salvatore, battled a faction led by DiGregorio and supported by Magaddino, Colombo, and the rest of the Mafia Commission. After a further absence, Joseph Bonanno reappeared in May 1966, and was charged with failing to appear before a grand jury and was released on bail. He sent word that he intended to retire, but would remain in New York until the conflict within his organization was ended. Mafia Commission support for DiGregorio melted away. By 1970, outside meddling in the Bonanno organization ended, and Bonanno entered a semi-retirement in Tucson. However, authorities believed Tucson became the operations base for a still busy Bonanno criminal empire.

ABOVE Thomas "Three Finger Brown" Lucchese swears before the Senate Labor Rackets Committee that he is not a member of any Mafia crime syndicate.

MAFIA COMMISSION

Joseph Bonanno said of the Mafia Commission: "We replaced leadership by one man with leadership by committee. We opted for a parliamentary arrangement whereby a group of the most important men in our world would assume the function formerly performed by one man. This group became known as the Commission."

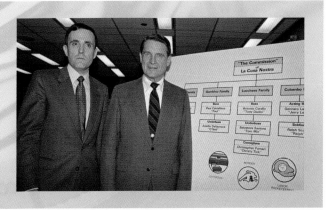

US Attorney General, Rudolph Giuliani (left), and FBI Director, William Webster, reveal the chart of the Mafia Commission hierarchy.

OPPOSITE The funeral of Joseph "Crazy Joe" Gallo, who was gunned down on his 43rd birthday in Manhattan, NY.

Removing a Boss

It quickly became evident to the Mafia Commission that Joseph Colombo did not have the temperament to be a successful Mafia boss. His quest for publicity and his antagonism of law enforcement initially cost him the support of the Mafia Commission and ultimately cost him his life

Profaci Family

In the 1950s, Colombo was welcomed into the Profaci Crime Family. Colombo became an effective enforcer for the underworld clan, but he did not wholeheartedly join in Profaci's fight against the rebellious Gallos. Colombo's links to the Gambino Crime Family continued. Beginning about 1960, Colombo became a real estate salesman for a Brooklyn company run by Gambino associate Anthony Cantalupo.

After Profaci's death in 1962, new boss Joseph Magliocco assigned Colombo to set up the assassinations of rival bosses Gambino and Tommy Lucchese. Rather than perform the hits, Colombo betrayed his superior's intentions to Gambino. Magliocco was forced into retirement. Gambino used his influence over the Mafia Commission to install Colombo as head of the old Profaci Family early in 1964. The appointment caused some resentment in that organization and in other regional Mafia units.

Publicity

Unlike most other crime bosses—certainly unlike his camera-shy mentor Carlo Gambino—Colombo was comfortable with fame. He loudly and publicly protested FBI action against *Mafiosi*, accusing the Bureau of an institutional bias against Italians. When Colombo's son, Joseph Jr., was arrested in spring 1970, Colombo arranged for hundreds of sign-carrying picketers to circle the FBI offices at 69th Street and Third Avenue. The picket was repeated for days. Rather than dissuade the FBI from battling organized crime, the protests drew additional Bureau attention to Colombo and his underworld associates.

Colombo discussed the FBI's alleged anti-Italian bias with the media, even granting an interview to television's Dick Cavett. Playing down his frequent arrests, his ongoing troubles with the IRS, and recently released surveillance tapes confirming his position

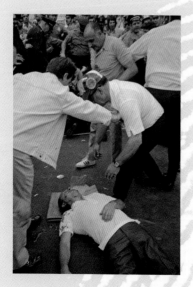

JOE COLOMBO

Colombo was born in Brooklyn in 1923. He grew up in Brooklyn's Gravesend section, not far from Coney Island. While Joe was still a teenager, his father Anthony, a member of the Profaci Crime Family, and his girlfriend were found strangled to death in a car in 1938.

As a young man, Colombo joined the Coast Guard. He served three troubled years, being recorded as absent without leave several times and earning a one-year sentence in a military prison. His prison term was cut short by a diagnosis of a nervous disorder, and Colombo was discharged from the Coast Guard. Colombo then tried his hand at a few occupations, including salesman for a meat company run by the Castellano Family, relatives of Carlo Gambino. It was likely in this period that Colombo became acquainted with Gambino.

Joe Colombo after being shot in the head at the Italian-American Unity parade. He was shot by a black man who in turn was shot by another gunman, probably part of the Gallo Crime Family.

as crime boss, he stated that the FBI created myths about the Mafia and *La Cosa Nostra* in an effort to cast all Italians in an unfavorable light. He founded the Italian-American Civil Rights League, a high-profile group designed to combat any anti-Italian bias. The league quickly grew to 45,000 members across the country. Among the league's other accomplishments, it managed to have the word "Mafia" removed from the 1972 film, *The Godfather*, and from the television series, *The FBI*.

Silenced

Gambino distanced himself from Colombo. When Colombo scheduled an Italian Unity Day for New York's Columbus Circle on June 28, 1971, Gambino ordered his associates to stay away. Less than an hour before the event was to begin, Colombo was shot in the head in front of thousands of witnesses.

His alleged attacker, an African-American man named Jerome Johnson, was then immediately shot to death by another gunman. Police always suspected that Johnson was associated with the Gallo group.

The shooting left Colombo almost completely paralyzed. He spent his remaining years under constant care at his upstate New York vacation residence. In 1975, doctors found that he had control only over two fingers on his right hand. He died of a heart attack May 22, 1978, at age fifty-four.

In April 1972, the underworld caught up with Gallo faction leader "Crazy Joe" Gallo. He was killed by a gunshot to the back during a birthday celebration at Umberto's Clam House on Little Italy's Mulberry Street.

BELOW Joe Colombo (holding sign) minutes before his assassination, as he walks in the Italian Unity Day parade with his son, Anthony, in 1970.

Union Gangs

From the late nineteenth century on, Mafiosi have been linked with longshoremen, laborers, garment workers, seafood workers, restaurant workers, bakers, and other unions. While legislative committees and prosecutors looked into all of those union links, the greatest attention was paid to the International Brotherhood of Teamsters.

That union, comprised mostly of truck drivers, was large, wealthy, and powerful when the Senate's McClellan Committee and its counsel Robert Kennedy first began investigating it in the late 1950s. The focus of that investigation became Teamsters official, James Riddle "Jimmy" Hoffa.

Hoffa

Hoffa had worked his way up from business agent for a Teamsters' local office in Detroit to head of the union's Central States region. In that capacity, he had dealings with mobsters in Detroit, Chicago, and Cleveland. About 1950, Hoffa began to invest heavily in the mob. He approved secret loans from the Central States Teamsters' benefits funds to underworld casino projects.

Underworld Ties

Anthony "Tony Ducks" Corallo and Johnny "Dio" Dioguardi, significant figures in New York's Lucchese Crime Family, helped Hoffa expand his influence into the Eastern Region. Russell Bufalino, boss of the northeastern Pennsylvania Mafia after

ABOVE Teamster boss, Jimmy Hoffa, confronts Robert Kennedy, chief counsel at the Senate Labor Rackets Committee, during hearings in 1958.

BELOW The last issue of the NY *Daily Mirror* hails the testimony of Joe Valachi before the McClellan Committee in 1963.

the 1959 death of Joseph Barbara, worked with Hoffa through his Delaware associate, Frank "the Irishman" Sheeran. Anthony "Tony Pro" Provenzano, a New Jersey-based lieutenant of the Genovese Crime Family, also became a close Hoffa ally.

The racketeers helped create Teamster union "paper locals"—offices of the union that had voting power but no actual membership. Dioguardi reportedly aided the Hoffa cause through wiretapping, acquiring information to use against Hoffa's New York rival, Martin T. Lacey.

Hoffa vs. Kennedy

Teamsters International President Dave Beck departed the union in disgrace at the end of 1957, and Hoffa was elected to lead the Teamsters. In 1960, John F. Kennedy was elected US President, and he appointed his brother Robert, to the post of Attorney General, setting up a major confrontation with the Teamsters boss.

Under Robert Kennedy, the Justice Department vigorously pursued legal action against Hoffa and his Mafia-aligned administration. In 1963, while McClellan Committee counsel, Kennedy was responsible for the disclosures of Joseph Valachi. Hoffa was convicted in 1962 of jury tampering, and in 1964 of improperly manipulating the union pension fund. Hoffa was sentenced to 13 years in federal prison. Between his two convictions, President Kennedy was assassinated in November 1963. Hoffa's lack of grief over the President's death caused five members of his staff to resign.

Hoffa avoided prison through legal appeals until March 1967. Just before starting his sentence in Lewisburg, Pennsylvania, he selected longtime friend, Frank Fitzsimmons, to succeed him as union president. One year after his incarceration, Presidential candidate Robert Kennedy was shot to death after celebrating a primary election victory at the Los Angeles Ambassador Hotel.

Within Lewisburg's penitentiary, Hoffa reportedly met up with one of his allies, Anthony Provenzano, also imprisoned there. The relationship between the two men deteriorated over time, as Hoffa's deep resentment toward the *Mafiosi* who infiltrated his union became evident.

Disappearance

In 1971, President Richard Nixon pardoned Hoffa. The former Teamsters boss was released from prison on the condition that he not engage in any union activity before 1980. Four years after his release, he made an effort to repair his relationships with his old allies. He called for a meeting with Mafia representatives in summer 1975.

In the afternoon of July 30, 1975, Hoffa was seen waiting in the parking lot of the Machus Red Fox restaurant outside of Detroit. He telephoned his wife from a pay phone there at 2:15 p.m., telling her that a planned meeting hadn't occurred. He said he would wait just a few minutes longer.

Jimmy Hoffa was never seen or heard from again.

BLOOD FEUDS

While many underworld conflicts occurred as gangs vied with other gangs for the control of territory and rackets, some conflicts were far more personal. Blood feuds between families could last for years, decades, or even generations.

The Bonanno clan brought along its vendettas when it crossed the Atlantic. The family, and its Magaddino and Bonventre relatives, long had been at war with the Buccellato family. The Bonannos and the Buccellatos were from Castellammare del Golfo, Sicily, and both established colonies in Brooklyn and Detroit. "They were archenemies in Castellammare, and archenemies they remained in Brooklyn," Joseph Bonanno noted in his autobiography. The Bonanno faction eventually emerged victorious after a number of assassinations of Buccellatos. The victory came with a price. With authorities on their trail for one of the killings, two of the Bonanno faction leaders were forced to flee Brooklyn.

Joe Bonanno's son, Salvatore (right), talks to an FBI agent following his arrest. The FBI want to question him regarding his father's alleged kidnapping and he is being held on $25,000 USD bail.

BELOW John Dioguardi being booked after his arrest in 1953. Part of the Lucchese Crime Family, he assisted Hoffa with wiretapping.

The Skim

Casino gambling held enormous attraction for racketeers. Generating a vast amount of relatively small wagers, the income from casino operations was beyond calculation until proceeds were actually collected and counted. Taxable income was the figure produced in casino counting rooms. Money that did not make it into the official count was known as "the skim." It represented untaxed profits for casino operators and their underworld partners.

Before government regulators stepped in, gambling income could be skimmed right in Las Vegas counting rooms, without trickery or subtlety. Gross receipts, the underworld's share, and the figure reported to state and federal tax agencies could be calculated openly. In the early days, Mafia representatives would show up at a gaming establishment, walk right into the counting room and pick up skimmed cash.

As government became wise to skimming and more closely watched the count, racketeers devised different methods to skim profits either outside of counting room doors or right under the noses of officials. One method was to inflate reports of casino losses through fraudulent paperwork. Phony "fill slips," documenting transfers of gambling chips from the cashier's cage to gaming tables, were used for that purpose.

Slot Machines

In 1976, an investigator with the Nevada Gaming Commission discovered that employees at the Stardust Casino were skimming proceeds from coin-operated slot machines. As the machines handled too many coins to be hand counted, the casino calculated their income by weighing the coins. The Nevada official discovered that counting room scales were designed with a secret switch. When the switch was on, scale weights would be lower, undervaluing the worth of the slot machine income and providing untaxed proceeds to the casino operator.

Watching Investments

Over the years, the "Chicago Outfit" sent members to Las Vegas to look after its many investments, particularly the Stardust and Fremont casinos. Johnny Roselli was then appointed to handle the skim and maintain order during the 1950s. By 1960, Roselli had been replaced by Marshall Caifano. Anthony Spilotro, a hotheaded Chicago killer, became the Outfit's man in Vegas in the early 1970s.

The Black Book

In 1960, Nevada gaming authorities attempted to crack down on the Mafia presence in casinos through a "List of Excluded Persons", also known as "the Black Book." That book, including the names, faces, and backgrounds of those deemed threatening to the state's interests, continues to this day. Individuals named in the Black Book are forbidden from entering gambling establishments in the state, and casino operators wishing to keep their licenses are responsible for seeing that the individuals do not gain access. Chicago racketeer, Marshall Caifano, was one of the first entries in the Black Book. While the Black Book has not eliminated mob influence in Las Vegas, it has made it very difficult for experienced gambling racketeers to ply their trade.

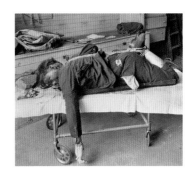

ABOVE The body of Walter Sage, club owner in the Catskills, was found floating in a local lake despite being weighted down with a slot machine.

Strawman

Mafia power within the Teamsters union was not ended with the jailing of Jimmy Hoffa. Approval of Teamster pension fund loans to the Las Vegas casino developers and management firms required the cooperation of a number of crime families. Allen Glick and his Argent Corporation used Teamster cash to take nominal control of the Stardust and the Fremont in 1974. Glick initially believed himself fully in control of the casinos but quickly learned that he was a screen—a strawman—covering the activities of Mafia-appointed managers.

In the late 1970s, FBI bugs of Kansas City *Mafiosi* picked up conversations relating to the Argent Corporation and skim-sharing agreements among the Kansas City, Chicago, Cleveland, and Milwaukee crime families. Raids in 1979 captured an $80,000 USD skim payment to Kansas City and documentation on how Vegas gambling proceeds were divided up.

Brothers Nick and Carl Civella, bosses of the Kansas City mob, were convicted of racketeering in 1984's "Strawman Case." They and others in the crime family leadership received long prison sentences. A related case in 1986 resulted in prison terms for much of the Chicago Outfit leadership, including boss Joseph Aiuppa, as well as Cleveland racketeer Milton Rockman, and Milwaukee crime boss Frank Balistrieri.

MORE LIKE GUIDELINES THAN RULES

Upon entrance into the Mafia fraternity, new members are told the rules—they must never provide information to authorities, they must never kill without permission, they must honestly report all income and provide a healthy percentage to higher-ups, they must refrain from affairs with married women, and they must avoid dealing in narcotics. The stated penalty for violating any of those orders is death.

Michael "Mikey Scars" DiLeonardo, former *capodecina* of the Gambino Crime Family, branded the rules as hypocrisy. Testifying in federal court in 2006, itself a violation of the Mafia's rule of silence, DiLeonardo noted that the higher-ups who explained the rules to him had already violated most if not all of them.

"The hierarchy itself… just killed a boss [Paul Castellano] without Commission approval. So it was a lot of double standards and hypocrisy there." DiLeonardo also told of secret side deals made by mobsters to avoid paying their superiors as well as widespread drug dealing within the Mafia.

Surrounded by supporters, Paul Castellano leaves court after posting bail in an indictment as one of the overlords of the "Mafia Commission."

ABOVE Vincent Gigante, head of the Genovese Crime Family, is escorted by detectives. He spent years pretending to have a mental illness as a disguise.

Bonanno's Tell-All

In 1983, aging Mafia boss Joseph Bonanno's autobiography was published. In the book, Bonanno focused his attention on the activities of deceased crime bosses, like Luciano, Genovese, Chicago's Sam Giancana, and Bonanno's cousin, Buffalo crime boss Stefano Magaddino. He detailed the Mafia links between Sicily and the United States, the Castellammarese War, and underworld rackets during Prohibition.

However, Bonanno also revealed the formation, membership, and functions of the Mafia Commission where members jointly considered the value of certain rackets, like drug smuggling, and also met to approve or reject plans for high-level assassinations.

RICO

Those details caught the eye of Rudolph Giuliani, US Attorney for the Southern District of New York. Giuliani spotted a continuing criminal conspiracy that he could prosecute using the Racketeer Influence and Corrupt Organizations (RICO) laws.

RICO laws passed in 1970 allowed entire groups to be charged with wrongdoing. They also provided for the seizures of property and cash generated through illegal enterprises and for hefty prison terms on those found guilty of racketeering.

Bosses on Trial

In 1985, Giuliani went after all the perceived heads of New York's five major Mafia clans—Gambino boss Paul Castellano, Colombo acting boss Gennaro Langella, Lucchese boss Anthony "Tony Ducks" Corallo, Bonanno boss Philip "Rusty" Rastelli,

PAUL CASTELLANO

Paul Castellano was born in 1915 to Sicilian immigrants in Brooklyn. He followed his father Joseph's footsteps into the butcher business and into the Mafia. In 1957, his cousin (and brother-in-law) Carlo Gambino became a Mafia boss, replacing the murdered Albert Anastasia as chief of New York's largest criminal clan. Also in that year, Castellano attended the underworld conclave at Apalachin and was among those gathered up by New York State Police. Castellano later served time in prison for refusing to discuss the purpose of the gathering.

On his deathbed in 1976, Gambino named Castellano his successor, offending a faction loyal to underboss Aniello Dellacroce. Dellacroce had been a protégé of Anastasia, and his followers assumed their faction would return to power after Gambino's reign. In November 1976, Dellacroce put a stop to the grumblings by pledging his loyalty to Castellano.

Under Castellano, the crime family moved away from vice-related crimes and into legitimate business enterprises. Castellano himself expanded his butcher shop into a meat distribution network, which had chicken industry giant Frank Perdue as a client.

In 1985, Castellano was charged with overseeing a car theft ring and with being part of the Mafia Commission. As arrests of alleged Mafia Commission members were made in February, the press learned that Castellano's mansion in the Todt Hill section of Staten Island had been bugged by the FBI since 1983. Within Castellano's Crime Family, there was anger that the boss's lack of caution had allowed so many secrets to fall into government hands, and there was growing resentment over his appointment of Thomas Bilotti, a relatively minor Mafioso, as his underboss.

On December 16, 1985, Castellano and Bilotti were shot to death by members of their own organization. They died on the sidewalk in front of a Manhattan restaurant.

Mug shot of Paul Castellano after his arrest for loan sharking in 1975. Castellano had no qualms about ordering murders, including one of his paid hitmen who he was afraid would betray him.

and apparent Genovese boss Anthony "Fat Tony" Salerno. Prosecutors did not know at the time that Salerno was providing cover for the actual boss, Vincent "the Chin" Gigante. Four other high-level crime family members were also named as defendants in the case—Gambino underboss Aniello Dellacroce, Colombo member Ralph Scopo, Lucchese underboss Salvatore Santoro, and Lucchese member Christopher Furnari.

When the nine defendants were charged, the public learned that much of the government's evidence had been obtained through electronic eavesdropping at Castellano's home and in the Jaguar driven by Corallo confidant, Salvatore Avellino Jr.

Colombo Family boss Carmine "the Snake" Persico and Bonanno Family member Anthony Indelicato later were added as defendants in the case. Three original defendants were removed. Castellano and Dellacroce did not live long enough to stand trial. Dellacroce died on December 2, 1985, after a long illness while a band of his former supporters led by John J. Gotti conspired in the assassination of Castellano and his underboss, Thomas Bilotti, outside a Manhattan restaurant on December 16, 1985. Rastelli was removed as a defendant from the Mafia Commission case and was convicted of racketeering in a separate trial. All remaining defendants were found guilty of racketeering conspiracies and all except Indelicato were sentenced to 100-year prison terms. Indelicato got 40 years.

In the wake of the Mafia Commission case, John Gotti emerged as the boss of the Gambino Crime Family. Without Salerno as cover, prosecutors soon identified Gigante as boss of the Genovese clan. Called to testify against New York bosses, octogenarian Joe Bonanno refused, citing health concerns, and was jailed for contempt of court.

BELOW A smiling senior "Joe Bananas" (Joseph Bonnano), who, at 26, was one of the youngest crime family bosses. It's believed that his funeral parlor was used to dispose of bodies.

Yakuza Modern Samurai

In the last 20 years of the twentieth century, the Japanese economy went on an extraordinary ride, and the Yakuza rode the tide adeptly, making profits in the economic highs and lows.

ABOVE A priest sits serenely before stacked jars of sake in a temple. Sake is sometimes used in initiation ceremonies in Yakuza.

Driven Underground

In the twentieth century, the Yakuza proved to be an extraordinary organized crime group, engaging in street racketeering as well as manipulation of national politics. Despite the fall in public influence, connections between politics and the Yakuza remain pervasive. However, the public aversion to gang-influenced politics forced the corruption deeper underground.

Marching towards the twenty-first century, the gangsters no longer confined themselves to street rackets. They brought their extortion schemes to financial markets and corporate and real estate business. To meet the challenge in the age of global economy, they transformed themselves into economic gangsters—both financial and corporate racketeers. Much of the Yakuza's story—their strength, devotion, and success—must be told in the context of their culture, customs, organizational structures, as well as the unique relationships they maintain with the public.

Structure

The traditional Yakuza power structure, like that of Italian Mafia, is pyramid. Clans are organized in families, with a godfather at the top and new members coming to the clan as older brothers, younger brothers, and children.

The Yakuza system, however, features a unique Japanese relationship known as *oyabun-kobun. Oyabun* means "father role" and *kobun* means "child role." The *oyabun* is obliged to provide protection and advice to the child. In return, the *kobun* promises unyielding loyalty and unquestioning obedience to the *oyabun*. The *oyabun-kobun* relationship is a mirror of the traditional Japanese family in which the father holds the paramount authority. Within the Yakuza gangs, the relationship produces strength, cohesion, devotion, and a trust unknown to other criminal groups in Western countries.

Initiation

In the early Yakuza years, a very elaborate ceremony was developed to initiate new recruits into the organization. The ceremony, which continues today, is characterized by a formal exchange of sake (rice wine) cups, symbolizing the blood connection. During the ceremony, the *oyabun* and the initiate sit face-to-face as the sake is prepared and poured into cups. The cup of the *oyabun*

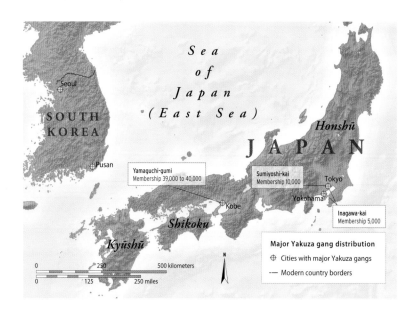

Sea of Japan (East Sea)

Seoul

SOUTH KOREA

Pusan

JAPAN

Honshū

Yamaguchi-gumi
Membership 39,000 to 40,000

Sumiyoshi-kai
Membership 10,000

Tokyo

Yokohama

Kobe

Inagawa-kai
Membership 5,000

Shikoku

Kyūshū

0   250   500 kilometers
0   125   250 miles

Major Yakuza gang distribution
⊕ Cities with major Yakuza gangs
-- Modern country borders

is full, while the initiate's gets much less, befitting their respective status. They drink a little, then exchange cups, drinking the sake from the other's cup. The initiate, now a *kobun*, has made his commitment to the family. From this moment on, the *kobun* regards the *oyabun* as his parent and he must follow him through "fire and flood."

Expulsion

The Yakuza requires the members to follow a set of rules including strict adherence to secrecy and obedience to the *oyabun-kobun* system. Cowardice, disobedience, and revealing gang secrets are dealt with severely.

Short of death, the most severe punishment is expulsion. Upon expulsion, special postcards are sent to all Yakuza gangs with which it has friendly relations, informing them of the expulsion. To honor a long-standing tradition, no Yakuza groups would accept the expelled member. Expulsion carries severe consequences, for the expellee is usually deprived of the opportunity of both legal and illegal employment. Being a gang member, the expellee may find it hard to find employment in the legitimate sector and he is forbidden to take part in illegal activity in the Yakuza's territory. An expellee who violates the understanding may be challenged, beaten, or even killed if the warning is disregarded. By conducting himself properly outside the gang and showing remorse for his past transgressions, the expellee may be reinstated, after a length of time. Postcards will be sent to relevant Yakuza groups with the notification of reinstatement of the member.

ABOVE Modern-day samurais in their traditional costume, prepare to fire their guns signaling the opening of the Musha Gyorestsu Festival that takes place in the seventeenth-century Odawara Castle.

1960 Socialist Party Secretary-General Inejiro Asanuma is assassinated by a right-wing fanatic, presumed a member of Yakuza.

1970 The amphetamine "speed" accounts for almost half the income of Yakuza.

1990 Yamaguchi-gumi have over 40 offices in Tokyo.

1996 Loan sharking—*sarakin*—is held responsible for the suicide of over 3,000 people in Japan.

THE BIG THREE

Currently, there are about 85,000 Yakuza members nationwide and 22 Yakuza syndicates. More than 70 percent of the Yakuza members belong to one of the three largest Yakuza syndicates.

ABOVE Nagasaki Mayor, Hitoshi Motosima, after being seriously injured by a right wing gang, affiliated with the Yamaguchi-gumi.

BELOW Police fire tear gas at radical university students who had paralyzed the campus for over a year with support of the Yakuza.

Yamaguchi-gumi

Yamaguchi-gumi is the largest Yakuza organization with about 40,000 active members. Its membership makes up 47 percent of the entire Yakuza population. The size of the organization also makes it the largest criminal syndicate in the world.

Yamaguchi-gumi was founded in 1915 and named after its founder Harukichi Yamaguchi. In the early days, the organization was nothing but an ordinary mob. The group owed its growth to its able leader and the underworld giant Kazuo Taoka. Kazuo Taoka was born in 1913 and grew up in Kobe. As a teenager, he began his association with the Yamaguchi gang earning the nickname "the bear" for his signature move of gouging out his opponents' eyes with his fingers. At age 23, he was sentenced to eight years for murder. After his release in 1943, he went back to his old gang and became the new boss three years later when police arrests and military draft had reduced the ranks to only 25 members. Using intrigues as well as violence, he incorporated some Yakuza gangs and squeezed others out of the Kobe area. Under his reign, the gang soon expanded the territory to the entire Kobe-Osaka area. In the 1960s, Yamaguci-gumi's ranks swelled to 10,000 members. Taoka brought 343 different gangs under the Yamaguchi umbrella.

In 1978, while watching a limbo dance and with five bodyguards surrounding him, he was shot in the neck by a rival gang member. Taoka survived the assassination attempt but died of a heart attack three years later in 1981. After Taoka's death, despite difficulty and confusion surrounding his succession, Yamaguchi continued to grow. Yamaguchi-gumi currently is under the rule of the sixth-generation boss, Shinobu Tsukasa. Its operation area centers in Kobe area, but the gang has territory all over Japan, including Tokyo.

Sumiyoshi-kai

Sumiyoshi-kai is the second largest Yakuza syndicate with about 10,000 members in 2009. It was founded in 1958 and its current leader is Shigeo Nishiguchi. Sumiyoshi-kai is a confederation of smaller gangs, rather than the traditional pyramid structure of Yama-guchi, with enormous control vested at the top. As a federation, the godfather has less authority and individual gangs have greater autonomy. Nishiguichi is godfather of the organization, but he shares the power with several other bosses. Monetary tributes to the top from individual gangs need not be as much as they would be in a centralized organization.

Sumiyoshi-kai's operational territory is in the Tokyo region. In recent years, its turf is being threatened by ambitious Yamaguchi-gumi. In 2006, gang violence between members of the two groups broke out with increased frequency. Concerned that the violence

ABOVE Gangs, armed with sticks, march in protest against the building of a new international airport in Narita, in 1967.

might escalate into a full-scale turf war, the police cracked down on both groups. They raided the gang offices and arrested gang members suspected of involvement in the violence. To avoid further police raids, the two groups reportedly have made peace and agreed to a truce.

Inagawa-kai

Inagawa-kai is the third largest Yakuza group with about 5,000 members. The group is based in Kanto and operates mainly around the nation's capital, Tokyo. Sumiyoshi-kai is Inagawa-kai's main rival, for the two groups operate in the same region. Like Yamaguchi-gumi, Inagawa-kai has a traditional pyramid organizational structure, with a godfather sitting at the top and wielding the utmost power. The group's smaller size allows it to maintain greater discipline, tighter organization, and more operational flexibility. Inagawa-kai has the reputation of being the most efficient Yakuza organization.

Inagawa-kai was founded in 1945 by Kakuji Inagawa (1914–2007). Like his contemporary Taoka, Inagawa was one of the most powerful Yakuza godfathers of the twentieth century. After Taoka's death, Inagawa became the most senior statesman of the Yakuza. After his retirement, Susumu Ishii took over and through loan-shark operations, banking deals, and real estate scams, Susumu Ishii accumulated assets of over $1.5 billion USD. With Susumu Ishii at the helm, Inagawa was among the first Yakuza groups to extend overseas. After his retirement, Toi Inagawa, son of Kukaji Inagawa, became the third-generation boss. Toi Inagawa died in 2005. Ever since, no clear leader has emerged. It seems that Hideki Inagawa, Kukaji Inagawa's grandson, is the most likely candidate to be the next boss of the group.

ABOVE A member of Yakuza watches video surveillance screens. His missing fingers are part of Yakuza ritual.

Activities

Like mobsters worldwide, the Yakuza are engaged in all typical gang activities. These include extortion, gambling, prostitution, drug trafficking, arms dealings, and human trafficking. But the Yakuza are among the most resourceful and ingenious gangsters in terms of coming up with scams and tactics.

Gambling dens

The Yakuza are veterans in running gambling dens. Despite the tightening of the anti-gambling laws, the gangs continue to extract huge profits from gambling. To ensure smooth operation, the Yakuza have developed a highly effective advance-warning system by establishing connections within the police. The warning system enables them to evade many police raids.

To cater to the needs of wealthy gamblers, the Yakuza sponsor luxury gambling trips and take the wealthy to private country villas, hot-spring resorts, and even abroad, returning huge profits to the Yakuza. The Yakuza also attempt to buy their way into the foreign casino ownership.

Sex Industry

For much of Japan's history, prostitution was not illegal. From the feudal times on, the rulers viewed prostitution as a way to preserve social peace. Prostitution was not made illegal until the passage of the Prostitution Prevention Law in 1956. Its criminalization brought in the Yakuza and ever since, the sex industry has become the Yakuza's bread and butter. Besides profits from distributing pornography and operating prostitution rings, the Yakuza are involved in organizing sex tours to East and Southeast Asian countries. The sex tour was born in the late 1960s and 70s, and by the 1980s, sex tours to countries such as Thailand and the Philippines became so popular that the invasion of Japanese sex tourists incurred great anger and protests. To stop national embarrassment, Japanese travel associations and the government condemned the trips and took steps to halt the sex tours.

Not wishing to lose revenue, the Yakuza began to import foreign women. Most women are brought to Japan from countries like Thailand, the Philippines, Malaysia, Indonesia, and more recently China and some from South America. Various scams are used to lure the women including the promise of jobs such as receptionists, entertainers, factory workers, waitresses, and nannies. Once in Japan, the women are sold to Yakuza gangs and turned into deeply indebted sex slaves. The complex and sophisticated trafficking network not only involves the Yakuza but also the immigration fixers, forgers, recruiters, translators, and travel agents. The trafficked women must bear the full cost of the operation and turn in a profit for the Yakuza. Not all are forced into the industry and some enlist voluntarily. There are about 100,000 foreign sex workers in Japan. With such strong demand for foreign prostitutes, the sex industry will continue to deliver handsome income to the Yakuza.

BELOW The inner streets of big cities are usually the home of the sex industry, involving workers and merchandise.

...a majority of companies listed on the Tokyo stock exchange had either resumed payoffs or begun to seriously consider doing so.

Asian Wall Street Journal, 1984, commenting on the influence of the Yakuza.

TATTOOS

During the feudal period in Japan, the tattoo was a mark of punishment. The criminal was tattooed with a black ring around his arm for each offense he had committed. Tattooing, however, has a nobler side. The tradition of tattooing dates back to the third century and over the years it developed into a form of art. With its elaborate designs and brilliant colors, many consider Japanese tattooing as the world's finest. The feudal authority eventually banned tattooing but the prohibition did litter to curb its popularity. The tattoo has ever since become the great Yakuza trademark.

Traditional tattooing, involving hand-pricking skin with a cluster of needles dipped in ink, is painful, but going through the process is seen as a test of strength. Today, even with the advent of modern tattooing machines, many still opt to do it traditional way. The full-body tattoos cover the entire torso and legs to mid-calf.

An estimated 70 percent of the Yakuza members have tattooing. The tattoo marks signify a person's identity as a Yakuza. The public aversion to the Yakuza is evident in the fact that many public bathhouses and gymnasiums ban people bearing large and graphic tattoos. However, the Yakuza are proud of their status as outcasts from society. The parade at local festivals such as Sanja Matsuri offers a rare chance to display their body art. They carry a shrine through the streets, while proudly showing off their elaborate tattoos. Tattoos, however, also bear evidence of Yakuza's involvement in transnational crimes, for there is no shortage of tattooed Yakuza members in various Asian prisons.

Extortion and Protection

Extortion is the oldest and most typical gang business. The Yakuza, without exception, are involved in it. The schemes range from demanding fees from street vendors for permission to operate, to coercing business owners to buy goods from gang-owned businesses at inflated prices. In Japan, however, a notable aspect of Yakuza operation is that business owners often voluntarily enlist the Yakuza service rather than being forced to accept the Yakuza protection. The request for Yakuza protection is especially common in entertainment industries. Establishments such as restaurants, bars, night-clubs, and massage parlors are vulnerable to disruptions caused by bad customers, employees, and predators. Business owners find it worthwhile to enlist the Yakuza service to ensure a smooth business operation.

In Japan, enlisting service from the underworld does not carry such stigma as it does in Western countries. The use of Yakuza service is fairly common. A police survey in the Tokyo-Yokohama region shows that more than 70 percent of entertainment enterprises paid the Yakuza for their protection.

Yakuza protection is also very significant in industries with a high concentration of unskilled workers. Construction, trucking, and package delivery companies often pay the Yakuza to ensure trouble-free business. The Yakuza help these companies to prevent pilfering of materials and delays caused by labor disputes.

Civil Involvement

The Yakuza's ingenuity in coming up with moneymaking schemes is best illustrated in the so-called Yakuza intervention in settlement of civil affairs. The Yakuza intervention includes debt collection, eviction by threat and harassment, bankruptcy management, and disruption of companies' shareholders meetings.

ABOVE Strong-arm tactics and business disruption are some of the methods used to extort payments by the Yakuza.

FINGERCUTTING

Fingercutting is an atonement ritual in Yakuza culture. Although often a form of punishment, it is frequently performed by a Yakuza transgressor preemptively to show his penance or apology for a serious mistake, embarrassment to the gang, or costing the gang money. He may perform the ritual to end a feud or settle a dispute and avoid a division in the ranks. The ritual is also used by gang bosses when meditating conflicts between rival gangs. The mediating gang bosses may perform the ritual to show their sincerity to both sides and their commitment to resolving the disputes between the conflicting gangs.

The fingercutting ritual was once widely practiced. In 1993, a government survey revealed that 45 percent of Yakuza members had missing fingers, and 15 percent of them had performed the ritual at least twice. With the weakening of the traditional Yakuza ethos, the ritual is becoming less prevalent among younger Yakuza members. They prefer to offer money, not their fingers, to express apology or settle a dispute. In recent years, some Yakuza members wear prosthetic fingertips to hide the telltale sign.

ABOVE To hide fingercutting and thus Yakuza membership, members often wear prosthetic fingers disguising the joins with large gold rings.

Debt Collection

In Japan, lawyers are the only authorized debt collectors. Nonetheless, using the legal channels is often ineffective and time-consuming and many creditors find it advantageous to hire Yakuza debt collectors. The law prohibits debt collection by explicit intimidation but the gangsters are skillful in avoiding legal trouble and rarely need to resort to explicit intimidation or physical violence. Debt collection invariably starts with polite requests and patient negotiations. The debtors, confronted by people with tattoos and missing fingers, cannot fail to know whom they are dealing with and are willing to settle with the Yakuza debt collectors.

Insurance

Business owners are not the only ones that use the Yakuza service. Ordinary citizens use them as well. The Yakuza service is often requested in traffic disputes involving insurance companies. Claimants, unwilling to get mired in the time-consuming claim process, may subcontract their claims to the Yakuza. The pressure brought to bear by the gangsters often makes the insurance companies pay more quickly. However, the effectiveness in collecting insurance payment also creates an incentive on the part of the Yakuza to engineer incidents and file false claims.

Street Rackets

Beyond insurance fraud, the Yakuza engage in other ordinary street rackets. They may extract money from an owner of a dry cleaner by claiming the store has "damaged" their boss's expensive suit, or from a store owner by complaining about the "quality" of the goods they purchased. These old-fashioned racketeering schemes continue to deliver income while the more educated and business-minded Yakuza direct their attention to bigger moneymaking schemes in business and finance.

ABOVE The busy streets of Shibuya, near Hachiko Square in Tokyo, are the home of the youth culture area, an ideal recruiting ground for the Yakuza.

RIGHT Alleged racketeer, or *sokaiya*, Kaoru Ogawa. The *sokaiya* gather negative information in order to disrupt corporate shareholders' meetings.

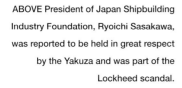

ABOVE President of Japan Shipbuilding Industry Foundation, Ryoichi Sasakawa, was reported to be held in great respect by the Yakuza and was part of the Lockheed scandal.

Property Development

The mob-run eviction service, known as *jiage*, is one tactic fashioned by the Yakuza to grab a share of profit in the real estate industry. *Jiage* is a form of land-sharking. In delivering the service, the Yakuza help real estates developers to force small landholders to sell up their adjacent plots or force the leaseholders to give up their leases. The purpose of the eviction is to obtain sites at a more reasonable rate.

The common eviction tactics involve harassment phone calls, the playing of loud music, pressing home owners' door bells in the middle of the night, crashing cars into targeted property, pouring glue into keyholes, spreading manure on the targeted property, infesting the property with poisonous insects, death threats, abduction, and arson. The *jiage* business proves to be far more lucrative than street rackets with gangs typically charging a percentage of a property's sale price, often bringing in thousands of dollars in a single *jiage* job.

Bankruptcy Management

Bankruptcy management is another Yakuza moneymaking scheme where creditors and debtors both may feel the need to enlist the Yakuza service. Managers of bankrupt companies may hire the Yakuza to protect them from the wrath of angry creditors. The creditors may find it advantageous to sell their debts to Yakuza and let them handle the debt collection. As legal bankruptcy proceedings may take years to complete, some creditors find it worthwhile to sell their debts to the Yakuza at a rate much lower than the debt's face value.

Another common tactic is to identify a company on the verge of bankruptcy and move in to extend it a short-term loan. When the company is unable to pay back the loan, the Yakuza managers show up to take charge of the company.

In a bankruptcy proceeding, the largest creditor stands to receive the largest portion of the bankrupt company's liquidated assets. Once taking charge of the company, the Yakuza managers may forge promissory notes and documents to make them appear to be the company's largest creditor. If they choose not to take over the company, they still profit from being the largest creditor to receive payment at bankruptcy.

Corporate Blackmail

The Yakuza also have ways to extort money by corporate blackmail. The most common form of corporate blackmail is by threats to disrupt the company's annual shareholders' meeting. The Yakuza specialized in this line of business are called *sokaiya*.

Prior to the Commercial Code Revisions in 1982, the *sokaiya* would buy one share in a company's stock—at any par value per share—to earn the right to attend the shareholders' annual general meeting. They would show up at the meeting to extort money by threatening to disclose a company's sensitive information, ranging from its financial status and management irregularities, to corporate executives' personal scandals.

Japanese law does not require companies to publicly release such detailed financial reports as required in other industrial countries, forcing investors to judge a company's financial wellbeing by indirect means. Investors often regard a prolonged shareholders' meeting as a sign of trouble. Prolonging the shareholders' meeting thus becomes a Yakuza tool of extortion. Ironically, concerned about the disruption and unable to pay off all the *sokaiya*, companies often find it necessary to hire other Yakuza to fend off the threat of the *sokaiya*. The Yakuza thus stand to make money from companies either by threatening to cause disruption or protecting the companies from the threat of disruption. Companies also hire the Yakuza to deal with protesters and their own shareholders. When a company is the target of public protest for environmental violations, it may hire the Yakuza to prevent protesters from disrupting its shareholders' meeting. When the company has a non-profitable year it may also find it convenient to enlist the Yakuza service to ensure an orderly shareholders' meeting.

Since 1982, the law requires that a person must have a threshold of ¥5,000.00 worth of stock before they have full voting rights and can attend the shareholders' annual general meeting. The law also makes it illegal for companies to pay for *sokaiya*. The law, however, is not a success as it has not stopped criminal operations. Not all Yakuza extortionists have the money to meet the ¥5,000.00 threshold. Unable to make the extortion by disrupting the shareholders' meeting, these Yakuza shift tactics by threatening to publish unfavorable information in the newspapers and magazines. The companies meanwhile continue to enlist and pay for *sokaiya* service.

ABOVE A Japanese motorcycle gang in 1985. Gangs such as this were the base of many Yakuza groups as they offered members a sense of unity.

BELOW Major sites like this in Osaka, are the ideal operations for *jiage*, a form of land-sharking, where Yakuza force out established tenants to allow for new development.

Cultural Acceptance

The Yakuza represent Japan's criminal underworld but in comparison with organized crime in other industrial countries, it enjoys a much greater degree of tolerance and acceptance in Japan's larger society. The existence of Yakuza has become a way of life in Japan. They can legally open their offices with the gang's symbol displayed. Association with the Yakuza or enlisting the Yakuza services seems to be normal. The explanation of the greater public acceptance of the Yakuza probably lies in both the Japanese culture and the country's social structure.

The Yakuza see themselves as chivalrous gangsters who will help rather than harm ordinary people. This claim seems to have gained a high degree of acceptance. The fairly common reliance on the Yakuza services on one hand shows that the Yakuza perform a useful function in society while on the other it reveals the inadequacy of the social services in Japanese society, which leaves comfortable room for the Yakuza to survive and grow. Most Japanese try their best to avoid dealing with the Yakuza but they often find that there are no other alternatives. Inadequacy and inefficiency of the legal channels to provide protection and to resolve disputes have rendered the Yakuza services a reasonable source of alternative dispute resolutions. The opinion polls find that a striking number of Japanese agree that hiring gangsters to collect debts or settle disputes is not bad or is acceptable.

Japan has one of the lowest crime rates among Western industrial countries. The Japanese police take pride in being called the world's best cops. But one can not help wondering why the world's best cops are unable to eradicate the Yakuza underworld. The answer to the question is that the police have never had the intention to eradicate the Yakuza. To the Japanese authorites, including the lawmakers, prosecutors, and the police, the solution to the Yakuza problem is not eradication but containment.

BELOW Police guard the headquarters of Aum Shinrikyo. In 1995, the cult attacked the Tokyo subway with Sarin gas, killing 12 people.

CELLULOID MAFIA

Black Rain

Set largely in a turbulent and dangerous Osaka, the film *Black Rain* tells the story of two New York cops escorting a Japanese gangster from New York to Osaka, who escapes and disappears into the vicious underworld of the Yakuza.

The Story

Michael Douglas plays Nick Conlin, a motorcycle-loving, morally flexible homicide detective under investigation by Internal Affairs. He is also divorced from his wife who has custody of their two children, and is in financial trouble. His partner, Charlie Vincent, is played by Andy Garcia. On arrival in Osaka, two Yazuka men masquerading as police take their prisoner, Sato (Yusaka Mutsada), before the real police arrive. The chase begins, and the New Yorkers are allowed merely to "observe" the hunt under the guidance of a Japanese officer, Masahiro Matsumoto (Ken Takakura). Things get pretty rough very quickly, as the Yakuza capture and decapitate Charlie while a helpless Nick looks on from behind a car park grill door.

Through American nightclub hostess, Joyce (Kate Capshaw), Nick learns that Sato is fighting a gang war with a notorious Yakuza boss, Sugai (Tomisaburo Wakayama). Sato, once a Sugai soldier, wants his own territory. Sato was in New York to disrupt a meeting with American Italian gangsters about a counterfeiting scheme being set up by Sugai, when the meeting turned bloody and Nick and Charlie intervened—the scene which triggered the entire plot.

Near the end of the film, Nick's already established motorcycling skills are used during a dirt bike chase in which Nick pursues, and triumphs over, an escaping Sato.

Awards

Nominated for Best Sound and Best Sound Effects at the 1990 Academy Awards, Ridley Scott's *Black Rain* won the Best Foreign Language Film Award at the Japanese Academy and is a highly popular film even today

ABOVE Nick Conlin (Michael Douglas) and Charlie Vincent (Andy Garcia) take a ride on Nick's beloved motorcycle.

THE YAKUZA

Grizzly alpha male Robert Mitchum (left) plays Harry Kilmer in *The Yakuza* (1974), written by the acclaimed Paul Schrader and Robert Towne, of *Chinatown* fame, and directed by Sydney Pollack. Kilmer is hired by his World War II army buddy, George Tanner (Brian Keith), now a successful shipping executive, to rescue his daughter from the Yakuza who are holding her for an alleged default on a business deal.

Ken (Ken Takakura), who owes Kilmer a favor from the past, must honor the request to infiltrate the Yakuza. Takakura also has a support role in *Black Rain*.

RIGHT Japanese biker gangs continue to be a constant source of criminal activity throughout the country.

ABOVE Despite the constant police presence on Japanese streets, the acceptance of Yakuza by both citizens and law enforcement continues.

Police Tolerance

Police tolerance of the Yakuza comes from the unique relationship between the two. The police stage regular crackdowns on the Yakuza and they come down hard especially when there is an escalation of gang violence. Through connections within the police, the gangs usually receive warning before police raids. The warning allows the gangs to conceal contraband and send their bosses into hiding. To help the police save face, they leave behind a few guns for the police to confiscate. The police do round up thousands of gang members each year but release most of them after a short detention because of insufficient evidence.

Police Bribes

The Yakuza have a long history of bribing the police and undoubtedly, endemic police corruption forms part of the police-Yakuza relationship. Scandals involving officers receiving Yakuza payments erupt from time to time and these scandals bring disgrace to the police and sometimes result in the suicide of involved officers.

Joint Cooperation

Many police officers sincerely believe that not all Yakuza are bad. In a unique Japanese way, there is mutual respect and understanding between the Yakuza and the police.

The Yakuza understand the police duty to enforce the law and to ensure that the police properly perform their duty, it is not unheard of that guilty Yakuza members would turn themselves in and make full confessions for crimes under police investigation. It is also common for the Yakuza to help the police solve crimes by providing information needed for convictions.

Modern Samurai

To a certain extent, police believe that the existence of the Yakuza may not be a bad thing. They see that the existence of the Yakuza may serve as a deterrent to unorganized crime, for the Yakuza would not tolerate others to commit crimes in their turf. Some police officers, and even criminologists, attribute the low street crimes to the existence of the Yakuza. Many believe that breaking up the Yakuza and turning the members into freelance criminals may increase, rather than decrease, the challenge faced by the police. Most police officers share the conservative view held by the Yakuza. Moreover, both police and the Yakuza take the feudal *samurai* as their role models and consider themselves a kind of modern day *samurai*.

ETHNIC KOREAN YAKUZA

While ethnic Koreans comprise 0.5 percent of the total population, they make up about 15 percent of the Yakuza membership.

Discrimination

The prominent presence of Koreans in the Yakuza ranks is attributable to discrimination experienced by Koreans in Japan where they were not allowed to hold government jobs and suffered discrimination in housing, education, and employment in private sectors. The Korean outcast status fits in well with Yakuza's self-image. Although Korean numbers in the Yakuza are subject to controversy, no one disputes that they are well in excess of the ratio to the general population.

Tosei-kai

Hisayuki Machii (1923–2002) was the most famous Korean-Japanese Yakuza godfather. Born in Japanese-occupied Korea, Machii settled permanently in Japan after the war. He formed his own gang, *Tosei-kai*—Voice of the East Gang—in 1948, composed of largely ethnic Koreans. Outnumbering the police in manpower and strength, it soon took over Tokyo's famed Ginza entertainment district earning him the title "the Ginza Tiger" and his gang the name of "Ginza Police." His vast empire included entertainment, tourism, prostitution, and even oil importing. In 1965, under police pressure, Machii disbanded *Tosei-kai* and then established two legitimate companies as the gang's front.

Foreign Diplomacy

Machii was a Yakuza godfather of national stature. He had a long and profitable relationship with Yoshio Kodama and formed an alliance with Yamaguchi-gumi's powerful godfather, Kazuo Taoka. His talent brought him to the stage of foreign diplomacy where he and Kodama played an active role in promoting the normalization of relationships between Japan and Republic of Korea. Because of his connections, he was granted the right to operate the major ferry line between Japan and South Korea.

Korea

Machii's greatest legacy was his introduction of Yakuza operation into his homeland Korea. Thanks to his path-breaking effort, South Korea has become Yakuza's home away from home. Fugitives from Japanese justice have also found an ideal safe haven in Korea.

Towa Yuai Jigyo Kumiai

Machii retired in the 1980s and died in 2002. His gang, made up of still mainly ethnic Koreans, is currently called Towa Yuai Jigyo Kumiai—East Asia Friendship Enterprises Association. The gang has about 1,000 members and ranks as the fourth largest Yakuza syndicate in Japan.

BELOW The Ginza shopping district in Tokyo became almost totally under the control of the *Tosei-kai* during the middle of the twentieth century.

Triads Going Global

All successful Triads operate on a global scale. Their activities consist of counterfeiting, smuggling people, and most importantly, drugs.

China White

During the 1950s and 1960s, the Triads became masters at flooding Western Europe and North America with heroin. Their product was known to be of superior quality, at least 90 percent pure. On the streets it was called "China White" and though it was expensive, it was a very wanted drug.

The members of Triads are not always gangsters. As long as they are patriots, concerned with maintaining the prosperity of Hong Kong, we should respect them

Tao Siju, Minister of Public Security, People's Republic of China, 1993.

Opium poppies growing in Burma are harvested for distribution. Burma is the world's second largest producer of opium and is a major player in the "Golden Triangle."

THE GOLDEN TRIANGLE

The so-called Golden Triangle in Southeast Asia, an area of 150,000 square miles (390,000 sq km) is where "China White" heroin originates. Farmers have huge fields where they grow the opium poppy. Each year the opium is harvested from the end of December to the beginning of March. The farmers then sell their crops to the army, middlemen, or directly to traffickers, who pay them in cash, or goods like clothing and food. Several countries are part of this heroin triangle, namely the western fringe of Laos, the four northern provinces of Thailand, and Burma. During the 1970s, an estimated 70 percent of all the world's heroin came from here. Triads were directly involved in getting the heroin from Southeast Asia to the backstreets of New York, London, and Amsterdam.

Chinese Roots

The Triads called on their roots when it came to making contact with heroin suppliers. When Chiang Kai-shek's Chinese forces were defeated, two of his armies that were stationed in the southern Chinese province of Yunnan fled into the Shan States of northern Burma. There farmers with Chinese roots dating back 3,000 years were growing and harvesting the opium poppy.

Processing the Poppy

With Chiang Kai-shek's former army controlling the growing of opium in Burma, and Triad groups in Hong Kong looking for a good supplier, the contact was easily made. The middlemen would smuggle the raw opium to refineries in Burma near the border with Thailand, where the opium was converted into morphine.

As morphine the opium package was reduced to one tenth of its original bulk. From these refineries it was smuggled into Thailand, which was used as a go-between because of its large port in Bangkok from where large drug shipments could be sent to anywhere in the world.

Making the Deal

Before shipment a deal has to be made between supplier and buyer. These deals were made in Thailand's second largest city, Chiang Mai, situated over 400 miles (650 km) north of Bangkok. In the 1970s, Chiang Mai was a popular tourist destination, but it was also a favorite among drug traffickers looking to set up a deal, or for those on the run from authorities. Many Chinese traffickers would eventually settle in Thailand, and even trade their Chinese name for a Thai one. The heroin business was booming, and the Triads had the global contacts to introduce the world to "China White."

ABOVE Chinese drug trafficker, Han Yong-wan, goes on trial in 2000. Four drug traffickers were put to death in a crack-down by Chinese authorities.

BELOW Packets of opium were openly sold in markets throughout Burma. The merchant is about to weigh a packet for prospective buyers.

ABOVE Hundreds of Chinese, guarded by troops, crouch under arrest after riots throughout Hong Kong in 1956. The riots were allegedly begun by secret societies from the Kowloon side of Hong Kong.

BELOW Hong Kong harbor police search a junk for narcotics and illegal immigrants commonly smuggled on board.

Leading Triads

World War II had made the Triads richer and more powerful than ever before. Three Triads were especially strong—the Wo Shing Wo, the 14K, and the Sun Yee On.

Wo Group

The Wo Shing Wo is part of the so-called Wo group. During the war years, this group consisted of 41 societies, some of which were larger and more involved in crime than others. Important societies within the Wo group, beside the Wo Shing Wo, were the Wo On Lok, Wo Shing Tong, and the Wo Shing Yee. Though they were part of the same group, they still competed for the same territories causing frequent wars between them. The Wo Shing Wo eventually came out on top and began operating worldwide.

14K

The 14K was founded by Kot Sui-wong. Kot was a lieutenant-general in the army of Chiang Kai-shek, which was fighting the forces led by Mao Zedong. Kot was given orders to organize all the Triad societies in Guangdong. Each of these societies was given a code name that included the number 14 because the society's headquarters was based at 14 Po Wah Road. It wasn't until much later that, for unknown reasons, the letter K was added. When Kot and his Triad forces were defeated by Mao, he fled to Hong Kong where his 14K quickly made its presence felt by fighting wars for control of the Kowloon area of Hong Kong. After Kot's death in 1953, the 14K grew rapidly to around 80,000 members. Just like the Wo Shing Wo, it started looking for new markets, finding them in other parts of Asia and Europe.

Sun Yee On

The Sun Yee On had a troubled past. Part of the Teochiu societies, it started out as the Yee On. The society went off the radar during World War II, appearing again in 1946 after Japanese forces left. In those years following the war, some members then started informing on their leaders and several Yee On bosses were arrested. In the turmoil that followed, the Yee On split into two groups. Several years later it emerged again under the name Sun Yee On. Despite this troubled past, the Sun Yee On is now considered one of the most powerful Triads in the world.

CELLULOID MAFIA
Shanghai Triad

Chinese filmmaker Zhang Yimou's 1995 exploration of Shanghai drug gangs, *Shanghai Triad* is based on a traditional Chinese lullaby.

Screenplay

The screenplay is adapted from a novel by Li Xiao and stars one of China's most internationally successful actresses, Gong Li. Zhang Yimou blends the genre origins of the work—about organized crime—with the observation of lifestyles of the rich and infamous in 1930's Shanghai.

The Plot

Set over the course of seven days in Shanghai, the story is seen through the naive eyes of Shuisheng (Wang Xiao Xiao), a dumbstruck peasant boy brought to the city to serve Jewel (Gong Li), herself once a peasant girl, but now the spoilt mistress of the gang boss, Tang (Li Boatian). Tang's men pay lip service to the boss's moll, but in private they consider her a whore. What Tang doesn't know is about to bite him—she's having an affair with the Boss' No 2, Song (Sun Chun), and Fat Yu (Liu Jiang) is plotting to overthrow him and take over leadership.

While the film deals with the violent world of the Triads, the violence is mostly off screen, as Zhang Yimou examines the emotional and ethical elements of the story. Some have said it's more a spiritual film than a gangster movie—a response no doubt influenced by the film's strikingly handsome visuals. The reason is that while the film was originally intended to be a straight adaptation of the Li Xiao novel, *Gang Law*, the tone changed with Gong Li's character becoming more important and the story's viewpoint shifting to that of the young boy, Shuisheng.

Awards

The international film community embraced the film's cinematic achievements with an Academy Award nomination for Yue Lu's cinematography—an award both the New York and Los Angeles Film Critics bestowed on him. The film had Official Selection at Cannes, and won the Grand Technical Prize, and a Best Foreign Language Film nomination at the Golden Globe Awards.

REEL TO REAL The shift in character emphasis from the original novel to the film, *Shanghai Triad*, is perhaps explained by the fact that filmmaker Zhang Yimou and Gong Li had been off-screen partners for some time.

When the film was completed, the two agreed to end their relationship both professionally and personally. They would not work together for 11 years—until 2006, on *Curse of the Golden Flower*.

BELOW Jewel (Gong Li), the beautiful mistress of a gang boss, is having an affair with his second-in-charge.

THE UNICORN MAN

Chung "Unicorn" Mon was born on September 10, 1920, in the city Po On in the Guangdong province of China. He arrived in the Netherlands when he was 18 years old. He was a cook on a freighter that made a quick stop in Rotterdam. During the stop Chung Mon vanished into the tight knit Chinese community there.

On May 10, 1940, the German army invaded the Netherlands. Hitler's troops would occupy the small country until it was liberated on May 6, 1945, and during the war Mon played a very shady role as informant for the German Gestapo. Mon was a survivor first and foremost, and instead of being a victim of the Nazis, he decided to help them out in return for favors.

After the war he managed to escape punishment for his assistance to the Germans, and went on to become a very successful businessman. He owned several restaurants that were doing very well. But he also owned several illegal gambling houses. Such an influential figure is always helpful for foreigners who are looking to tap into a new market.

At some point the 14K knocked on Mon's door and made him a member. He was soon the man responsible for accepting and distributing almost all heroin shipments destined for Western Europe.

This 1960 shot shows the sea front at Scheveningen, in the Netherlands, where casinos flourished, mostly controlled by Triads as well as the Chinese who immigrated from China in the 1920s. Many of these casinos were fronts for heroin distribution.

1975 Over 200 Triad suspects are arrested in Singapore

1977 Triads fire bomb a nightclub in Hong Kong, killing 17 people

1986 Triad gang named Big Circle Boys move into the Netherlands.

1995 The Golden Triangle is producing more than 1,500 tons (1,300 kg) of opium per year

Going Global

The city of Amsterdam in the Netherlands is known for its lenient legislation regarding drugs and prostitution. Tourists from around the world flock to the city, where it is legal to buy and smoke hashish and weed in so-called "coffee shops." Back in the 1960s, Amsterdam was filled with hippies, who were enjoying the decade of freedom and love while getting high. And despite all the drugs, things were relatively peaceful.

Easy Pickings

In Amsterdam, arguments were settled with a fistfight and executions were unheard of. But this changed during the 1970s. In the late 1960s, the Chinese Triads picked Amsterdam as the first European city where they would sell their heroin. Their choice was obvious. Amsterdam had the largest Chinese community in Europe, soft legislation, and its own port—with Europe's biggest port nearby in Rotterdam. It was the perfect place to begin a campaign for control of the drug market in Western Europe. The man chosen to undertake this important task was Chung Mon.

Western European Operations

Chung Mon's status as 14K boss for Western Europe was reflected in his entourage of bodyguards and his bulletproof Mercedes. He was considered the main authority within the Chinese community, and would help fellow Chinese out by providing them with jobs, and giving them advice. Because of his business acumen, he was even decorated by the Dutch government. But Mon's drug deals were drawing attention and law enforcement in Europe and the United States were beginning to see through the façade that Mon had created.

By 1973, several drug couriers had been arrested at various European airports. They all had one thing in common—their final destination was 106 Prins Hendrikkade in Amsterdam. Interestingly, this was the address of one of Mon's restaurants. His explanation for this was that he was known as an influential Chinese man who could help newly immigrated Chinese settle in Europe. But he didn't fool law enforcement and the DEA officially labeled him the head of the 14K Triad in the Netherlands.

ABOVE A customs inspector in San Francisco reveals packages of hashish, smuggled in from Amsterdam inside the panels of this foreign-made mini bus.

Muscling In

As head of the 14K, and in charge of the importation of heroin into Western Europe, he is alleged to have taken a 5 percent cut out of every heroin deal that was set up by the Triads. But with so much money at stake it wasn't long before other Triad societies tried to muscle in. The most serious threat came from nearby Rotterdam, where the Wo Shing Wo Triad had established a branch.

Payback

Mon dealt with this threat in the same way as he had done during World War II—he started giving information about his rivals to Dutch police. Though this gave him some space in the short run, it would turn out to be disastrous in the long run. By informing on his fellow Triads he broke a golden rule, and his end was near. On May 3, 1975, three Chinese men assassinated Mon as he stepped out of his restaurant in Amsterdam. His successor was murdered precisely one year later. These bloody executions shocked the citizens of the Netherlands, who had never seen this type of violence before. But the Triads had not just shocked the Netherlands with their criminal operations and violent behavior operations. They had also drawn the attention of the world.

RIGHT The body of a Tong victim lies in Mott Street, New York, the result of a Tong war in Chinatown.

ABOVE Eddie Gong, leader of the Hip Sing Tong, displays his cleavers. He allegedly has a history of being a "hatchet man" for the New York Tongs.

Welcome to America—Tongs

The first wave of Chinese immigrants in the United States came during the 1840s, and was followed by a flood when the Americans needed laborers to build the great railroad from the East to the West Coast. These Chinese workers were treated as second-class humans, and were given the most dangerous work. In the decades that followed, the situation for the Chinese immigrants did not improve. In order to survive, they stuck together, creating societies that offered food and rent money to those in need. These first societies were legitimate organizations that did a lot of good. In the United States these societies did not go by the name "Triad," but were called "Tong" instead. "Tong" translates as "Town Hall," indicating exactly what its function was.

Laying Low

As their power grew, so did the stakes and the possibility of easy profits. Just like in China, wars broke out between the various Tong societies. During the 1950s, the calm returned and the Tongs focused on laying low and making money. Their main activities were prostitution, narcotics, gambling, and extortion. Because the Chinese kept to themselves, it was impossible for authorities to know the extent of the criminal acts being committed. No one went to the police, and if the Tongs kept the violence at a minimum, the police had no interest.

Violent Additions

From the 1960s on, there was a huge influx of Chinese immigrants and among these immigrants were violent Triad members, who quickly made

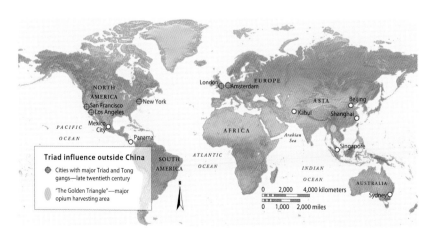

Triad influence outside China
⊕ Cities with major Triad and Tong gangs—late twentieth century
"The Golden Triangle"—major opium harvesting area

SAVING FACE

During the 1990s the most important gangs in New York were the Chinese Ghost Shadows, Flying Dragons, Tung On, Fuk Ching, Green Dragons, White Tigers, Hung Ching, the Taiwan Brotherhood, and the Vietnamese Born-To-Kill gang. All these gangs were fighting for their piece of the city rackets and things regularly got out of hand. A couple of incidents involved Wing Yeung Chan, leader of On Leong Tong and Ghost Shadows and his brother, Wing Lok.

In January 1992, during a night out at the Triple 8 nightclub, members of the rival Tung On gang attacked Wing Lok and beat him to a bloody pulp. Wing Lok needed to save face, so a few days later he killed a Tung On gang member on East Broadway. The revenge attack by the Tung On, where they opened fire inside a pool-hall, left an innocent bystander dead, and authorities in shock.

On July 12, 1992, members of the Ghost Shadows beat and robbed Shui Bao, the leader of the rival Flying Dragons. Shui Bao had to retaliate immediately. When Wing Yeung Chan, Wing Lok Chan, and six other Ghost Shadow members arrived for a supposed peaceful meeting, they were met by 20 Flying Dragon members armed with knives and guns. In the ensuing battle, one Ghost Shadow was shot to death, while Wing Lok barely made it out alive after being stabbed.

The constant beatings, stabbings, and frequent murders brought much attention from law enforcement. By the mid-nineties, the entire leadership of both the Ghost Shadows and the Tung On was in prison. Wing Yeung Chan and his brother Wing Lok both agreed to testify against their underlings in return for a second chance at life outside prison.

contact with the Tong societies, which welcomed them with open arms. Also among the new immigrants were young Chinese and Vietnamese boys, who, once in the United States, formed violent street gangs. As the Tongs started working closely with these violent Asian youth gangs, law enforcement started taking notice.

Prominent Gangs

During the late 1980s to the mid-1990s, the most prominent Tong in New York was the On Leong Chinese Merchants Association. The On Leong Tong used a gang named the Ghost Shadows as muscle and protection. For over a decade the Ghost Shadows terrorized New York. According to the FBI, almost 75 percent of businesses in Chinatown paid them extortion money. They also ran betting parlors and a scheme where they scammed 300 Asian investors out of $10 million USD. The main power behind the On Leong Tong and Ghost Shadows gangs was Wing Yeung Chan.

Tong activity in the United States is mostly confined to the West Coast, namely California, and the East Coast, primarily New York. With scores of Chinese immigrants settling in the Big Apple every year, Chinatown expanded rapidly. Currently it is even larger than the famous Little Italy.

BELOW This parade at the opening of the Hip Sing and On Leong national conventions involves potential clashes between the Tong gangs.

ABOVE Poster on the wall in Soho, in London's Chinatown, appealing for any witnesses to a murder in a Triad turf war.

London Bound

As the Triads brought their heroin to Amsterdam, they also introduced it to London. The quality stunned the British junkies, and it became an instant hit. Up until the late 1960s, the 14K was the dominant Triad in Britain, with branches in London, Liverpool, and Bristol. But as happened in Amsterdam, other Triads were looking for a piece of the heroin pie. And just like in Amsterdam, the main threat was the Wo Shing Wo.

In Britain, a man known by the nickname "Georgie Pai" would become the most important Triad boss. The British Wo Shing Wo groups were disorganized, and Pai saw it as his task to organize all the groups into one strong Triad.

He assembled a group of 80 loyal followers, whom he used to defeat the 14K and take over criminal operations in London. With London under his control, he continued his crusade for power and money. He ran protection rackets in and around Manchester, Birmingham, Southampton, and Portsmouth. Only Liverpool was out of reach because it was still under control of the 14K. According to British law enforcement, Georgie Pai would stay in charge of the Wo Shing Wo until the new millennium.

Macau

Chinese Triads based in Hong Kong and Taiwan did not have to travel far to make a lot of money. Their potential biggest moneymaker was very close to their home territory: Macau. Like Hong Kong, Macau, too, was a colony. Where Britain ruled Hong Kong, Portugal ruled Macau. Macau remained under Portuguese rule until December 1999, when sovereignty was handed back to China, which placed it under the so-called "one country, two systems" principle. Under this principle, Macau has a high degree of autonomy in all areas except in defense and foreign affairs. The Triads had already discovered Macau by then, and ruled the island's prostitution and gambling industry thanks to widespread corruption.

RIGHT This old photograph shows the entrance to a high class gambling house in Macau, during Portuguese possession.

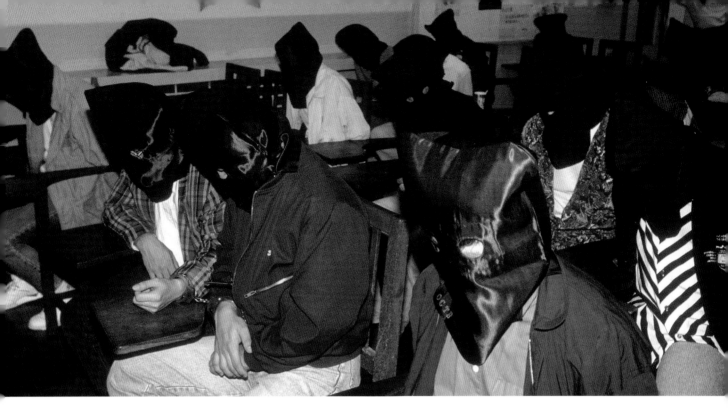

In the mid-1990s, a war between the 14K and Wo On Lok rocked the gambling paradise. Both groups were fighting for more power, mainly over who would control the VIP gaming rooms, which attracted the high rollers. After several murders caused the number of visiting tourists to drop, both sides agreed to attend peace talks, but they could not come to an agreement and the war continued. When the tourism number was down 23 percent, authorities decided they needed to get tough. An anti-Triad bill was ratified, which enabled authorities to hand out tough sentences for Triad crimes.

The 14K of Macau was led by Wan Kuok-koi, nicknamed "Broken Tooth" after losing nine teeth during an attempted hit by the Wo On Lok. He had fought his way to the top of the 14K by winning an internal power struggle against his former boss, and taking over his operations.

In May 1998, Wan was charged with a long list of Triad crimes and pleaded not guilty, claiming he made a living as a high stakes gambler and real estate investor. But the prosecution used 50 witnesses and Wan's own words against him during the trial, after which he was found guilty and sentenced to 15 years in prison.

During the 1990s, many high-ranking Triad members were sent to prison after receiving heavy sentences for their crimes, while other members died in a hail of bullets. Even though these men were removed from the scene, the Triad groups continued their criminal operations. Every fallen boss, or soldier, was replaced, so business would continue as usual.

Moving to the new millennium, the Triads were still heavily involved in crime all around the world. There were billions of dollars and Euros to be made with the smuggling of drugs, and humans. Operating from the safe confines of the Chinese com-munities, the Triads and Tongs largely remained safe from law enforcement, and continued to grow stronger. Like all organized crime groups, they also saw the potential profits from forming alliances with other ethnic groups.

ABOVE The Organized Crime and Triads Bureau in Hong Kong arrest a group of gang members in 1993. Their faces are covered to protect their identities.

THE NUMBERS

By the 1990s, it was said that of Macau's population of 500,000, a staggering 10,000 people were Triad members. The 14K, with an estimated 5,000 members, controlled seven casinos, while the Wo On Lok, with an esti-mated 3,000 members, controlled two other casinos. The Sun Yee On was also involved in gambling establishments, but did not wield as much influence as the other two groups.

Russian Mafia
Crime Superpower

As a general rule, organized crime tends to thrive when a government is weak and unable to perform its functions. In highly authoritarian societies, by contrast, organized crime can be successful only when government allows it to be. Patterns of organized crime in Russia provide ample support for this general rule.

1985 Gorbachev introduces a restriction on the amount of alcohol available to consumers, resulting in black market alcohol.

1991 The Belavezha Accords dissolve the Soviet Union and establish the Commonwealth of Independent States, opening up smaller states to corruption by criminal organizations.

1993 The number of people employed in the fight against organized crime in Russia grows to 15,000.

Communist Party

The proclaimed superior Soviet system was dominated by the Communist Party that had a right of appointment to all posts of importance in society, and the authority to supervise everyone.

Under the planned economy, a production target was set for each industrial enterprise. The state bureaucracy was persistently unable to deliver raw material supplies on time or in the required quantities and quality. To secure the much-needed supplies, alleviate the burden of hard-to-meet production quotas, and to make superiors turn a blind eye to the falsified production reports, industrial managers felt the need to cultivate and maintain favorable relationships with higher-level party and government officials.

Illegal Pay-offs

Once the connection was established, the bureaucrat would perform illegal favors for relatives, members of his ethnic group, close friends, or those who made pay-offs. Because of party officials' power to monitor and control all aspects of Soviet life, it was impossible for the illegal favors to be made without party figures' assistance or acquiescence. A system of tribute came into being where party officials regularly received gifts in return for favors.

RIGHT Communist Party members register their votes by holding up cards, negating any chance of voting against the party.

Institutionalized Corruption

Originally, the establishment of the network of personal favors was intended, at least in part, to overcome the inadequacy of the poorly articulated administrative system. The network soon turned into a system of personal gain and racketeering. Bribery became a lubricant of the function of the entire Soviet society. Bribes were given for selling off state resources, for granting permits for costruction, for allocating consumer goods, for granting pensions, for obtaining promotion, for admission to higher educational institutions, and for the awarding of diplomas. Bribes were also given to cover up falsified production reports and to conceal large-scale embezzlement and theft. Because of the dominant position of party officials in Soviet society, bureaucrats were forced to collude in the perpetration and concealment of the illegal act. There thus developed an institutionalized corruption and an alliance of comrade criminals.

Black Market

The ill-managed Soviet economy created a chronic shortage of consumer goods, which in turn created ample opportunities for comrade criminals to rake in profits. Speculation and profiteering on "deficit" goods became a standard way of racketeering. The consumer goods, instead of being shipped to state-run outlets, were smuggled out of warehouses and factories to the black market and sold to the highest bidder. For the goods that did arrive at retail stores, managers would take their share running their own rackets. The criminal underworld happily served as the middlemen, shipping the goods stolen or illegally diverted from the state allocation systems to the black market. All those involved in the illegal schemes needed to pay tribute to the party officials to ensure that they would turn a blind eye. The party bosses thus became the ultimate beneficiaries of all rackets and from there developed a form of organized crime—the Soviet Mafia. Powerful party bosses and officials occupying key positions in the state bureaucracy became the real organized crime figures in Soviet society.

ABOVE Moscow residents rally in streets in favor of the continuation of communism, May Day, 1991.

TOP LEFT Russian life after communism was harsh with scarce food supplies and a rife black market keeping prices high. These Moscow residents are bargaining over the cost of meat.

ABOVE The Russian tax police pull no punches when it comes to breaking into premises to seize illegal vodka near Moscow.

Endemic Corruption

The social and economic conditions in Russia were such that everybody understood that you had to manipulate the system or you and your family would suffer. The mentality greatly blurred the line between right and wrong and legal and illegal. It turned virtually everyone into a thief of some kind. Peasants stole fodder, workers stole tools and materials, physicians stole medicines, drivers stole gasoline, and truck drivers diverted freight. All stolen goods found their way onto the black market. The schemes allowed the participants to pocket extra cash as a supplement to their meager salary. The participants found justification for their acts in the reasoning that stealing from the state was not a crime, for the people after all were the masters of the state.

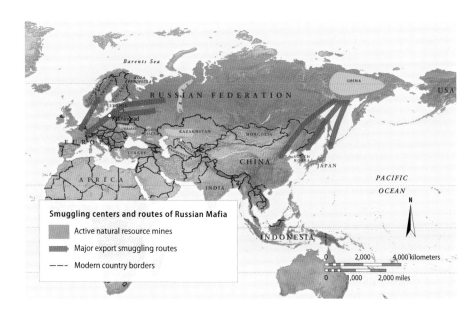

Within a relatively short period of time the crime world has made the transition from separate groups of disparate gangs to a set of intellectually and technically secure and well-disguised criminal communities.

MVD (Ministry of Internal Affairs, Russia), February 20, 1997

Mafias by Industry

The black market economy also gave rise to a multitude of Mafias. With the right connections, individual entrepreneurs could gain control over many specific goods or services. They exercised the control for their personal economic gains but to the detriment of the interest of the consumers of those goods or services. There thus was a fruit Mafia, a vegetable Mafia, a cotton Mafia, a caviar Mafia, a transportation Mafia, a hotel Mafia, and so on. All these Mafias reported to and made tribute to the party chiefs in exchange for their assistance or acquiescence of the rackets. Soviet citizens rightfully blamed these Mafias for the half-empty shelves and long lines at state stores and the high price they had to pay on the black market. The citizens, on the other hand, had no choice but to participate in the black market economy, for no one could live a normal life without black market goods and services.

Shadow Economy

The shadow economy became an integral part of Soviet economy and it employed thousands of people. Among those who profited from the shadow economy were peasants who cultivated private plots and sold their products on the black market, private manufacturers of consumer goods in short supply, common criminals who sold whatever they could lay their hands on, well-connected entrepreneurs who dealt with commodities stolen or diverted from state supply systems, foreign currency dealers, and prostitutes. By 1990, an official estimate showed that more than 50 percent of Soviet citizens purchased a variety of goods from the black market. The ones who stood to rake in the greatest profits in the shadow economy were the party bosses and those who occupied key positions in the state bureaucracy, for no individual racketeers could survive or prosper without first paying their dues to the people who held the ultimate authority in Soviet society. The real racketeers were none other than corrupt party bosses and self-seekers occupying key positions in the state bureaucracy. The unique conditions of life in the Soviet Union, characterized by endemic corruption and the burgeoning black market economy, became the training and breeding ground for the organized crime groups that rose to power in post-Soviet Russia.

BELOW Middle-class Russian women attempt to sell liquor they have just bought in a store, on the black market. Shortages on the shelves made this a lucrative business.

RED GODFATHERS
Life and Death as a Powerful Vor

On April 5, 1994, as Otari Kvantrishvili, one of Russia's most powerful Mafia bosses, was stepping out of the Krasnopresnenskaya baths in Moscow, he was brought down by three bullets from a sniper's gun. Meanwhile in the United States, Kvantrishvili's friend, Vyacheslav Ivankov, was reaching the peak of his criminal career in Brighton Beach, a Russian immigrant enclave in New York City.

Otari Kvantrishvili

A Georgian native, Kvantrishvili started his criminal career in the late 1960s, joining a major criminal group. In 1966, he was charged with rape but was released after being diagnosed as a schizophrenic—a common tactic to avoid conviction.

Connections

After working as a wrestling coach for a police team, he befriended famous athletes, especially boxers, wrestlers, and martial arts specialists and served as chairman of Lev Yashin Fund for the Support of Athletes. As chairman of a high profile "charitable organization," he traveled with Gorbachev to Europe. Just before his death, he had even received authorization from President Yeltsin to open a national sports center.

Thanks to his government connections, he had obtained numerous favorable deals, including facilities and fiscal discounts, export quota for cement, metals, naphtha, titanium, and aluminum. He controlled many hotels and restaurants and indirectly owned several casinos in Moscow. He made frequent television appearances, championing for charity and other social causes. His celebrity life nonetheless was cut short by a sniper.

Celebrity Death

His mourners represented a cross section of his life, including government officials, the criminal underworld, entertainers, athletes, law enforcement officers, veterans of the Afghan War, bank executives, and officers of various social organizations. At his burial, luxury foreign-made cars tied up traffic around the cemetery for hours. As an underworld figure, he earned his distinction more because of his ability to attain an influential position in the legitimate world than his power in the underworld.

In all likelihood it will never be known who ordered Kvantrishvili's murder. His life, and possibly his death, provides a good illustration of the interweaving of the criminal underworld and the legitimate world.

ABOVE Cockroach races are popular in Moscow. Here the winners of the Cup of Moscow celebrate in a casino many of which are owned by gangsters.

BELOW A member of the Russia of Justice party kicks a slot machine in protest while holding a sign reading "Down with a gambling Mafia."

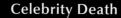

Vyacheslav Ivankov

Vyacheslav Ivankov was born in 1945 in Georgia and grew up in Moscow. In his early career, he and his gangs allegedly ransacked black marketeers' homes and confiscated their valuables.

Prison Camp

In 1974, after a gun battle over extortion, Ivankov disappeared. Six months later, he turned himself in, claiming he was a paranoid schizophrenic. He was confined first in a mental institution and then sent to a penal colony. After his release, he supposedly resumed his extortion schemes and was caught again in 1982. This time he was sentenced to 14 years in a maximum-security prison in Siberia where he was initiated as a *vor v zakone*. In 1991, after his early release, he launched a gang war against Chechen gangs. While happy with his success, in 1992 a ruling council of the *vory* decided to send him to the United States.

New York Expansion

He settled in Brighton Beach, New York City, where he became involved with gambling, prostitution, drug sales, and gasoline tax fraud. He obtained shares in legitimate businesses such as strip clubs, restaurants, and real estate and purchased a used car dealership as a money-laundering instrument.

Eyeing the huge profits from a cocaine importation route, he negotiated with the Russian gangsters back home to purchase it. The group refused his offer, but conveniently, within three months, all the top three bosses involved in the cocaine business were murdered in Moscow.

ABOVE A heavily armed Chechen rebel stands ready for battle. Ivankov ran a war against Chechen gangs.

US Prison

Ivankov's downfall involved his henchmen kidnapping two bank investors and forcing them to sign a contract promising to pay $3.5 million to one of his associates. The FBI became aware of the extortion scheme and in 1995, agents arrested Ivankov. He accused the FBI of inventing the myth of Russian Mafia. In July 1996, he was convicted of extortion and sentenced to imprisonment of nine years and seven months.

Extradition

On July 13, 2004, the US authority deported Ivankov to Russia to face murder charges. On July 18, 2005, the jury found him not guilty after five witnesses, including a police officer, testified that Ivankov was not the one involved. Ivankov remains a constant presence in Russian organized crime.

Revival of *Vory v Zakone*

By the end of the 1950s, the *vory* society had been almost entirely destroyed during the "bitches' war." Realizing that it was impossible to survive without some form of protection from the prison authorities, the *vory* modified their code to allow certain collaboration with the authorities. Even at the time of forced collaboration, the *vory* understood how to take advantage of the situation. A team leader was in a position to save food for his brothers, and barbers had access to razors and scissors, which would be invaluable weapons for self-protection. The loosening of the rigid thieves' law paved the way for the growth of a new generation of *vory*.

Money Talks

In the 1960s, law enforcement authorities were happy to believe that the *vory v zakone* were all but destroyed. The *vory*, however, were not to be written off easily. There emerged a new generation of *vory* who was more practical. They strived to stay out of prison. To them, one day spent in prison was one day wasted in their race to make money. Traditional *vory* took pride in their extensive body tattoos. The symbols of achievement for the new generation of *vory* were their fancy clothes, foreign cars, and luxurious apartments. The more successful *vory* owned a series of restaurants, hotels, retail outlets in Europe, and purchased some luxurious homes there.

The *vory*, however, remained faithful to many core requirements in the traditional thieves' law, fulfilling their obligation to provide moral and material support to their brothers. Following the *vory* tradition, a common monetary fund was set up in each group and was used to bribe the prison authorities and to buy food, alcohol, and drugs

ABOVE The beaches of Crimea have become the leisure haunts of Russian mobsters during the summer months.

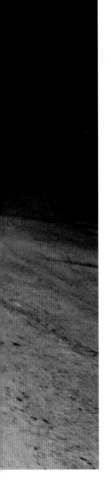

for incarcerated thieves from the group. Outside, the fund was used to bribe law enforcement officials and other public officials, to plan and carry out crimes, and to support the families of incarcerated thieves. The size of the fund carried great significance in the thieves' world. The respect a *vor* and his thieves commanded among fellow groups was proportionate to the size of the fund.

Vory v zakone supposedly occupied the highest level of the criminal hierarchy. Their elite status was recognized both within and outside prison. Within prison, the *vor* occupied the most comfortable space in a cell, usually the space that was near the window and far away from the commune toilet. Outside, the *vor* acted as the organizer or inspiration for a crime rather than personally participating in the crime. This mode of operation often hindered the successful prosecution of *vory*.

The new generation of *vory* still dutifully fulfill their obligation to recruit the young, and difficult economic conditions make the *vory*'s lifestyle even more attractive. The *vory* are known to have provided jobs and money to young men struggling in unemployment and hard economic conditions after the fall of the communist regime. "The family helps you" has become a typical line of recruitment.

Currently, there are about 400 *vory* operating in Russia. Disagreement exists as to the role of *vory* in contemporary Russian organized crime. Some dismiss them as old-fashioned gangs that could not adapt to the changed conditions. There are nonetheless signs that the *vory* have adapted well. It is said that to ensure profit taking is well regulated, *vory* groups have divided the world into power spheres, with separate groups assigned different countries for operation. The *vory* are key players in not only Russian organized crime but also in global organized crime.

ABOVE One of Russia's new rich stands outside his *datcha*. Once considered a simple country house, this *datcha* is valued at over $1 million USD.

TOP LEFT Police in the Irkutsk region of Siberia investigate a murder. The frozen body is of a man who has been badly beaten. His tattoos suggest he was a *vor*.

CELLULOID MAFIA

Dirty Pretty Things

BELOW Okwe (Chiwetel Ejiofor) chats with Senay (Audrey Tautou) on a London street.

Directed by Stephen Frears, with a script by Steven Knight, *Dirty Pretty Things* is a tense film that explores the challenges facing illegal migrants and the risks they sometimes feel compelled to take to survive.

The Plot

Formerly a doctor in Africa, Okwe (Chiwetel Ejiofor) is an illegal Nigerian immigrant working a double shift as a mini-cab driver and night porter at The Baltic, a backstreet London hotel, with a Russian doorman. When Okwe stumbles across a human heart blocking the toilet in a room at the hotel, he is unsure what to do, and confides in the arrogant entrepreneurial hotel manager "Sneaky" Juan (Sergi Lopez), a Chinese morgue attendant friend, Guo Yi (Benedict Wong), and the hotel maid Senay (Audrey Tautou) who is working illegally and letting him share her tiny flat. Sneaky is part of a criminal ring, controlled by the Russian Mafia, that uses illegal migrants for body parts—selling one of their kidneys, say, for a passport and thus obtaining a new identity.

When immigration authorities close in on the desperate Senay, she agrees to exchange a kidney for a passport. Juan forces her to have sex with him before permitting her to undergo the operation. Discovering Senay's plan, Okwe convinces Juan to let him perform the operation to ensure her safety. But Okwe and Senay drug Juan, harvest his kidney, and sell it to Juan's contact—having also obtained their new passports from Juan.

Awards

Dirty Pretty Things was nominated for an Academy Award for Best Original Screenplay and won a British Independent Film Award for Best Independent British Film in 2003. Frears made his name with the internationally acclaimed *My Beautiful Laundrette*, which also explores the lives and problems of migrants in London.

LEFT Pressured by her boss, Senay gives in to his demands and agrees to sell her kidney

Eastern Promises

Eastern Promises depicts the morality-challenged world of the Russian Mafia that callously exchanges people for goods.

The Plot

Russian-born Nikolai Luzhin (Viggo Mortensen) is a driver for one of London's most notorious East European organized crime families, headed by Semyon (Armin Mueller-Stahl), whose front is a Trans-Siberian London restaurant. Semyon's volatile son Kirill (Vincent Cassel) does the dirty work, while Nikolai quietly and efficiently cleans up the mess. It is Christmas time, and Nikolai crosses paths with Anna Khitrova (Naomi Watts), a midwife, who is affected by the death of a 14-year-old girl who dies while giving birth. In a bid to find the baby's relatives, Anna looks for answers in the girl's personal diary, and while Anna's mother Helen (Sinéad Cusack) is ambivalent, her Russian-born uncle Stepan (Jerzy Skolimowski) is concerned, as the diary revealed secrets about the criminal *vory* brotherhood that will put them all at risk.

Gruesome Climax

Mortensen wears Armani suits and a deadpan expression for much of the film, but in the climactic scene set in a bathhouse, he wears nothing but his descriptive, Mafia-badge tattoos, in a spectacularly choreographed conflict that includes bloody stabbings and a graphic eye-gouging.

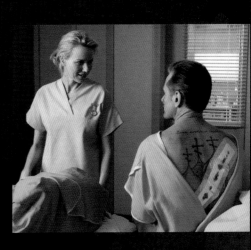

Awards

The film is directed by the iconoclastic David Cronenberg. *Eastern Promises* won the Audience Prize for best film at the Toronto International Film Festival and the Best Actor award for Mortensen at the 2007 British Independent Film Awards. The film received 12 Genie Award nominations, three Golden Globe Award nominations, and Mortensen was nominated for Best Actor at the Academy Awards.

ROOF

Protection has long been the specific commodity the Mafia sells. However, a noteworthy phenomenon was the emergence of a more profitable level of protection service known as a *krysha* or "roof." The service of "roof" was controlled by powerful criminals composed of traditional crime bosses and party-bosses-turned-entrepreneurs. Former KGB agents and army officers, out of work or receiving low pay, were more than willing to offer their services to the crime bosses.

Pay-offs to government officials were needed for obtaining business licenses and permits. The Mafia also needed to be paid off. The Mafia demanded protection money from businesses and then used the money to bribe government officials and the police. The Mafia thus placed itself in a position of total control. The pervasive corruption, a legacy of the Soviet era, made it impossible to draw a clear distinction between criminal enterprises and the government.

As corrupt officials and oligarchs pocketed millions of dollars, young police recruits earned only $200 USD a month. The harsh reality made the police ranks vulnerable to corruption. In 1994, the Moscow police chief estimated that 95 percent of his men were on the take.

A more vicious form of organized crime involved police and KGB officers arresting entrepreneurs on real or trumped-up charges. They would take over their enterprises and confiscate their property. It was estimated that this fate befell more than 200,000 entrepreneurs.

A scene at an early 1929 corruption and pay-off trial of 147 Soviet government employees in the Winter Theatre, Astrachan.

ABOVE An official of the Moscow State Drug Control Committee inspects syringes found in a surprise raid on the Zima Night Club.

Rise of Russian Mafias

The unique conditions of life and the transition to a market economy in the post-Soviet era produced the most fertile soil for the growth of organized crime.

The recognition of the right to private property enabled the underground tycoons and party barons to find a legitimate outlet for their secret wealth. The capital accumulated in the black market economy found its way into stock exchanges, joint ventures, cooperatives, banks and stock companies. Crimes like theft, robbery, embezzlement, forgery, fraud, and counterfeiting increased manifold. But the criminal organizations found the best fit for their talent in providing protection.

Smuggling

As Russia experienced the painful transformation to capitalism, party barons and crime bosses found two simple ways of accumulating wealth—smuggling of raw materials and looting state industries.

Former party bosses and self-seeking industrial managers allowed enormous quantities of minerals and precious metals to be stolen or purchased at extremely low prices from state-run mines and factories. The income from the smuggling trade formed the financial foundation of Russian organized crime.

Looting

Looting state-run industries was another way to accumulate wealth. In 1992, Russia began to privatize state property. With ill-gotten wealth, the former party bosses shed the useless party cards and turned into entrepreneurs and capitalists. Gangland murders, bomb explosions, kidnappings, and gun battles became frequent occurrences in some Russian cities. The extreme form of violence that was employed is illustrated in an incident in which a criminal gang hijacked a T-90 tank and drove it to the local market to fire upon a rival gang that was taking protection money from the wrong turf.

Contract Killing

The most pernicious feature of the criminal violence was contract killing. In the chaotic years after the fall of the communist regime, Russia saw about 10,000 fatal shootings each year. A considerable number of these were contract killings. Desperate for money, assassins would take out a contract for as little as $1,000 USD. From 1992 to 1998, 95 bankers and 13 journalists fell victim to assassins' bullets.

Money Laundering

To carry out their money laundering schemes, organized crime organizations realized that they would have to infiltrate or take over banks and financial institutions.

Assassination was their ultimate weapon to get rid of anyone who stood in their way. The disproportionate number of assassination attempts against top banking officials throughout Russia proves the determination of criminal organizations to control these monetary institutions.

At the close of the 1990s, the rapacious former party bosses and oligarchs emerged as Russia's new class of entrepreneurs and capitalists. With their enormous wealth and possession of many legitimate businesses, they gained a commanding control over the Russian economy.

ABOVE Chechen commander Sulim Yamadayev (right) was dismissed in 2008 over the alleged blackmail and abduction of a Chechen businessman.

BELOW The largest amber mine in the world in Kaliningrad Oblast. This region is a major smuggling route out of Russia.

Drug Cartels
South America

ABOVE Members of the Revolutionary
Armed Forces of Colombia (FARC) hide
in the jungle. FARC is considered
a terrorist organization because
of its actions against civilians.

**The multi-billion dollar cocaine exporting business began in the
mid-1970s with a handful of marijuana smugglers operating out
of small makeshift conversion laboratories and transporting the
product on their person or in luggage across international borders.**

Domestic Crops

During most of the twentieth century and up until the late 1990s, Bolivia and Peru
were the primary producers of coca. Both of these countries have a large indigenous
population of Indians who have been cultivating the coca plant for domestic use for
hundreds, if not thousands, of years. In the early to mid-twentieth century a large
portion of Bolivia's tax structure was based on the cultivation of coca.

In fact, coca cultivation and processing were responsible for hundreds of thousands
of jobs in these two countries where unemployment in the mid-1970s was high. The
rise in the cultivation of coca coincided with an huge increase in demand, widespread
economic problems, and the evolution of the major Colombian drug cartels.

Peru

In Peru, the Upper Huallaga Valley became a major coca producer in the late 1970s and a major trafficking hub in the 1980s. Planes destined for Colombia and loaded with coca paste would depart each week from numerous airstrips located throughout the area.

This area was effectively under the control of the Maoist insurgent group, Sendero Luminosa, or Shining Path. This group essentially protected the coca-producing valley, insuring that peasant cultivation of coca proceeded uninterrupted. Sendero Luminosa was able to extort millions of dollars per year from peasant farmers and Colombian drug cartels by imposing a revolutionary tax on coca paste. Like their Colombian counterparts—the Revolutionary Armed Forces of Colombia (FARC)—Sendero Luminosa financed their insurgency mainly from the illegal drug trade.

As in Bolivia and Colombia, corruption of public officials was part of the political landscape. In the 1980s, the US government and Peruvian officials attempted to manually eradicate the crop but these efforts failed due to ongoing violence perpetuated by Peruvian insurgents and the efforts of Sendero Luminosa. Bi-lateral eradication efforts also increased popular support for Sendero Luminosa

Bolivia

Unlike Colombia, Bolivia, at first, did not engage in the international trafficking of cocaine. This had more to do with geography and a lack of business acumen compared to their Colombian counterparts. However, in the 1980s Bolivian trafficking organizations did form operational alliances with Colombian traffickers and other international drug trafficking networks. The Bolivian government had developed a symbiotic relationship with narco-traffickers and coca became Bolivia's most valuable export commodity at that time. Thus, its influence penetrated all facets of economic and political life including the judiciary.

Indeed, in the late 1990s, dozens of judges were removed by the Bolivian Judicial Council, an oversight body with broad powers established in 1998 to address corruption among members of the judiciary. These judges were dismissed for accepting bribes in regard to drug-related cases and the disposition of convicted traffickers. During the latter part of the twentieth century, Bolivian trafficking groups were often allied with law enforcement and frequently both groups worked in unison.

Systematic efforts to rid the country of coca through eradication met with very stiff resistance especially in the Yungas, a coca-growing region in central Bolivia, and have consolidated public sentiment and sparked mass demonstrations from farmers and trade unions that constituted a large percentage of the national population. This strong opposition from pro-coca lobbies was more of a destabilizing factor in Bolivia than the presence and activities of cocaine-producing and trafficking cartels.

ABOVE An armed anti-narcotics police helicopter patrols the Upper Huallaga Valley in Peru searching for illegal crops.

Colombia is in a risky position. They've got a peace process that's going nowhere, and a drug production problem that's skyrocketing.

Barry McCaffrey, retired US Army General

ABOVE Colombian anti-narcotics police oversee the destruction of six tons of cocaine, illegally processed in the jungle.

BELOW Police clear debris placed on the road by Bolivian farmers who were protesting over the government's plans to eradicate their coca crops.

Major Employer

Various estimates of the numbers employed in the cocaine trade surfaced in the 1990s. In Peru and Bolivia estimates ranged from 2 to 4 percent of the total work force in Peru, and approximately 3 percent of the Bolivian work force were thought to be involved in the cocaine industry. These figures would undoubtedly be a lot higher if ancillary employment was included and the number of public officials, who are collecting revenue for disregarding legislation designed to curtail the trade, failing to take the appropriate legal action against individuals involved in the trade, or simply turning a blind eye to the illegal activity that they know is occurring, were factored in.

Production Levels

It is difficult to determine how much coca is produced on an annual basis. It is even harder to determine how much cultivated coca is processed into cocaine. The coca-rich regions of Bolivia, Colombia, and Peru, or the Andean region as it is referred to, account for nearly 100 percent of the world's illicit cocaine supply. Given the furtive nature of the trade of trafficking in cocaine, as well as other controlled substances, and the fluid dynamics of this enterprise, reliable data is difficult to assess. The UN, using primarily ground surveys and imagery from commercial satellites, and the USA that relies on satellite surveillance technology, are probably the most reliable sources for information on the cultivation of coca and the processing and production of cocaine and other illicit substances.

Eradication Methods

Since the early 1990s attempts have been made to eradicate coca manually and by aerial spraying of herbicides. A successful eradication process usually kills the plant within 2–3 months. Eradication efforts involved the US Department of State operating out of the embassy in Bogota, the Colombian National Police, and the Colombian army that secured the targeted area prior to the operation.

It can be expected that if aerial eradication proved successful, coca cultivation and production processes would migrate to other areas within the country or spill over into neighboring states.

ABOVE US Army cargo plane delivers helicopters to the Colombian government to aid its battle against drug trafficking by the Medellin cartel.

SEIZURE DATA

Seizure data—the amount and type of drug intercepted by various local and national interdiction agencies—provides monitors with a somewhat skewed picture of the trafficking dimension of the drug problem.

BELOW US Customs agents unload a massive haul of cocaine seized from the ship *Barlovento*, off Key West.

Success of Interdiction Methods

Successful drug seizures do not necessarily reflect the magnitude of the drug trafficking problem but rather the activities of law enforcement and the priorities attached to the interception of illegal drugs within a given agency. It provides law enforcement with a gauge to measure the effectiveness of their interdiction methods. Seizure data also reflects the types of drugs that are being trafficked and is a good indicator of the specific drug demand—usage trends, purity level, and source country. Seizure data also provides information relative to methods of conveyance and concealment.

Purity Levels

A primary indicator of increased drug production is the purity level. A decrease in the purity level of a narcotic is generally an indicator of reduced supply; the higher the purity of the drug the greater the availability and the lower the price. If supply is diminished the purity level goes down and the price escalates based on demand. A reduced supply can be attributed to a number of factors such as increased law enforcement activity or low crop yields due to environmental factors.

Trafficking Methods

Government efforts to curtail the flow of drugs are often countered with equal and novel production and trafficking methods. Drug trafficking organizations are inventive. For example, law enforcement successes at curtailing the flow of precursor chemicals used to convert coca into cocaine or opium into heroin are very often thwarted by the use of alternative, more accessible chemical agents. Additionally, in efforts to circumvent law enforcement interdiction strategies, drug traffickers have employed a variety of innovative smuggling techniques such as maritime containerized shipping and the

ABOVE The Colombian army raids the house of Medellin cartel chief, Pablo Escobar, in 1989, after his arrest.

Colombian Drug Production

Colombia is the world's largest producer of coca and cocaine and serves as the principal transportation hub. Without a doubt, the criminal groups in Colombia dominated the international trade in cocaine from late 1970s to early–mid 1990s. While Asia supplies most of the world's heroin, Colombia has made some small but significant inroads into this area most notably in the US market over the past several years. Colombia accounts for approximately 2 percent of the world's heroin supply, and is the largest producer and distributor of opium/heroin in the Western Hemisphere. The heroin trade is a recent phenomenon in Colombia created by declining demand for cocaine in North America and a growing demand for heroin.

Medellin Cartel

The Medellin cartel originated in Medellin, Colombia, and operated in the 1970s and 1980s. The group was formed by Pablo Escobar, a violent street criminal who became the group's leader; Carlos Lehder, an ex-convict and small-time marijuana trafficker; Rodriquez Gacha, who had been involved in the illicit trading of precious metals; and the Ochoa brothers—Jorge, Juan David, and Fabio. The group shipped cocaine directly into the United States by plane as demand for the drug increased. Because of their propensity for extreme violence, US and Colombian law enforcement officials considered the Medellin cartel a more serious threat to the government than the rival Cali cartel.

Cali Cartel

The Cali cartel was founded by Gilberto and Miguel Orejuela and Jose Santacruz Londono in the early 1970s. Initially, the group trafficked in marijuana but became involved in the more lucrative cocaine market that was expanding in North America, and eventually diversified into the heroin market. Operating in small cells the Cali cartel soon established itself as the most powerful drug syndicate in the world. Cali's operational sophistication and business acumen set it apart from other more violent drug organizations. Cali drug lords formed alliances with European criminal groups to reduce their risk and expand their market.

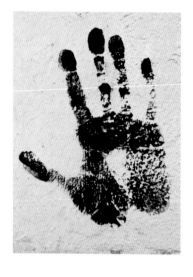

ABOVE The black handprint on a white wall or background is the symbol of the Cali cartel.

RIGHT Gilberta Orejuela, head of the Cali cartel, is deported to the USA after his arrest in 2004.

Additionally, in an effort to eliminate competitors, specifically the Medellin cartel, Cali was known for cooperating with US and Colombian authorities.

The Cali cartel met its end in the mid-1990s. Prior to its downfall, its annual profits exceeded $8 billion USD. The Orejuela brothers were arrested in 1995 and extradited to the United States. They are both serving time there. Londono was killed by police in Medellin in 1996, after his escape from prison.

CELLULOID MAFIA
Maria Full of Grace

The 2004 film, written and directed by Joshua Marston, is a painstaking depiction of the grueling nature of the mule's task, as we see Maria desperately swallowing 62 pellets of heroin.

You have the pellets back!

Maria (Catalina Sandino Moreno)

Exactly, we have them back and we don't need you anymore.

Felipe (Charles Albert Patiño)

ABOVE Maria (Catalina Sandino Moreno) slumps on the desk at the thought of having to swallow pellets of heroin.

Typical Victim

Maria Alvarez (Catalina Sandino Moreno) is portrayed as a stereotype victim of Colombian drug cartel operators, who prey on vulnerable young women and persuade them to take great risks for the sake of their family's financial survival.

Drug Mule

Maria is a typical 17-year-old girl in rural Colombia—typically poor, typically caught in a dead-end job stripping rose stems along a conveyor belt, alongside her best friend Blanca (Yenny Paola Vega). When she gets pregnant to her gutless boyfriend, Juan (Wilson Guerrero), and her boss is unsympathetic, she quits on the spot. Now jobless and ostracized by her family, Maria is offered a way out through a chance meeting with a nice looking young man Franklin (John Alex Toro), who has contacts.

He arranges a meeting in which Maria is offered a job as a drug "mule," carrying 62 pellets of heroin to the USA—inside her stomach. Once in New York, the simple plan is made complicated by a fellow mule's violent death. Maria needs to learn how survive in a hostile environment, and fast.

BELOW Trying to forget her troubles, Maria takes a ride with Franklin (John Alex Torro), who will lead her down a deadly path of hopelessness.

Realism

Moreno and Marston agreed that it would be more realistic for her to try swallowing the pellets for the first time on-camera. The pellets were made of easily digestible substances but neither Moreno nor Marston will reveal what that is.

Awards

Catalina Sandino Moreno was nominated for a Best Supporting Actress Oscar for her role—the first actress to be nominated for a role spoken entirely in Spanish—after win-

Global Domination

During the 1980s, the Medellin and Cali cartels dominated the global traffic of illicit cocaine, supplying most consumer demand in the North America and Europe.

Colombia's evolution to major drug producer began in the 1970s. Before that time Colombia did not play a dominant role in the international drug trade. While both groups were powerful and held tremendous influence in Colombia's government and political and social institutions, they had different *modus operandi* or protocols they used to achieve the influence they sought in order to conduct their illegal activities.

Extradition Treaty

During the 1980s, the threats and violence against members of the Colombian judiciary escalated with dozens of officials, including Supreme Court justices, being murdered. Threats against sitting judges escalated further after the US–Colombian extradition treaty entered into force in 1982. The treaty signaled cooperation between the two governments in their bilateral fight against illicit trafficking of drugs. The major cartels, through bribes and intimidation, attempted to influence legislative action taken by the Colombian government. Consequently, mass violence ensued and many Colombian citizens, public officials, and police officers were murdered.

In 1986, this treaty was invalidated by the Colombian Supreme Court, although numerous Colombian-born traffickers were extradited pursuant to this treaty during the period 1982–1986 and continued by executive degree until 1990. In 1997, the extradition of Colombian nationals to the USA for prosecution relative to drug trafficking became law when the Colombian constitution was amended. However, the law only allowed extradition for crimes committed after December 1997. Shortcomings in the new legislation were that crimes committed prior to this date did not fall under the mandates of the revised law and the law only applied to certain types of offenses.

BELOW Demonstrators in Medellin, Colombia, display photos of human rights workers kidnapped by paramilitary forces in the area.

Cartel Kidnappings

Another issue that commanded unified action by the major cartels was the kidnapping of wealthy drug barons and their family members by Marxist guerrillas, mainly the Revolutionary Armed Forces of Colombia (FARC), M-19, and the National Liberation Army (ELN). These groups, which have been at war with the Colombian government for decades, generate a large portion of their

revenue by kidnapping. Colombia has a long reputation for being one of the world's foremost places for kidnapping which is a cottage industry in Colombia and is second only to the drug trade in terms of revenue generation. Colombian government officials, rich landowners, foreign nationals, and powerful members of the major drug cartels have been the targets of such violence. Many kidnap victims are held captive for many years prior to their release.

FARC, the largest guerrilla group in Colombia with between 15,000 and 20,000 members, is the considered the most prolific kidnapper. FARC units are dispatched along wide swathes of the country, usually in rural and lightly populated areas.

ABOVE Mourners carry the coffin of Colombian presidential candidate Carlos Pizarro after his assassination by a Colombian paramilitary group in 1990.

DEATH TO KIDNAPPERS

In an effort to counter the kidnapping threat among cartel members, a 1981 meeting of the major drug traffickers led to the formation of the Muerte a Secuestradores (MAS) or "Death to Kidnappers" group. The sole purpose of this army of mercenaries was to stop the kidnapping for ransom of cartel members and their families. MAS engaged the guerrilla forces and often worked in conjunction with the Colombian army and national police. This death squad was initially spawned following the kidnapping of a sister of the Ochoa brothers by M-19, a Colombian guerrilla group, which demanded a ransom of $15 million USD. The woman, Marta Nieves Ochoa, was released following violent retaliation by the major cartels.

Supporters of M-19, shout in rage after the funeral of their previous leader, Carlos Pizarro. He was one of the founders of M-19 after disagreements caused him to leave FARC.

1969 Richard Nixon identifies drug abuse as "a serious national threat."

1972 By order of the Nixon administration, all vehicles crossing from Mexico to the United States are checked for drugs. Drug trafficking does not decrease.

1985 The Pentagon spends $40 million USD on drug interdiction.

1986 Boris Yeltsin states that there are over 3,700 registered drug addicts in Moscow.

RIGHT Customs agents in Mexico dump packages of illicit drugs into a container ready for disposal.

OPPOSITE Thousands of paratroopers return to Fort Bragg after the US invasion of Panama, designed to seize and arrest Manuel Noriega for drug trafficking.

Narcoterrorism

The term narcoterrorism implies a direct or indirect financial benefit accrued to terrorist/extremist groups based in or operating from Colombia and other Andean drug-producing states by their involvement in any aspect of the cocaine/heroin trade. More specifically, in Colombia as well as Afghanistan, the term narcoterrorism denotes a linkage or an alliance of convenience between groups—Marxist guerrillas and terrorists/insurgents—with disparate long-term objectives but short-term financial and logistical needs.

The term narcoterrorism also applies to the use of violence by insurgent forces against drug trafficking groups in drug cultivation and production areas controlled by revolutionary forces. The use of terror tactics by drug criminals—the Medellin cartel employed these tactics against state judiciary and other government officials—also falls under the term narcoterrorism.

Mexican Drug Trafficking and Corruption

Mexico became a major player in the trafficking of cocaine in the 1980s. Today approximately 90 percent of all the cocaine that reaches consumers in the United States enters through Mexico. Mexico's geography and terrain make it an ideal smuggling corridor. According to Mexican government officials, seven major trafficking cartels control the drug trade in Mexico. In addition to cocaine, these organizations are responsible for transporting heroin, methamphetamines, and marijuana.

The major drug players in Mexico are the Tijuana, Senaloa, Juarez, Guadalajara, and Gulf cartels. The Tijuana group has a reputation similar in style to Colombia's Medellin cartel and is known for its violent tactics, ability to traffic huge amounts of cocaine, and the corruption of state and public officials. The Tijuana cartel is considered by many in the law enforcement community to be one of the world's most violent drug crime organizations.

As in Colombia, government corruption in Mexico is rampant especially among police officials, the military, and members of the judiciary. It is estimated that millions of dollars are spent each year by Mexican cartels in the bribery of public officials at the local as well as national levels. In fact, the involvement of Mexico's military in the illegal drug trade has had heavy international repercussions specifically with regard to the United States.

Western Europe
Global Markets

The second half of the twentieth century was even more interesting and dangerous than the first in terms of the development of organized crime, with a worldwide expansion in global markets, activities, and threats. The focus, however, was on the United Kingdom and the Balkans.

BELOW Organized crime is evident in areas such as this, where poverty creates a hotbed of crime and violence.

The Fruits of War

In the field of organized crime as elsewhere, World War II was one of the defining events of the twentieth century, reshaping many underworld organizations and newly empowering others.

Two international organizations were particularly empowered—Italian crime families and Chinese organizations. World War II was when the distribution of power changed, with organized crime groups seizing opportunities to become truly international. The war also developed new markets and began global trade in others—drug trafficking, money laundering, and fraud. It also increased black market activities such as prostitution and slave labor. Other events that affected crime in the latter half of the twentieth century included the Cold War, the de-colonization efforts of many countries around the world, the growth of terrorism, the fall of the Berlin Wall, and the collapse of the Soviet Union. All of these events led to the destabilization of governments and the opening up of opportunities for organized crime to become established. Wars also continually shape the face of existing and active organized crime groups. Local wars—the Indochina war, the Vietnam War, the Afghanistan War, the Algerian War, and the first Gulf War—all contributed to the success of organized crime through the disruption of power and the explosion of opportunities for corruption and illegal profit.

Society prepares the crime, the criminal commits it.

Henry Thomas Buckle (1821–1862), English historian

Chemicals, Computers, Narcotics

OPPOSITE Pakistani Customs officials burn piles of confiscated narcotics and smuggled goods. Pakistan straddles the narcotics trade route from Afghanistan to the Middle East and Europe.

Historical events have not been the only cause of criminal progression. Technologies, including the development of the chemical industry and the computer industry, have had a major impact on the existence of illegal markets and trade and on the organized crime groups that are active today. But the one single illegal market that has dominated all the others during this period is narcotics.

ABOVE Notorious Jewish gangster Jack "Spot" Comer (second from left) with his wife Rita after acquittal, 1955. For years, Comer was crime lord of London's East End.

Opportunity Knocks

World War II opened up a whole new set of possibilities to organized crime groups operating in the United Kingdom, thanks mainly to the shortages and rationing of essential goods during and immediately after the war. Billy Hill, for example, became a major crime boss in and around London at that time, mainly running black market operations in food and gasoline.

Boss of the Underworld

Born in 1911, Billy Hill began his career in 1920 when he went to work as a small-time housebreaker. As his experience grew, he began to tackle jewelers.

World War II gave him the opportunity to begin successful black market operations in restricted commodities like rationed food and scarce gasoline. After being charged with breaking and entering, Billy fled to South Africa to avoid sentencing. There he became heavily involved in the underground control of nightclubs in the Johannesburg area. However, once again, he was arrested and charged, this time for assault. He was extradited to Britain where he served a jail sentence until 1947.

Upon his release, Billy went back to the nightclub business with a partner, Jack "Spot" Comer. He also started another lucrative business in big-time robberies. The first in 1952, from a postal van, reaped somewhere near £250,000. Two years later, he hit again, this time robbing a van carrying bullion worth about £40,000. Known for his entrepreneurial flair, he also organized the smuggling of cigarettes from Morocco—no doubt helped by his girlfriend, who owned a nightclub there. He continued his gambling and property scams until the 1970s when he more or less retired. He died in 1984, still a wealthy man.

RIGHT Billy Hill (1911–1984), the United Kingdom's first celebrity gangster, is said to have planned a heist that set the template for the Great Train Robbery.

BROTHERS IN ARMS

The Torture Gang

World War II brought many new opportunities for illegal enterprises to flourish, particularly when it came to the business of dealing with the waste of war—building materials and scrap metal. The Richardson brothers were ready.

Born in the 1930s, Charles and Eddie Richardson began their crime careers by stealing goods quite literally from the backs of passing trucks. By the age of 19, Charles had taken on the leadership of the team when he opened a scrap yard, dealing mainly in stolen goods and metal recycling. His brother, Eddie, meanwhile, was marketing "fruit" machines—a form of slot machine. He would convince pub owners to install his machines in exchange for his protection.

Charles bought or built up small companies using a legitimate-looking frontman. He would then approach banks for credit facilities, but as soon as they were in place the business would disappear, together with the money. Charles did not disappear, however. He was arrested and charged with fraud.

With World War II underway, Charles was made to join the army as punishment. After the war, he returned to scrap metal, and by 1956 he owned five yards as well as several nightclubs. Once again, he was charged with selling stolen scrap but this time he escaped to Canada. Immediately, he set up a successful business that he was able to sell before returning to the United Kingdom, where, after a very generous donation to the Police Fund, he was acquitted of all charges against him.

During the restructuring of his empire, Charles, in association with "Mad" Frankie Fraser, held "kangaroo courts" where they would decide what punishments they would mete out to various conmen. Their gang, known as the Torture Gang, soon gained a reputation as sadistic.

In 1966, after a nightclub fight in which Dickie Hart, a Kray associate, was murdered, the entire Richardson Gang was arrested. Charles received a 25-year sentence while Eddie and their cohort, Frankie Fraser, received lighter sentences. Eddie was released in 1976, but was charged and sentenced again in 1990, receiving another 25-year sentence for drug smuggling. Charles was released in 1984 and took up legitimate business.

BELOW Charles and Eddie Richardson outside their Brixton scrap-metal yard. The brothers had a long-running gangland feud with the Kray twins.

RIGHT The truth, the whole truth, and nothing but the truth. The author, "Mad" Frankie Fraser, with a copy of his book, 2000.

ABOVE Police officers watch the crowd during the funeral of Ronald Kray (1933–1995), a huge public event that saw hundreds of people lining the streets.

The Krays

Organized crime in the post-war years in the United Kingdom was dominated by the Kray twins, Ronald "Ronnie" and Reginald "Reggie," born in Hoxton, East London on October 24, 1933. They had an older brother, Charlie, but he was less well known. Their own status eventually rose beyond the criminal underworld and into the world of celebrity as they mixed with the famous.

Violent Beginnings

Greatly influenced by their grandfather, Jimmy "Cannonball" Lee, who had been a bare-knuckle boxer in his youth, the boys entered amateur boxing leagues, a popular pursuit for the young working-class boys of West End London at the time. Renowned for their boxing skill while still young, they both turned professional at the age of nineteen.

During their teens they became famous locally for their street gang, and their reputation for toughness was enhanced when they were called up for National Service, an event that ended their boxing career and pushed them firmly into crime. Their reaction to authority and its various representatives was harsh, even bestial, especially if these representatives were police officers. It is reported that at this time, Ronnie began to show signs of what is known now as "paranoid schizophrenia." Prison guards and police officers thought he was a dangerous psychotic.

"The Firm"

The Krays' criminal activities included a protection racket, hijacking, robbery, murder, and the counterfeiting of documents to gain National Service exemption or jobs on the docks. They learned their trade from Jack "Spot" and Billy Hill, and also worked for them as bodyguards before acquiring a whole series of clubs.

One of the clubs the twins took over was Esmeralda's, a nightclub in Knightsbridge, and this increased their fame and influence in West End London. They expanded by taking over clubs that had mysteriously been bombed, while at the same time investing in their other illegal businesses. The Kray gang was so entrenched in London crime that it became known as "The Firm." They were assisted by the banker Alan Cooper who was seeking protection from threats by the Richardson brothers.

CELEBRITY STATUS

The Kray brothers' very well-publicized clubs were frequented by celebrities and people of means, and the twins were photographed with lords, members of parliament, and famous actors and actresses such as George Raft, Judy Garland, Barbara Windsor, and Frank Sinatra. During the "Swinging Sixties" in London, the Kray twins became very influential. They were introduced to a peer of the realm, Lord Boothby, at one of the gay parties they attended, an association that proved fruitful.

Ronnie, second from left, and Reggie, third from right, with Charlie Kray (right), George Raft, and Rocky Marciano, c. 1965.

A Higher Authority

Ronnie and Reggie both preferred to keep a low profile on the criminal side, letting other members of "The Firm" do the dirty business. When they were arrested in 1965 for forcing protection on a club owner named Hew McGowan, the length of their detention was questioned by Lord Boothby in the House of Lords, causing a minor media sensation. They were cleared of all charges and, less than a month later, they took over McGowan's Hideaway club, renaming it El Morocco.

Who Killed Who

In 1966, the Krays attempted to infiltrate the Richardsons' territory in South London. Allegedly, there was also trouble over profit-sharing from a pornographic film racket. Whatever its various sources, the friction came to a head in a gun battle at a club called Mr Smith's that resulted in the killing of Dickie Hart. It is not known for certain who killed Hart. Some have said it was Frankie Fraser, others that it was George Cornell, an associate of the Richardson gang. It is known, however, that Ronnie shot Cornell through the eye in the Blind Beggar Public House.

Decline and Fall

At the end of 1966, the Krays organized the escape of Frank "Mad Axeman" Mitchell from Dartmoor Prison. Mitchell was killed some months later, and from that time on the deteriorating mental and physical health of the Kray twins had a destabilizing effect on The Firm, culminating in the murder of Jack "The Hat" McVitie. On May 8, 1968, the twins were arrested and sentenced to life. Ronnie died in 1995, Reggie in 2000.

ABOVE The Kray twins enjoy a cup of tea and a cigarette after 36 hours of questioning by the police over the murder of George Cornell, 1966.

The Clerkenwell Crime Syndicate

One of the largest, and still active, crime families in London during the 1990s was the Clerkenwell crime syndicate. The British press regard it as the most powerful criminal organization in the United Kingdom.

The syndicate, an Irish Catholic group also known as the Adams Family or the A-team, is based in Islington, London. Their activities allegedly include drug trafficking, armed robbery, extortion, fraud, money laundering, and murder. They are also linked to the Jamaican Yardies and the Colombian drug cartels. Media reports have linked the A-Team to more than 25 murders, and to wealth of more than £200 million.

In the 1990s the gang was supposedly ruled by Terry Adams, along with his two brothers Tommy and Patrick. It was said that they had a Conservative MP in their pocket, but if this is so it did not save Terry, who pleaded guilty to money laundering in 2007 and is serving a three-and-a-half-year sentence. The syndicate has also been linked to the shooting of Frankie Fraser, a former associate of the Richardson brothers.

Brindle and Daley

Another gang active in the United Kingdom during the 1990s was the Brindle Family. They engaged in a gang war with their rivals the Daley Family in South London. Both were allegedly involved in drug trafficking and had links with Turkish families—especially the Arif brothers who were convicted in April 1991. The head of the Brindle Family, Anthony Brindle, survived despite being shot three times by a former IRA assassin, and just a month after Brindle and his associates had tried to extort money from one of the Daley brothers, a Brindle associate was shot seven times by a Turkish gunmen linked to the Arifs. He too survived, but the gunman was killed in March 1991.

BELOW Detectives dust a stolen car for fingerprints after it was used to hijack gold bullion from a lorry near London. The raid took only twenty seconds.

The Noonans

The head of the Noonan Crime Family, Desmond "Dessie" Noonan, born in 1959, was a well-known organized crime figure in Manchester in the 1990s. The Noonans, of Irish descent, ruled for more than 20 years and are thought to be responsible for more than 25 unsolved murders. At his peak, Desmond Noonan was regarded as one of the major crime bosses in the United Kingdom.

The Noonan Crime Family took control of organized crime in the Manchester area after the 1991 gangland murder of Anthony "White Tony" Johnson, the leader of the rival Cheetham Hill Gang. Desmond and his brothers Dominic, Damian, and Derek, had interests in nightclubs in other cities such as Liverpool, London, and Newcastle. This expansion beyond the family's original territory brought the Noonans into contact with other leading crime bosses including the alleged Liverpool drug baron Curtis Warren, Dave Courtney in London who claimed to be a friend of the Krays, and the head of the family ruling Newcastle's organized crime, Paddy Conroy.

Glasgow and Globalization

Scottish gangsters were experts in the explosives used in coalmines and plied their talent blowing up safes for a living. During the 1950s and 1960s, Glasgow was allegedly controlled by Mendel Morris, and he later passed his empire to his protégé. Despite the fact that he must have been busy running a criminal empire, it is said that Thompson also worked for MI5, the British intelligence agency.

During the last years of the twentieth century, the financial benefits of globalization were felt by a number of Scottish clans, including the Daniel clan, considered one of the richest families in Scotland. Though active in tobacco and drug smuggling as well as money laundering, they became powerful only thanks to the many of Italian clans that settled in Scotland, especially those from Calabria and Naples, who taught the Scottish criminals how to manage a truly professional international organized crime business.

BELOW Dave Courtney at the Kerrang! Awards at The Brewery in London, 2005. The former gangster has now become an author and film-maker.

Funding the IRA

The war in Northern Ireland had a deep impact on the British underworld as the IRA sought financial support there. The vast resources they needed could only be funded illegally—through weapons, explosives, and narcotics trafficking. Special units of the IRA in charge of such lucrative businesses dealt with the English crime families and Scottish clans and it was not long before these units turned into true organized crime units rather than political terrorist outfits or liberation teams.

Yardies

Jamaican gangs are known as Yardies—a slang term for the occupants of government yards in Kingston, Jamaica. Jamaicans migrated first to the United States and then to Britain where most of them moved to the London districts of Brixton, Halesden, and Hackney. Yardies culture is characterized by a strong tendency to violence. Yardies gangs are renowned for this tendency, and often do jobs called "muscles" for other gangs and organized crime groups throughout the United Kingdom.

In 1998, the British police launched the famous "Operation Trident" in the London area in order to combat gun crime committed by Yardies and black gangs. The gun problem had escalated from the mid-1980s to the 1990s with an estimated 300,000 weapons in circulation in Britain, many of them in Yardies' hands.

In the United States, similar Jamaican-based gangs called Posses can be found, mainly in New York City. These gangs are known for their drive-by shootings and their gunrunning. One of the most notorious is the called Shower Posse because of its method of "showering" its opponents with bullets.

THE JAMAICAN INFLUENCE

Organized crime in the United Kingdom includes gangs formed among neighborhoods of mainly Jamaican descent. In the mid-1980s, Jamaican Posses migrated to the United States and then to England after the terrible devastation of Hurricane Charlie and the poverty that came in its wake. Their activities have included the control of prostitution, illegal drinking clubs, gambling, and drug trafficking—mainly marijuana, though beginning in the 1980s, the trade in crack and other cocaine derivatives has been booming in the United Kingdom.

When depression hit Jamaica in 1952, nearly 10,000 West Indians migrated to the United Kingdom.

A Matter of Classification

The British police are reluctant to classify Yardies as organized crime gangs because of their loose structure. In the United States, however, the police don't hesitate to do so, given that the Posses claim control of drug trafficking—especially cocaine and its derivatives—in all major US cities, and have strong structures and close links with Jamaican bosses. The Pennsylvanian Crime Commission reported that "at the national level, Posses have one or more top leaders, sometimes called 'Generals'."

Posses and Parties

In Jamaica, the Shower Posse has been linked to the Jamaica Labour Party (JLP). Other alleged politically linked Posses include the Trenchtown Massive, Southside, One Order Gang, Precinct 13, Banton Po, and Montego Bay Posses. According to Jamaican security forces, the political opponent of the JLP, the People's National Party (PNP), is supported by the Spangler Posse, Jungle, Gully, Mountain View, Clansman, Tel Aviv, Dog, Rat, Cuban, Brown, Jae Bone, British Luni Up Crew, and 90s Posses.

Headquarters and Beyond

The Shower Posse has one leader in Jamaica and one in the United States. The first region of the country in which a Posse operates may evolve into "headquarters," or a base of operations from which subsequent expansion is directed. From headquarters, the Posse leader may send out "captains" or "lieutenants" to establish operations in new regions. These representatives of the national leadership are responsible for recruiting supervisors to manage workers—often illegal aliens smuggled from Jamaica into the United States.

The connection and subsequent power of the Yardies in both the United States and Britain are due mainly to their strong ties with the Colombian Drug Cartels. They also maintain strong ties with Irish gangs active in the United Kingdom and with Italian clans in both the United States and the United Kingdom. Yardie enclaves can be found in almost every large British city, especially Bristol, Birmingham, and Nottingham.

OPPOSITE A potential member of the Low-Down Posse is beaten up as part of an initiation rite in Dallas, Texas, c. 2000.

BELOW Police use their new Stop and Search powers to do just that to youths at Notting Hill Carnival, London, as part of an initiative to combat knife crime.

CRIME SCE

4 THE NEW MILLENNIUM

The New Millennium
Crime Reinvention

ABOVE Opium pickers in Afghanistan are guarded by armed men, protecting the crop more than the workers.

As the twenty-first century dawned, traditional Mafia activities were being severely curbed by improvements in law enforcement and the cross-boundary cooperation of agencies. There was no choice but to reinvent some enterprises and create transnational endeavors to combat law enforcement.

Evolving Enterprises

The bread-and-butter endeavors of extortion, gambling, and prostitution have been running for a long time. However, organized crime has evolved and expanded these staples to include drugs and embezzlement. Now, at the start of the twenty-first century, different types of organized groups have emerged bringing new crimes into the fold, including kidnapping, human trafficking, and arms dealing.

The industry that is the most profitable and with the least amount of trouble conducting business will always be the primary industry of organized crime. Like any other business, organized crime groups look for high profits and low overheads.

New and Old Crimes

Not all major crimes are committed by organized crime groups. For instance, the first decade of this century saw a renewed world awareness of the Ponzi/pyramid scheme, in particular that run by the leading American investor, Bernard Madoff. Though not strictly part of organized crime, this is an example of how the old crimes are still more than viable in a technologically advanced world. Bernard Madoff, using his status on Wall Street, convinced investors that big returns could be made in a short amount of time with little or no risk.

At the same time, some of the less sophisticated crimes are organized. Over the last few years, piracy has been reprised in some areas of the world, particularly off the coast of Africa. While piracy on the open seas is not what individuals may think of when they hear of organized crime, it is nevertheless a type, as it is a framework for committing illegal acts. Piracy is actually one of the first types of organized crime.

Mafia and organized crime groups make the most profit from a very simple and straightforward philosophy—if it is not broken, do not try to fix it. While some new criminal organizations attempt to be innovative and creative, the majority just copy ideas that have been shown to work by others.

ABOVE African immigrants clash with police in Naples after six had been shot by Camorra hitmen in 2008. Violence in the Naples region is escalating dramatically.

Sicilian Mafia
The New Wave

The Mafia phenomenon has demonstrated quite incredible resilience throughout history, somehow managing to exploit every historical development or event to its own advantage.

Historical Continuity

The Mafia, particularly in Sicily, has survived a great many historical transformations, from feudalism to an administrative state, from the unification of Italy through to its involvement in two World Wars, from the Cold War to the recent trend toward globalization—including globalized crime—and the war on terror that has more recently diverted the attention of many countries from the repression of organized crime.

The main features of such historical continuity have been the use of organized crime by entire political castes for protection and for purposes of political and social control; the consequent implicit impunity enjoyed by members of the Mafia and especially their institutional protectors; and the continual attempts that political powers have made to control, subjugate, influence, and interfere with the judiciary.

Consequently, those at all levels—politicians, judges, mediators, and the like—who have seriously attempted to combat the situation have been subjected to defamation and humiliation, brought into disrepute, and often ultimately murdered.

BELOW In December 2008, Italian police arrested over 90 alleged *Mafiosi* who were in the process of re-organizing their command structure. Benedetto Capizzi, shown here with a police escort, was allegedly in line for the top job.

AIDING AND ABETTING

In 1993, at the height of the massacres, the boss of *Cosa Nostra*, Totò Riina, was arrested. It is normal practice for the police to search the houses of suspects—even of minor drug pushers—yet it was almost a month before the *Carabinieri* arrived at Riina's house. By then, all compromising documents had disappeared; even the furniture had been rearranged and the walls repainted. The colonel of the Special Operations Task Force in the *Carabinieri*, Mario Mori, a secret agent, was held responsible for the delay and was later accused of aiding and abetting the Mafia. According to his accusers, in 1995 he had also hindered the capture of Provenzano, whose hiding place had been disclosed to the *Carabinieri* by an informer. The informer, named Ilardo, had accepted protection under a state scheme and was about to collaborate with the forces of justice, intending to reveal connections between the Mafia and various institutions. He was killed the day before his interrogation by the police was to start. The Italian media, however, barely mentioned the Mori case. Even before the magistrates reached their judgment of acquittal, Colonel Mori was hotly defended by various sources through a series of declarations issued to the press and television.

Business Expansion

The Sicilian Mafia entered the new millennium weakened on its armed front, but reinforced on its political front and in important economic spheres. Organized crime, sometimes referred to as The Mafia Ltd., including the four main Italian Mafia groups, is now the largest business in Italy. According to a report issued in November 2008 by the Confesercenti, the Italian association which represents workers in the commercial sector and tourism, the commercial branch of organized Mafia crime now has a value of well over 92 billion Euros, a figure which represents 6 percent of the nation's GDP and is the equivalent to income from almost five budget reforms. But these figures represent only part of the volume of Mafia affairs. If income from money laundering were to be included, the amount in question could well be over 150 billion Euros.

Globalization

Today's *Mafioso* is far removed from the image of Bernardo Provenzano, portrayed on Italian television immediately after his arrest as an unimposing shepherd. Now power is wielded by the Mafia bourgeoisie, a cast of managers, professionals, accountants, lawyers, politicians, engineers—none of them averse to using arms—who are rapidly moving the Mafia into the big business of globalization.

Political Saviors

In the 1990s, the armed Mafia was in genuine trouble, with informers and ex-Mafia members lining up outside the courts to give evidence. Known as *pentitismo* (turning evidence), this phenomenon represented a complete break with the past. A feeling of defeat—that the state had won—was spreading throughout the organization. State repression, however, concentrated only on the armed side of the organization. Political protection actually reinforced the political-bourgeois-business ranks of the Mafia, the level that really held the power. The organization was in effect "saved" by the politicians.

ABOVE Though accused in the early 1990s of aiding and abetting the Mafia, Mario Mori was absolved by the courts and went on to become head of the Italian intelligence agency (SISDE).

An entire people that pays protection money is a people without dignity.

Note posted on every billboard throughout Palermo's city center in 2004

GOTCHA!

The Capture of Bernardo Provenzano

On the morning of April 11, 2006, special units of the Italian police force were located at a distance of 1.2 miles (2 km) from an isolated farmhouse in the area of Contrada dei Cavalli, near Corleone.

Surveillance

Using a micro-camera hidden in a bush, the police watched for signs of movement around the farmhouse. They had been there for about two weeks. The farm consisted of two old houses. A shepherd lived in one of them; the other appeared uninhabited. However, a television antenna on the roof made the investigators suspicious.

Suspicious Bag

A policewoman had brought the place to their attention. She had noticed that a bag was often left outside the door of a house in Corleone where members of the Provenzano family lived, and realized that the bag could represent an important lead in capturing the head of *Cosa Nostra*, Bernardo Provenzano. Eventually the bag was collected by a passer-by and as he walked away he was followed. A couple of days went by and the bag was passed from the first man to a second. Another few days passed and it was handed to a third man. Finally, after a couple of weeks it was delivered to a shepherd who lived in the isolated farmhouse outside Corleone.

One morning the shepherd approached the apparently empty building. The door opened, an arm reached out and the bag was taken.

"Congratulations"

It was decided to carry out a raid immediately as a secret passage may have existed and if the suspect really was Provenzano, he could make an escape. Just a few days before, the super boss's defending lawyer had made a declaration stating, "It is pointless for the police to continue looking for him, he died some years ago." The interview was shown on television and was almost certainly a message in code for Provenzano meaning, "your cover is blown."

The first policeman to make a move was Renato Cortese. Flinging open the door of the house, he found a man standing upright and motionless inside. His appearance was very different from the computer-generated identikit based on information from state witnesses that police had circulated a few weeks before. On the table, however, was some chicory, a vegetable known to be part of the Mafia boss's diet due to his prostate problem. Cortese knew that after so many years he had finally captured his man. As the police squad surrounded him, Provenzano spoke only a single word: "Congratulations." Then, as he was being taken to police headquarters, he added, "You have no idea what this will start."

No technology of any kind was found inside the farmhouse. The Mafia boss had used neither a cell phone nor a computer. There was only a small television and an old typewriter for typing his *pizzini*, the scraps of paper by which he controlled his entire organization. They also found five bibles, one of which was much underlined, and some cassettes recorded with music to keep him company. One of these was the soundtrack of the film "*The Godfather*." The investigators succeeded in unraveling the connection between the *pizzini* and the bible—each *Mafioso* was associated with the number of a book in the Old Testament that was used as a code in the *pizzini*.

Life of Crime

Born there 75 years earlier, Bernardo Provenzano had rarely, if ever, left the his home town of Corleone. Since 1963 he had been in hiding from Italian justice, and the last known photo of him dated from the same year. Provenzano's nickname was U'Tratturi—the tractor, that destroys everything that stands in its way.

He was born on January 31, 1933, the third of seven sons, and left school after only a year to work in the fields. His criminal career began by stealing animals and corn from peasants. In the 1970s, the Mafia families of Palermo controlled drug trafficking, while the Corleone clan was forced to organize kidnappings to finance its activities. This changed in the early 1980s when the Corleone clan gained control of the entire organization in a violent takeover. When the prosecutors Giovanni Falcone and Paolo Borsellino were assassinated, the state passed a number of anti-Mafia laws and arrested Totò Riina, head of *Cosa Nostra*. At that point Provenzano took command. Following his orders, the massacres continued throughout 1993 in the rest of Italy—not in Sicily. The murders ceased at the end of 1993, but Provenzano continued to live in hiding until 2006 when at last he was betrayed—probably not by a simple bag, but by informers much higher up.

ABOVE This 2005 poster showed an approximation of what Provenzano might look like. He had been in hiding for such a long time that the police could only guess at his current appearance.

BELOW Provenzano after his arrest in Corleone in 2006. In 2009, Provenzano, together with Mafia boss Totò Riina, was given an additional life sentence, on top of the 12 he already faced, for the 1969 "Viale Lazio Massacre" between *Mafiosi*.

ACCORDING TO INFORMERS

At the same time as being tried for his alleged Mafia associations, Giulio Andreotti was also accused of instigating the murder of Mino Pecorelli, a journalist. In this case, too, he was fully acquitted, though on appeal he was later condemned to 24 years for having commissioned the murder. In 2003, the High Court of Cassazione annulled this sentence without deferment. The original acquittal therefore became definitive. According to informers, including Buscetta, the Salvo cousins—*Mafiosi* belonging to Andreotti's wing of the Christian Democrats—were given orders to carry out the murder by Andreotti himself. As a journalist, Pecorelli had come into possession of information regarding illegal financing of the Christian Democrats and the kidnapping and subsequent assassination of Christian Democrat politician Aldo Moro by the Red Brigades.

Nine of the 20 Red Brigades terrorists who were believed to have kidnapped former Italian Prime Minister, Aldo Moro.

The Trial of the Century

In late 1995 what was to become known as the "trial of the century" began. The most important politician in Italy during the second half of the twentieth century, seven times Prime Minister, Giulio Andreotti, was tried for collusion with the Mafia. In 1999, he was acquitted on all accounts but an appeal sentence on May 2, 2003, stated that Andreotti "had committed the offense of participation in a criminal association—being *Cosa Nostra*—factually proven until the spring of 1980."

The finding was much more serious than the accusation that had instigated the enquiry. The crime was, however, "barred by the statute of limitations," having been committed too many years before the actual pronouncement of a verdict. The law that had introduced the offense of criminal association with the Mafia dated from 1982, after the events of which Andreotti was found guilty. If the sentence had been delivered in 2002 instead of 2003, Andreotti would have been condemned for having belonged to *Cosa Nostra*. The slowness of the judicial system had worked in his favor.

Nevertheless, the *obiter dicta* to the sentence—the statement and comments incidental to the judgment—found that there was "an authentic, stable, and friendly

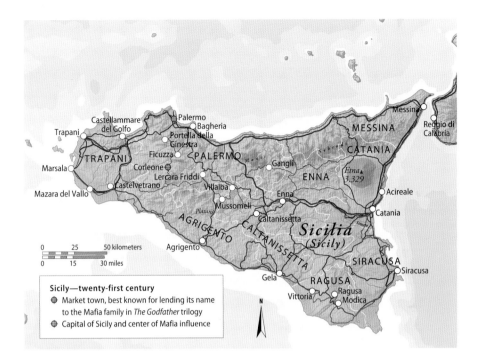

Sicily—twenty-first century
⊕ Market town, best known for lending its name to the Mafia family in *The Godfather* trilogy
⊕ Capital of Sicily and center of Mafia influence

relationship between the accused and members of the Mafia until the spring of 1980." Moreover, the motivation of the appeal sentence, later confirmed by the High Court of the Cassazione, "… recognized participation in the crime of association [that is, belonging to the Mafia rather than simply aiding and abetting it] not only in the limited sense of support, but in the wider and legally meaningful sense of concrete collaboration." In short, it alleged that from the end of World War II until the early 1990s, some Italian politicians had been judged to have had a close relationship with the Mafia until at least 1980.

Right-hand Man

During this same period other important figures of state were sent to trial. Senator Marcello Dell'Utri, right-hand man of Berlusconi and his close collaborator in founding the political party Forza Italia, was condemned to nine years' imprisonment in 2004 for complicity and collusion with the Mafia. The accusation was based on the declarations of criminals who had turned state's evidence. The sentence states:

"The motivation behind the range of activities created by Dell'Utri was to provide a genuine, deliberate, conscious, specific, and valuable contribution to the maintenance, consolidation, and strengthening of *Cosa Nostra*; moreover, Dell'Utri's mediation also provided opportunities for *Cosa Nostra* to enter into contact with important economic and financial spheres, thus facilitating the pursuance of its illicit ends, both economic and political."

In 2008, Dell'Utri was sentenced to five years' jail for aiding and abetting *Cosa Nostra* by passing on restricted information obtained from "moles" working within the Courts of Justice in Palermo. He is currently appealing against the judgment.

ABOVE Calogero Mannino, accused by police of involvement with the Mafia, was acquitted by the courts due to a lack of evidence and has now resumed his political career.

OPPOSITE In April 1985 thousands of people gathered for an anti-Mafia rally in Trapani, Sicily. At around this time, many high officials were being murdered for expressing similar views.

The Judiciary

In 2002, Judge Corrado Carnevale was acquitted by the High Court. When president of the first division of the Court of Cassation he had earned the nickname "the sentence-crushing judge" for his zealous application of procedural details, using them to quash numerous sentences of courts dealing with various matters. It has been alleged that many Mafiosi who had committed the most brutal murders and crimes were acquitted. Carnevale had previously been condemned in appeal to six years for complicity in collusion with the Mafia.

Political Hits and Misses

On February 26, 2006, the ex-head of Palermo's flying squad and later an officer of SISDE (Service for Information and the Safeguard of Democracy in Italy) was condemned to 10 years' imprisonment for collusion with the Mafia. In 2008, following a lengthy judicial procedure, Calogero Mannino, formerly a Christian Democrat minister, was acquitted of collusion with the Mafia.

Over the last 15 years, it would seem that the close relationship between the Mafia and politics, perhaps the main the reason for the incredible historical continuity of the Mafia, has been consolidated and reinforced as never before in the history of Italy. While the forces of order, despite severe difficulties, still pursue the armed wing of the Mafia, the rest seems to have guaranteed impunity. The most astute murder that has been committed has been that of the law.

Legal Measures

Numerous measures that have ultimately affected both political crimes and the Mafia have been approved since the mid-1990s. One worthy of mention is the reform of legislation concerning the falsification of accounts, lowering the bar under the statute of limitations from fifteen to seven and a half years. Given the slowness of trials in Italy this has meant that almost all trials for crimes of this kind are now considered lapsed. Another such measure is the "money amnesty" permitting capital illegally exported from Italy to be returned simply by paying 2.5 percent of the capital sum re-entering the country, while anonymity is guaranteed.

There are many other examples: The reduction of the time required for collaborators to provide state's evidence to 150 days, a measure approved as part of a package along with various others, making it more difficult for Mafiosi to collaborate with the police; the removal or reduction of escorts for magistrates and prosecutors involved in the fight against the Mafia, leaving them much more vulnerable to intimidation or worse; and last but by no means least, limitations to the use of phone tapping—an essential tool in the fight against the Mafia.

Silence

At the elections held in 2006 under the system of proportional representation, both the center-right alignment headed by Berlusconi and the center-left headed by Veltroni presented candidates in Sicily who had been tried for Mafia-related activities in the past. This was disturbing in itself, but the most disconcerting result, and the most worrying is the disappearance and/or isolation of any genuine anti-Mafia activity. Suffice to say that in the Italian political system there is an anti-Mafia commission that contains several members who have reportedly been condemned for crimes of various kinds.

Camorra & 'Ndrangheta
Italian Secret Societies

2000 A huge scandal regarding the milk industry is exposed. Large milk producers were said to be victims of extortion.

2002 Newspapers in Italy report that 'Ndrangheta has received a percentage of a multimillion-euro contract to build highways in Calabria.

2004 Eighteen people are arrested in Caserta after investigations into extortion by the Camorra.

2005 A massive stash of weapons, obviously part of arms trafficking, is discovered in Sant'Anastasia, near Mt Vesuvius, including machine guns, Uzis, and weapons capable of destroying tanks.

2005 Rotterdam authorities discover tons of English trash passed as recycling through Camorra clans' waste dumping racket.

BELOW The first official mention of the Camorra as an organization dates from 1820. Documents from 1842 refer to initiation rites and the provision of funds for the families of those imprisoned.

The Italian Mafia began in Sicily but other criminal organizations developed on the mainland. The most virulent are the Camorra and 'Ndrangheta, operating in the south and north of the country.

The Neapolitan Camorra

The origins of the Camorra can be traced to the modern period of history. In his tale *Rinconete Y Cortadillo*, the Spanish poet Miguel de Cervantes referred to a criminal association similar to those that developed in southern Italy at the time he was writing, the late sixteenth century. The word "Camorra," a corruption of "gumurra," signified a short red canvas jacket that was introduced to Naples by merchants from the Campidano region of Sardinia and continued to be popular until the late nineteenth century. The origins of the Camorra seem to be linked to the migration of this group of Hispano-Sardinian traders to Naples during the fifteenth century, a period when Spain ruled much of Italy. They brought with them not only the gumurra jacket but also criminal practices that probably gave rise to the formation of the Camorra.

Feeding on Poverty

The first study of the history of the Neapolitan Camorra was published in 1863. The author was Marco Monnier, a researcher at Geneva University, whose family had strong links with Naples. He referred to the Camorra as a "working-class secret society, whose purpose is evil." Monnier claimed that the main reason for the development of this criminal organization was the terrible poverty in which the working classes were forced to live under Bourbon rule. Subsequently, scholars were very influenced by this theory, which stated that the main, perhaps the only, reason for the emergence and development of criminal organizations in Italy was poverty. In fact, such organizations have also prospered in wealthy countries such as the United States and Japan.

Camorra and Mafia: Similarities

The organization developed both inside the prisons—where members of the Camorra practised extortion—and outside, and has many features in common with the Sicilian Mafia. These features include control of its territory—Naples was divided into 12 districts and control of them through extortion was complete; the support or consensus of much of the population; rituals of initiation inspired by Catholicism; and especially the infiltration of state institutions.

...And Differences

Certain important differences have, however, made the Sicilian Mafia a more enduring and permanent phenomenon. Despite the fact that Naples, and indeed all of southern Italy, was under the control of Spain, the city's history cannot be

Campania can get worse because you could cut into a Camorra group, but another ten could emerge from it.

Palquale Galasso (1955–), former boss of the Galasso Crime Family, part of Camorra.

compared to that of Sicily. The Camorra has not had the same degree of continuity throughout history as the Sicilian Mafia. There were scarcely any bandits in the region of Campania during the eighteenth century. In the preceding two centuries, the large landowners around Naples had never managed their own systems of justice as occurred in Sicily. On the contrary, Neapolitan judges quite often took sides against the powerful landowners.

Another significant difference in the origins of the two organizations lies in the fact that, although Palermo was the seat of political power and thus a point of reference for large landowners, the Sicilian Mafia mainly originated in the countryside, while the Neapolitan Camorra developed primarily among the city's lower classes. Moreover, the Camorra, unlike the Mafia, failed to maintain its original oligarchic structure.

State Sanction

As with the history of the Sicilian Mafia, the events leading to the formation of the Italian state and the years immediately following unification in 1861 represented an important period for the Camorra. The Prefects of the Kingdom of Italy—representatives of government in the various provinces of the state—had much difficulty in governing areas with a high density of criminal activity. They therefore made use of members of criminal organizations, often appointing them to the various police forces to contain the possibility of rebellion and control the lower classes. Thus both the Mafia and the Camorra reinforced their role of social control, or rather social domination, with the direct authorization of the Italian state.

ABOVE Giuseppe Setola, a suspected Camorra boss, escaped arrest in January 2009, through a tunnel underneath his house in Trentola Ducenta.

MAFIA WOMEN

Though historically the Mafia has been a male-dominated criminal society, some women have taken an active role in its illicit activities. Women participated in an early 1900s coin-counterfeiting racket of the American Mafia, with the New Jersey branch of the counterfeiters led by Stella Frauto. A Chicago branch of the operation allegedly included Mafia leader Antonio D'Andrea's wife Lena.

As successful prosecution and gang warfare have depleted the ranks of Camorra families in Italy, females have begun stepping into leadership positions. In the 1990s, police arrested Rosetta Cutolo, sister of jailed Camorra boss Raffaele Cutolo, charging her with managing a criminal empire. Other charges have been less dramatic. In 2007, UK housewife Ann Hathaway pleaded guilty in an Italian court to Mafia association. She was charged with acting as a courier for her husband, a jailed Sicilian Mafia leader.

In the United States, authorities charged Camille Serpico, wife of a Genovese Crime Family associate, of running a mob-affiliated chop shop for processing stolen car parts. Four of Camille's five husbands were linked to the underworld.

ABOVE Rosetta Cutolo, nicknamed "Ice Eyes," was once one of Italy's most wanted women. She was arrested in 1993 after being on the run for 13 years.

ABOVE Charles (Lucky) Luciano, former "New York vice king," did not seem unduly distressed at being placed under police surveillance. His deportation to Naples proved lucky for the Camorra.

OPPOSITE Aerial view of garbage at the Villa Literno site near Naples. Garbage crises have dogged the southern Campania region for years, due in no small part to the efforts of the Camorra.

Not Just Lucky

It was only much more recently however—after World War II—that the Camorra began to develop its present character. Its evolution was due mainly to two factors: The role of the Italo-American *Mafioso*, Lucky Luciano, whom the US government sent to Naples immediately after World War II, and collusion with members of the Christian Democrats beginning in the 1950s.

As one of the primary organizers of large-scale illegal trafficking, Lucky Luciano enabled the Camorra to be included in deals at an international level. They were involved mainly in trading contraband cigarettes in conjunction with the criminal bands of Marseilles. Meanwhile, collusion with administrators and politicians of the Christian Democrat party from the end of the war until the 1990s facilitated Camorra speculation in local businesses, the control of public tenders, and the creation of a network of contacts and relationships with businessmen, administrators, and politicians.

The Cutolo Clan

An attempt to centralize power within the organization was made during the 1970s by the boss Raffaele Cutolo. While in prison for committing murder, he tried to set up a hierarchical structure on the model of Sicily's *Cosa Nostra* by planning the creation of the *Nuova Camorra Organizzata*—New Organized Camorra. The purpose of this oligarchic structure was to organize drug trafficking more efficiently, but the project to centralize operations was opposed by the old clans who risked losing their power. These clans united in a single group named the *Nuova Famiglia*—New Family.

A ruthless gang war followed, ending in the defeat of the Cutolo clan and thus the failure of the oligarchic model. In the early 1990s, a further serious attempt to establish a vertical structure again failed and today the Camorra has a horizontal formation. Numerous clans thus compete for territory, often resulting in bloody feuds, the most deadly of which took place between 2004 and 2006.

Main Enterprises

The Camorra's main areas of activity are the control of public tenders (documented as early as the 1800s), contraband cigarettes, and drug trafficking (currently the most profitable). To these can be added exploitation of prostitution, usury, arms trafficking, waste disposal, extortion, and control of businesses, all of which combined produce an annual turnover which has been calculated at around 12 billion Euros but is probably much higher.

Other Clans

In addition to the Camorra in Naples and the surrounding region, there are several important clans in the province of Caserta, the foremost being the Casalesi clan, who manage a criminal cartel of international proportions. Their specialty is to re-invest income from various illegal activities—mainly drugs—in property in northern Italy and other parts of Europe.

Revelations

The Camorra has come to the attention of the world following the publication of books written "from the inside," and movies based on those books. These reveal the reality of life in the working-class districts of Naples and other areas in Campania under the influence of the Camorra. As one commentator puts it, "except as extras, the police are nowhere in sight and never seem to be on anyone's mind." Some maintain that such depictions send out a negative image; others that they merely reflect the reality of everyday life in much of southern Italy.

Caserta
The province of Caserta is the home of several important Camorra clans including the Casalesi clan which has international connections.

Gioia Tauro
Major port for the trafficking of cocaine and other drugs by the 'Ndrangheta.

Camorra and 'Ndrangheta controlled provinces
- Calabria
- Campania
- ⊕ Centers of Italian Mafia
- ----- Modern country borders

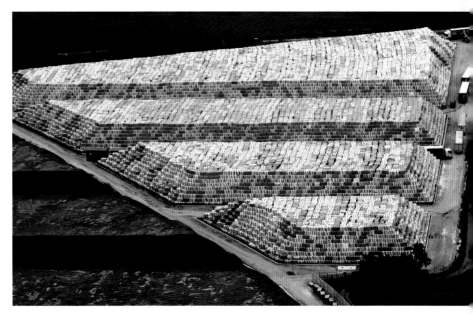

CELLULOID MAFIA

Gomorra (Gomorrah)

The title _Gomorra_ (_Gomorrah_) is a play on the name of the ill-fated, decadent, and lawless city of the Bible and the label by which the Naples criminal organization Camorra—said to be bigger and more powerful than Sicily's Mafia—is known.

Italian journalist and _Gomorrha_ author, Roberto Saviano, is under permanent police protection after receiving death threats from the Camorra for exposing their activities in his 2006 book, published by Arnoldo Mondadori Editore, and the subsequent film adaptation, produced by Domenico Procacci's Fandango Productions. The film's veracity is thus authenticated in a dramatic fashion and his book is often referred to as an exposé. Filmmaker Matteo Garrone approached Saviano after reading his book, and the pair collaborated on the screenplay. At its world premiere at Cannes in 2008, _Gomorra_ won the Grand Prix and went on to collect a number of other awards and nominations.

Research

The book's author, Roberto Saviano, worked as an assistant at a Chinese textile manufacturer and on a construction site, both controlled by the system, and as a waiter at a Camorra wedding as part of his research. Born in Naples, he recalls seeing his first murder at the age of 14, and how his own father, a doctor, suffered a brutal beating for trying to help an 18-year-old victim who had been left for dead in the street.

The film is set in the provinces of Naples and Caserta, where residents confront the system every day in matters large and small. In the film, directed by Matteo Garrone, five fictional stories are woven together, each rooted in brutal reality.

The Characters

The oldest of the film's protagonists, Don Ciro (Gianfelice Imparato), is "_il sottomarino_" who pays the families of the prisoners that are affiliated with his clan, a clan that has the undisputed command of the territory. He is sharp, discreet, and carries out his job without getting involved. But when the clan begins to crumble, he doesn't know who wields the power any more—a dangerous situation.

The youngest character, Totò (Salvatore Abruzzese), is 13 years old and keen to grow up. He begins his training in the school of life, one step at a time, until one day he has to make an irreversible and crucial decision.

Marco (Marco Macor) and Ciro (Ciro Petrone) think they are living in a Brian de Palma film, but in the eyes of the system they are like stray dogs whose acts of silly bravado are disturbing the orderly routine of business.

Roberto (Carmine Paternoster) is a university graduate looking for work. Franco (Toni Servillo) offers him steady employment with good earning prospects—a job in toxic waste management. But the ghastly reality of the task is too disconcerting for Roberto's conscience.

I can't consider them kids any more. They have to die, that's final. Giovanni (Giovanni Venosa)

You're right, but first let's tell the families.

Zio Vittorio (Bernardino Terracciano)

Pasquale (Salvatore Cantalupo) is a talented tailor who works surreptitiously for a small enterprise subcontracted by the *haute couture* industry. When Chinese competitors come to him wanting to learn the tricks of the trade, he is seduced into agreeing but his actions put his life in grave danger.

Realism

The film does not attempt show any of the big bosses who make the many millions in the Camorra, nor any of the spoils of the system. These characters live hard, oppressed lives. They are the pawns, easily dismissed, squashed, killed.

But while in the book Saviano is a central figure as the reporter, the film takes a more cinematic approach—albeit one that is naturalistic and largely devoid of glamor. Unlike romanticised movies about the Mafia where the dress code seems extravagantly stylish, these characters dress in sloppy casuals and live in housing that could well be mistaken for slums in some parts of the Western world.

Filmmaker

Filmmaker Matteo Garrone—who also frequently operated the camera—shot on actual locations, such as the housing complex called Vele di Sampi, where, as cinematographer Marco Onorato told Kodak's *InCamera* magazine "we could only shoot for a couple of hours in the morning because the effects of crack made the people aggressive and our safety would have been compromised."

Garrone, born in Rome in 1968, already has a number of award-winning films to his credit, including *Oreste Pipoli, Guests* (Ospiti), and *The Taxidermist. Gomorra* was Italy's official entry in the Foreign Language category of the 2009 Academy Awards.

ABOVE Critics have said of *Gomorra* that it finds "a strange kind of beauty in the ugly reality" of Naples and its surrounding regions. Here, Marco and Ciro go gunning down a river.

ABOVE Buff and bronzed, the men in the tanning booths joke and laugh together in the opening scene of *Gomorra*. And why not? Tomorrow, or sooner, they die.

ABOVE In February 1985, some 640 of Don Cutolo's Camorra operatives stood trial in what used to be the soccer field of Poggioreale prison.

ABOVE In 1981, Roberto Peci of the Red Brigades was assassinated by other members of the group after his brother collaborated with investigators.

"The Professor"

Known as "The Professor"—some say because he wears glasses, others because he is one of the few in the criminal underworld who can read and write—Raffaele Cutolo is one of the most important gangsters in the history of the Neapolitan underworld, despite the fact that he has spent almost his whole adult life in prison.

It is not altogether clear how his criminal career began. One version of the facts records that in 1963 he killed a boy from his own town who made lewd comments about his sister. A second version relates that one day, when his car ran out of petrol, he continued along in neutral but bumped into a girl walking along the road. A man complained on her behalf and an argument broke out during which Cutolo killed him. He disappeared but two days later gave himself up to the police. Whichever is the correct version, he was given a sentence of 24 years' imprisonment.

Establishing a Power Base

In 1970 Cutolo was released, as judgment had not been reached within the legal time limit. When the *Cassazione*, the Italian Supreme Court of Justice, confirmed the earlier sentence that same year, he went into hiding. He joined the Camorra and became involved in cigarette and drugs trafficking, but was arrested again a year later.

This time in prison he began the process of restructuring the criminal group and created the *Nuova Camorra Organizzata* (New Organized Camorra)—the NCO, introducing a ritual of initiation and coordinating the armed section.

In particular, however, Cutolo understood how best to exploit the great potential offered by the strategic importance of the port of Naples. In recent years the port had

become the most important in the Mediterranean for drugs and cigarette trafficking. The interests of the Sicilian *Cosa Nostra*, the 'Ndrangheta of Calabria, and the clans of Marseilles were all focused on the port. All were anxious to make agreements with the Neapolitan underworld—in other words to negotiate with Cutolo. His power was based on his ability to organize and to place himself at the center of negotiations.

Prison Connections

Cutolo's prestige grew in 1980 when many important Italian statesmen came to visit him in prison, including some ministers and secret services agents. The reason was the kidnapping of the regional councilor, Ciro Cirillo, a Christian Democrat politician. The kidnappers belonged to the *Brigate Rosse*, the extreme left terrorist group, and many of its members were in the same prisons as those of the Camorra, including Cutolo. The Camorra therefore represented a potential channel for negotiating with the terrorists. It has never been fully revealed if the Italian state did negotiate with organized crime, but following the meetings with Cutolo, councilor Cirillo was released.

Family Fragmentation

In 1981, the earthquake in Irpinia offered many opportunities for the criminal organizations of Campania and Naples and Cutolo's power was at first reinforced. The Camorra exploited the state of emergency to make money from the tenders for rebuilding and on the black market of funds for aid, rapidly becoming a veritable criminal holding company. However, the 50,000 billion Lire allocated by the Italian government to meet the state of emergency whetted the appetites of the old Neapolitan Camorra families as well as those in the surrounding region. They decided to form the *Nuova Famiglia* (New Family), giving rise to a violent conflict between the two factions that caused an astonishing number of deaths. The result was the defeat of Cutolo's NCO. The victorious *Nuova Famiglia* controlled the organization for a few years, but internal disputes provoked another violent power struggle, confirming the much more fragmentary and disorganized nature of Neapolitan organized crime compared to the Sicilian Mafia.

BELOW March 21, 2005. The body of Nunzio Giuliano, 57, lies in the street in Naples after he was shot dead as part of a war between rival Camorra factions.

The Calabrese 'Ndrangheta

Unlike the Sicilian Mafia, the 'Ndrangheta has never been very much studied. Yet today it is the most powerful and dangerous form of Mafia in Italy and one of the strongest in the world. According to a recent report issued by the Institute for Political, Economic, and Social Research (EURISPES), the organization probably has a turnover of 44 billion Euros a year. However, this figure does not take into account income from the money laundering and it is therefore probable that the actual turnover is closer to 60 billion Euros a year.

Origins

The only certainty concerning the word 'Ndrangheta is that it came originally from Greek, although the precise etymology is unclear. Most probably it derives from *andragathìa*, meaning "virility." It may also have derived from *Andragathia Regio*, a term used to indicate the region on the borders between Calabria and Basilicata.

The Calabrian Mafia began to take shape in the nineteenth century when many of the Sicilian Mafia were interned in the region. They came into contact with local criminals and encouraged them to set up the *'ndrine*—the Calabrian families. It is known, however, that some loosely organized form of criminal association already existed in seventeenth-century Calabria. As with the Sicilian Mafia, the origins of the 'Ndrangheta relate to the problem of land distribution. On one side were the landowners and bourgeoisie (a class between the owners and the agricultural laborers) and on the other were the farm workers. The intermediary between landowners and laborers was known in Calabria as the *industriante*; the same figure in Sicily was called the *gabelloto*. It was he who rented and managed the lands of the nobility, using armed guards to intimidate the peasants who, harshly exploited, survived at subsistence level.

Structure

The structure of the 'Ndrangheta was revealed by Serafino Castagna, a multiple murderer and member of the organization who began to collaborate with the forces of justice in 1955. Divided into families known as *'ndrine*, the 'Ndrangheta, he explained, was structured like a society, consisting of a head and 24 trustworthy men who lived in the Calabrian towns which had a court of justice, the most important being Reggio Calabria; the organization first began to develop in the surrounding province.

Although there was a general *'ndrina*, which consisted of the *'ndrine* of the various towns and was divided into a greater and a smaller *'ndrina*, this form of organization did not represent an oligarchic structure; it was in effect horizontal. Throughout its history the 'Ndrangheta has never adopted a vertical structure. Instead it is greatly fragmented and reflects the wide range of historical and cultural traditions that exist in the region of Calabria. The Italian parliamentary Anti-Mafia Commission describes it as having "a ubiquitous structure, lacking strategic direction but distinguished by a kind of organic intelligence." Like the al-Qa'eda terrorist organization, for example, it is more rhizomatic than pyramidal in structure; it has many cells that are not directly interlinked yet have an identical way of thinking and are capable of developing well beyond the region of origin.

ABOVE April 23, 1994. An alleged 'Ndrangheta godfather arrives back in Italy after being extradited from the United States, one of many to have made the return journey over the years.

BELOW Francesco Vottari is arrested following the murder of six Italians in the German city of Duisburg in 2007 as part of a blood feud between two 'Ndrangheta clans in San Luca.

Cocaine

Cocaine is the main source of income for the 'Ndrangheta. In the late 1970s and early 1980s, the Italian Mafia represented a serious problem for public order and was behind numerous murders and attacks that also involved members of state bodies and institutions. While the Italian state concentrated on repressing the Mafia, the gangs in Calabria made contact with Colombian narco-traffickers and South American paramilitary organizations and eventually succeeded in taking over a leading role in the international trafficking of cocaine.

This was a decisive period in the history of the organization as it represented the beginning of a process of expansion that led to it becoming one of the most powerful criminal organizations in the world during the 1990s. In order to finance the various operations connected with drug trafficking, the 'Ndrangheta stepped up its practice of kidnapping and ransoming rich people, mainly from northern Italy. Increasingly it began to resemble the Sicilian Mafia and in the 1990s, the volume of 'Ndrangheta's business overtook that of *Cosa Nostra*.

ABOVE On October 24, 1992, police seized 97 lb (44 kg) of cocaine in Rome, a drop in the ocean given the scale of 'Ndrangheta trafficking.

OPPOSITE *Carabinieri* arrest Giuseppe Nirta, alleged head of the Nirta-Strangio clan of the 'Ndrangheta, suspected of being behind the execution-style killing of six Italians in Germany in 2007.

Reggio Calabria

Only in the province of Reggio Calabria, the most important for the organization with some 73 *'ndrine*, do the gangs have a structure similar to that of *Cosa Nostra* with a central governing body known as "Santa." There are just over 150 *'ndrine* active in Calabria with about 6,000 members. One becomes part of a *'ndrina* either by birth or by baptism after the age of 14, and a ritual initiation binds the newcomer to the organization for life. The association is exclusive, elitist, and has established its own internal system of justice. It is not altogether old-fashioned, however. Formally, it is also open to women and legal records show that they too take an oath.

Blood Ties

Should a mistake or offense be committed, the tribunal of the clan sits in judgment and the entire family of the guilty person pays the price. Consequently very few members have turned state's evidence in the history of the 'Ndrangheta. Ties of blood are much more important than they are in the Sicilian Mafia and thus marriages take place between members of the various *'ndrine* specifically to create strong relationships within the organization. Each family controls its own area. Particularly significant is the fact that the organization has written codes that represent its statute.

Political Alliances

The fragmented, horizontal structure of the organization has also produced a similar fragmentation in the relationships between the various gangs and political parties. Alliances are made with different political parties according to the situation and the area. In the 1970s—in addition to contact with subversive forces of the extreme right—the *'ndrine* had links with members of the Christian Democrats and also with the rival Communist Party. Parts of the 'Ndrangheta were closer to agricultural workers and therefore tended to be associated with the Communist Party, while other parts of the organization were more closely identified with the middle class and thus preferred to associate with the Christian Democrats. The 'Ndrangheta is still not connected to any specific political party but makes deals according to the particular case in hand.

BELOW A *Carabiniere* searches a 'Ndrangheta bunker in Siderno, Reggio Calabria, as part of an international effort on September 17, 2008, that saw some 200 people arrested around the world.

A Multi-national Organization

The 'Ndrangheta is a mobile organization that has extended from Calabria to all continents. It is now a multi-national criminal group. It is particularly strong in Australia, Germany, and Canada—the countries to which Calabrians most frequently emigrated in the nineteenth and twentieth centuries.

Since the 1980s when it began to enter the cocaine market—now its main source of income—the organization has penetrated into almost all northern European countries, Britain, the Netherlands, Switzerland, and Austria. It is also particularly strong in the old communist states where the collapse of the former regimes created a void in which various criminal organizations were able to take

control with relative ease. The process of privatization of state agencies in particular provided a wide range of opportunities.

The 'Ndrangheta has established lucrative relationships with South American gangs such as the Colombian narcos and paramilitary organizations which are essential to cocaine trafficking. It has branches in all countries of South America, from Venezuela to Brazil, from Argentina to Paraguay, Peru to Chile, and from Uruguay to Bolivia.

In recent years the 'Ndrangheta has become known not only for the immense volume of its business, but also, more specifically, for the massacre in Duisburg in Germany in August 2007, in which six people were killed as the result of a feud between two rival gangs seeking power in the small town of San Luca in the province of Reggio Calabria.

In addition to its global expansion, the organization also has a strong hold now in the north and center of Italy. "Branches" of various bands of the 'Ndrangheta exist in many Italian provinces where they recycle money by buying and managing properties, hotels, discotheques, and commercial businesses.

In 1995, for the first time ever in the center-north of the country, a local council was disbanded for collusion with the Mafia. The phenomenon of dissolving a council for reasons of infiltration by the Mafia has become quite common in Sicily, Calabria, Campania, and Puglia—the four Italian regions where Mafia organizations originated—and is authorized by a law that was introduced in 1991.

ABOVE The flag of the Italian General Confederation of Labor (CGIL) flies over the Neapolitan suburb of Scampia.

American Mafia
The Information Age

As the world moved into the twenty-first century, discipline within crime families broke down as the harsh penalties of RICO served to loosen the tongues of indicted members.

Federal Intelligence

ABOVE Little Italy in Manhattan, all decked out for Christmas. This area was the center of Mafia crime in New York.

OPPOSITE TOP Like father, like son. John "Junior" Gotti, son of John J. Gotti, leaves court in 1999, after pleading guilty to bribery, extortion, gambling, and fraud.

As the twentieth century closed, a combination of much improved federal intelligence gathering and toughened anti-racketeering laws made life miserable for Mafia leaders.

In 1989, FBI listening devices captured an entire Mafia induction ceremony. Presided over by New England boss Raymond Patriarca Jnr., it became the first ever recording of a Mafia induction, and it led to racketeering charges against Patriarca and other members of his crime family.

An FBI bug installed in an apartment over the Ravenite Social Club in New York's Little Italy picked up important evidence against Gambino boss, John J. Gotti, during 1990. Gotti's knickname as "Teflon Don", due to his many escapes from arrest, was soon forgotten as Gotti's own recorded statements coupled with testimony of turncoat Salvatore Gravano resulted in a racketeering conviction against the Gambino boss.

Front Bosses

Some underworld bosses decided that their only protection from the law was to escape notice. Carmine Persico, alleged unofficial leader of the Colombo Crime Family, made himself second in command to acting boss Vincenzo Aloi in the 1970s. While Aloi held the title, Persico held the power. The misdirection was little help to Persico. He received a long prison sentence in the Mafia Commission case. Even from prison, however, Persico continued to call the shots through his son Alphonse and allies.

Philadelphia underworld leader Joey Merlino briefly used Ralph Natale as cover in the mid-1990s. Merlino's father Salvatore served as underboss to legendary Mafia chieftain Nicky Scarfo, so Merlino grew up in the Philly Mob. He supported Natale as acting boss, while taking the title of underboss for himself. When Natale turned coat at the end of the decade, Merlino was exposed. In 2001, he was convicted of racketeering and sentenced to 14 years in prison. He is still in jail.

On the Lam

Joseph Lombardo, a Chicago Outfit big shot with links to the Teamsters union, learned of an impending racketeering indictment against him in spring 2005. Lombardo's strategy for dealing with the situation was to disappear. He was a fugitive from justice for nine months, as he hid in locations in the Chicago area. Lombardo and other accused leaders of the Chicago underworld were tried in the Family Secrets Case in August and September of 2007. All the defendants were convicted of racketeering. Lombardo, Frank Calabrese Sr. and James Marcello also were convicted of racketeering murders.

Statute of Limitations

John Angelo "Junior" Gotti has found protection from law enforcement within the statute of limitations. He served time after a 1999 racketeering case, in which he pleaded guilty and admitted filling a supervisory role in the Gambino Crime Family during his father's imprisonment. He has since insisted that he severed his ties with the criminal organization in the 1990s. The statute of limitations will only allow prosecution of racketeering offenses committed after that time. Prosecutors failed in three subsequent trials to persuade juries that Gotti engaged in racketeering after 1999. Gotti was once again charged with racketeering offenses in 2008.

JOHN GOTTI

Born in 1940, John Gotti was involved in street gangs, which lead to his involvement in the Mafia. He took over leadership of the Gambino Crime Family in 1985 after the death of Paul Castellano, whom Gotti had plotted against. He married in 1962 and FBI tapes show him to have subjected his wife and five children to regular beatings. Publicity seeking and almost at celebrity status, Gotti earned the nickname "Teflon Dick."

After numerous attempts by federal agents to have him convicted, he was eventually imprisoned for murder and other charges in 1992. He developed throat cancer in 1998 and died in prison in 2002.

A smooth and charismatic John Gotti gestures as he chats to his lawyers during his assault trial in 1990, where the jury listened to secret tapes.

TRAITORS AND SPIES

Attempts by bosses to restore discipline by the murder of informants merely drove more fearful *Mafiosi* into the hands of law enforcement. At the same time, improved FBI infiltration was also of great help in anti-Mafia efforts.

Gregory Scarpa

Gregory Scarpa, Colombo Crime Family lieutenant and powerful ally of boss Carmine Persico, secretly aided the FBI through three decades until his death in 1994. While working with federal investigators, Scarpa led pro-Persico forces against Vittorio Orena's faction in a 1980s Colombo Crime Family civil war. Court testimony in 2007 indicated that Scarpa had assisted the FBI in breaking down a key witness to the 1964 murders of three civil rights workers in Mississippi.

Jimmy the Weasel

In the late 1970s, Aladena "Jimmy the Weasel" Fratianno began cooperating with federal investigators. Fratianno had experience with organized criminal enterprises in Cleveland, Los Angeles, San Francisco, and Las Vegas. He aided authorities in their attack on the Southern California Crime Family and provided a greater understanding of mob operations in Las Vegas.

Angelo Lonardo

Facing a lengthy prison sentence on a racketeering and drug conviction, Cleveland Mafia underboss Angelo Lonardo defected in 1983. As the son of 1927 mob hit victim Joseph Lonardo and as a longtime Midwest underworld leader, prosecutors found him particularly helpful in the Strawman and Mafia Commission cases.

BELOW "Sammy the Bull" Gravano opens the door for John Gotti as they leave the Ravenite Social Club. Sammy was the main rat in Gotti's conviction.

Sammy the Bull

Salvatore "Sammy the Bull" Gravano, a lieutenant in the Gambino Crime Family administration of John J. Gotti, became a government witness against his boss in 1992. Gravano's testimony helped federal prosecutors score a conviction and a life prison sentence against Gotti, who had escaped conviction in earlier racketeering cases.

D'Arco, Gaspipe, and Henry Hill

Two key members of the Lucchese Crime Family, Alphonse D'Arco and Anthony "Gaspipe" Casso, defected in the early 1990s. Casso had nearly become boss of the family after Anthony Corallo's conviction in the Mafia Commission case. D'Arco served briefly as acting boss of the clan in 1991. Though not an official member of the crime family, Lucchese associate Henry Hill's cooperation with authorities in the early 1980s brought down some powerful mobsters, including crime family lieutenant Paul Vario and top earning associate Jimmy Burke.

Joe Massino

The FBI won its most noteworthy convert in 2004, when Joseph Massino agreed to work with investigators. Massino, once a protégé of Philip Rastelli, had served as boss of the Bonanno Crime Family between 1991 and 2004. Facing the possibility of capital punishment for his role in mob killings, Massino agreed to provide information and to wear a listening device during a conversation with his successor, Vincent Basciano.

Big Billy

Late in 2008, the boss of the northeastern Pennsylvania Mafia agreed to work with authorities in exchange for a lesser sentence for money laundering and witness tampering. William "Big Billy" D'Elia, who once served as bodyguard for the late Russell Bufalino, was never charged with a crime until the indictment in 2006.

Spies

The best known of the FBI's undercover agents is Joseph Pistone. Acting the part of thief Donnie Brasco, he worked his way into the confidences of Bonanno and Lucchese Crime Family leaders between 1976 and 1981. After being pulled from his assignment, Pistone began a second career as a government witness. Information he accumulated during his undercover work triggered hundreds of racketeering indictments and more than 100 convictions. Pistone contributed to the breakup of the Pizza Connection heroin smuggling ring and to the Mafia Commission case. He testified against *Mafiosi* in Milwaukee and Tampa, as well as in New York City. His work also resulted in the assassination of Bonanno lieutenant Dominick "Sonny Black" Napolitano, who had escorted Brasco into underworld rackets.

Another noteworthy undercover FBI agent, Joaquin Garcia, was nearly inducted into a Gambino Crime Family crew run by Gregory DePalma before his assignment was ended in 2005. Garcia posed as an underworld "fence"—a seller of stolen merchandise—named Jack Falcone. DePalma was known to brag about his underworld ties, and some of his comments were captured on a recording device worn by Garcia. Garcia's testimony helped send DePalma to federal prison in 2006.

BLOOD ISN'T SO THICK

Kinship ties have been the foundation of many Mafia organizations. However, Mafia history holds numerous examples of family members turning on each other.

In the 1960s, the two crime bosses, Joseph Bonanno of Brooklyn and Stefano Magaddino of Buffalo, nearly entered into a shooting war with each other though they were cousins. When the Buffalo boss attempted to overthrow Bonanno as the leader of a crime family in Brooklyn, another Magaddino cousin betrayed the plan to Bonanno.

Chicago mobster Frank Calabrese Sr.'s conviction in 2007's landmark Family Secrets racketeering trial was based largely on testimony of his relatives. Frank Calabrese's brother Nicholas had been a hitman before turning informant.

Frank Calabrese's son, Frank Jnr., also testified. He recalled helping collect racket proceeds with his uncle and his father. Frank Sr. once found his son stealing from him. He put a pistol to his son's face, announcing, "I'd rather have you dead than disobey me."

Joe Bonanno was one of many *Mafiosi* who had no qualms about betraying family.

Corruption

Over time, American organized crime proved it was more than capable of infiltrating its opposition. Gangsters protected themselves from prosecution and limited the damage caused by underworld defectors by corrupting select individuals within the law enforcement community.

James "Whitey" Bulger, ruthless leader of the Irish Winter Hill Gang in the Boston area, cooperated with federal agents on their investigation of the New England Mafia. Bulger, brother to a Massachusetts state senator, developed a mutually beneficial relationship with FBI Agent John Connolly. When Connolly learned of a pending RICO indictment against the Winter Hill Gang leadership in January 1995, Bulger fled.

The details of Connolly's relationship with Bulger and of the FBI agent's criminal activity subsequently came to light. One of the more startling revelations was that the FBI helped convict New England *Mafiosi* Peter Limone, Louis Greco, Joseph Salvati, and Henry Tameleo for a murder that the FBI knew they did not commit. The four men were sent to prison in 1968. Tameleo and Greco died there. Limone and Salvati were released in 2001, after the FBI manipulations became known.

New England *Mafioso* Angelo "Sonny" Mercurio, who also had cooperated with Connolly, helped to convict the former FBI agent of racketeering in 2002. Connolly was sentenced to 10 years in prison. Late in 2008, Connolly was convicted of second-degree murder for leaking information about an anti-Bulger informant to the Winter Hill Gang. Acting on Connolly's information, the gang had the informant shot to death in 1982. A federal judge sentenced Connolly to 40 years for that offense, but noted that the conviction could be overturned due to the statute of limitations.

Mafia Cops

In 2006, a federal jury found that two highly decorated New York City Police Department detectives, Stephen Caracappa and Louis Eppolito, had aided the Lucchese Crime Family lieutenant, Anthony "Gaspipe" Casso, through the late 1980s. Caracappa and Eppolito were also convicted of conspiring with Casso in 11 murders and attempted murders while in the full-time employ of the police department. Prosecutors indicated that the pair accepted regular payments of $4,000 USD per month from Casso and additional money when killings were involved.

Shortly after the conviction, Judge Jack Weinstein said Caracappa and Eppolito deserved life sentences. However, the judge decided that the statute of limitations on the racketeering murders had expired and he overturned their convictions. Prosecutors appealed the decision. In September 2008, a three-judge appeals court panel ruled that Judge Weinstein's view of the racketeering conspiracy was too narrow. The panel reinstated the conviction against the so-called "Mafia Cops." At that time, defense attorneys said they planned to appeal.

OPPOSITE This ordinary liquor mart was secretly controlled by Whitey Bulger. It is alleged that here was where he won the lottery, yielding him $89,000 pa for 20 years.

FBI LEAKS

The Mafia had some luck battling the growing number of informants in the 1970s through offers of cash to low-ranking personnel in the FBI in exchange for the names of turncoats.

Shortly after he began secretly providing information to the FBI, Mafia big shot Jimmy Fratianno heard from Cleveland boss Jack "Blackie" Licavoli that the underworld had a female spy inside the FBI. Licavoli already had learned that recently murdered San Diego rackets boss Frank "Bomp" Bompensiero had been an informant for at least a decade.

"We've got a connection in the FBI office here through some broad," Licavoli told Fratianno.

Fearing discovery, Fratianno rushed into the Federal Witness Protection Program and disclosed all he knew of FBI leaks. In 1982, with assistance from his testimony, Cleveland mobster Anthony Liberatore was convicted of bribing a bureau clerk for a list of underworld figures cooperating in federal investigations. In the same year, Licavoli was brought down by a RICO conviction.

Turned federal witness, Jimmy "the Weasel" Fratianno, shrugs off any guilt in naming names.

THE KENNEDY ASSASSINATION

Whether the American Mafia had a hand in the November 1963 assassination of US President John F. Kennedy in Dallas, Texas, remains a controversy. As recently as 2009, new evidence surfaced linking the assassination to Mafia leaders. That evidence suggested that New Orleans crime boss Carlos Marcello worked with Tampa's Santo Trafficante Jnr. and Chicago Mafioso Johnny Roselli to set up the President. Their plan was to make the murder of Kennedy appear to be the work of Cuban Communists. Three assassination attempts were planned. The first two, in Chicago and Tampa, were aborted. The third attempt was November 22, 1963, in Dallas.

Authorities blamed the fatal attack on a single gunman, Lee Harvey Oswald, shooting at Kennedy's motorcade from the sixth floor of the Texas School Book Depository. Conspiracy theorists insist that Kennedy was shot to death by gunmen firing from another direction. Oswald never stood trial for killing Kennedy. While in police custody, Oswald was shot to death by Jack Ruby, an underworld figure connected to criminal organizations in Dallas and Chicago.

In 2008, files pulled from a forgotten safe at the Dallas County district attorney's office sparked new discussion about the relationship between Oswald and Ruby. A document presented as a transcript of October 4, 1963, conversation between the two men was found in the files. Within the document, Oswald and Ruby discuss killing the US President in order to bring to an end the Mafia investigations conducted by his brother, Attorney General Robert Kennedy. Ruby warns Oswald not to get caught or "the boys will make me follow you, wherever you go, and kill you."

After examination, JFK assassination experts dismissed the document as a fake, part of a collection of fictional material intended for a motion picture.

President John Kennedy and Mrs. Kennedy in the motorcade in Dallas on November 22, 1963. Moments later, the President was shot in the head and died a short time later. The Mafia are under constant suspicion for the assassination although nothing substantial has linked any members.

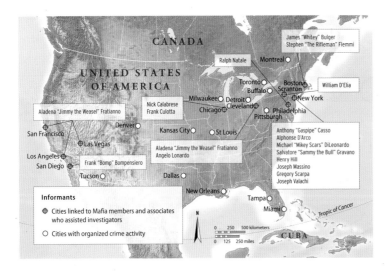

Unsolved

While the American Mafia has experienced over a half-century of exposure and decline since New York State Troopers broke up the Apalachin conclave, a number of crimes linked to the Mafia remain unsolved.

Hoffa's Disappearance

Mystery still surrounds the last moments of the former Teamster union boss Jimmy Hoffa's life and the location of his remains. Authorities have followed a number of leads since Hoffa vanished from the parking lot of the Machus Red Fox restaurant in 1974. Their efforts continue, though Hoffa was declared legally dead in 1982. During 2001, the FBI conducted DNA tests on some hair found in the back of a car used by Hoffa friend, Charles O'Brien, on the day the union leader disappeared. The hair was identified as Hoffa's.

Frank Sheeran confessed two years later that he had been involved in Jimmy Hoffa's demise. A longtime friend of Hoffa, Sheeran held positions with the Teamsters and with the northeastern Pennsylvania crime family led by Russell Bufalino. Sheeran's stories were inconsistent. He claimed once that he personally killed Hoffa on orders from Bufalino and Salvatore Briguglio, an underling of the New Jersey racketeer Anthony Provenzano. In another telling, Sheeran said he showed up after the killing and then helped dispose of Hoffa. Sheeran died in 2003, before his stories could be checked.

ABOVE A leading figure in the Pennsylvania crime family, Russell Bufalino was arrested in 1968 for alleged conspiracy to transport stolen television sets.

Some months later, investigators found blood beneath floorboards in a home Sheeran said was used for the Hoffa murder. Extensive DNA tests later indicated it was not Hoffa's blood.

The FBI conducted a massive dig at a horse farm in Milford Township, Michigan, in spring 2006. Acting on a tip, federal agents brought heavy digging equipment and "cadaver dogs" to the farm. They demolished a barn and dug into the ground underneath, spending hundreds of thousands of dollars in the process. Examinations found no evidence that Hoffa had ever been there.

BELOW Teamster boss, Jimmy Hoffa, making a statement to the press as he arrives at District Court. He is beginning his prison term for jury tampering.

The Search for Whitey Bulger

Since 1995, authorities have been looking for the New England gangster James "Whitey" Bulger. Bulger had worked for years as an FBI informant, while still racketeering as boss of Boston's Winter Hill Gang.

Working closely with Agent John Connolly, he aided the FBI with the dismantling of New England's Patriarca Crime Family. Connolly turned a blind eye to Bulger's criminal activity and warned Bulger of a January 1995 racketeering indictment against him. Bulger then fled. John Connolly later was convicted of racketeering.

Bulger is currently on the FBI Ten Most Wanted list and in 2008, the FBI offered a $2 million USD reward for information leading to his arrest of Bulger. It also released photos showing what an aging Bulger might look like today.

ABOVE Disposal of stockpiles of solid petroleum waste came under strict regulation in the 1970s, attracting the Mob to "assist" legitimate business.

2000 Federal prosecutors charge 120 people in New York with securities fraud linked to the Mafia.

2002 Seventeen members of the Gambino Crime Family are arrested for extortion.

2005 Two retired New York police officers are arrested for conspiracy in murders carried out by the Mafia. They are convicted in 2006.

2008 John A. Gotti Jr. is arrested on charges of links to three New York murders.

Protection

The Family Secrets Trial of 2007 showed that the Mafia of the twenty-first century still engages in a version of the nineteenth-century protection racket, in which business-men paid fees for underworld guarantees against harm. Trial evidence showed that Joseph "Joey the Clown" Lombardo assessed a street tax against operators of illicit enterprises within his territory. Prosecutors estimated that one gambling operation paid Lombardo up to $2,000 USD per month to avoid the wrath of Chicago mobsters.

Secret Monopolies

Mafia corruption of legitimate businesses allows the creation of secret monopolies that increase prices to consumers and provide opportunities for money laundering, no-show jobs, and other criminal activity. The Mafia Commission case showed that New York's crime families cooperated to drive up the price of construction materials. Testimony from Gambino Crime Family turncoat, Michael DiLeonardo, indicated that similar monopolies exist throughout the construction and demolition industries.

In 2006, dozens of people associated with ostensibly independent trash hauling businesses in western Connecticut and nearby New York State were charged with coordinating their efforts to defeat the bid process. Late that year, Matthew "Matty the Horse" Ianniello of the Genovese Crime Family pleaded guilty to participating in the scheme. He was sentenced to two years in prison.

THE MOB IN WASTE HAULING

Increased federal and state regulation of solid waste disposal during the 1970s, coupled with insufficient enforcement of those regulations, made the waste haul-ing industry a magnet for organized crime in much the same way that Prohibition drew mobsters into bootleg-ging. New regulations meant far greater expenses for legitimate businesses and, therefore, a huge financial incentive for them to engage in alliances with efficient criminal enterprises.

Investigators sample and test barrels of toxic waste ready for dis-posal. Organized crime worldwide makes millions from toxic waste.

CELLULOID MAFIA

Casino

Martin Scorsese's *Casino* (1995) has a strong claim on being authentic, even if, for the sake of filmmaking, it isn't always 100 percent accurate.

The Setting

The screenplay is based on the book by Nicholas Pileggi who co-wrote it with Scorsese. Robert De Niro stars as Sam "Ace" Rothstein, a Jewish chain-smoking, gambling handicapper called to oversee the Tangiers Casino in Las Vegas. The real life Rosenthal ran the Stardust, Fremont, and the Hacienda casinos in Las Vegas for the Chicago Outfit.

The Players

Joe Pesci plays Nicky Santoro, based on the real-life Anthony "Tony the Ant" Spilotro, an enforcer and psychopath. Sharon Stone plays Ace's wife, Ginger, a role that earned her a Golden Globe Award for Best Actress and an Academy Award nomination.

The Violence

Martin Scorsese stated that he created the "head in the vice" scene as a sacrifice, hoping this would draw fire away from other violent scenes. When the MPAA made no objection, he left it in, albeit slightly edited. In reality, that incident took place about 10 years before the setting of the film, and was the real reason why Spilotro became a "made" man.

The Characters

Most of the characters, not just Rothstein and Spilotro, are based on real people. For example, Sharon Stone's Ginger Rothstein is based on Geraldine Rothstein. Frank Vincent's Frankie Marino on Frank Cullotta (Cullotta plays Curly in the film); Don Rickles' Billy Sherbert on Murray Ehrenberg; and James Woods' character, Lester Diamond, on Leonard Marmor.

ABOVE Son of Teamster boss Jimmy Hoffa, James Hoffa, also Teamster Union President, marches in protest at the WTO meeting in Seattle in 1999.

Labor Racketeering

Despite the efforts of regulators and the many publicized successes of law enforcers, labor racketeering continues. A 1986 report from the President's Council on Organized Crime detected the influence of the Mafia network in major labor unions in America, including the International Brotherhood of Teamsters, the International Long-shoremen's Association, the Laborers International Union of North America, and the Hotel and Res-taurant Employees and Bartenders International Union. Federal officials worked with a reform faction of the Laborers union between 1995 and 2000 on a cleanup of corruption in that organiza-tion. This resulted in the removal of 220 corrupt union officials, more than half of whom were found to be members or associates of known organized crime groups.

In addition to stealing and misdirecting union funds, some corrupt officials and their underworld allies have been found acting directly against union interests in order to amass personal profits. A leading figure in the Genovese Crime Family admitted in 2006 that he arranged illegal pay-ments to leaders of a bus drivers' local in New York. In 2008, a former president of that local was sentenced to four years in prison after admitting that he accepted payments from non-union bus companies to direct his unionization efforts elsewhere.

The Internet

Worldwide networking of computers fosters the growth of a number of underworld industries. Gambling rackets have adapted well to the Internet. A 2006 investigation revealed links between an Internet sports gambling empire based in Costa Rica and the Bonanno Crime Family of New York. That gambling business was believed to have drawn more than $1 billion USD a year from US bettors while making regular payments to the Bonanno leadership. In 2008, New Jersey State Police broke up a gambling operation linked to the Genovese Crime Family that made use of offshore facilities in the Dominican Republic. Officials believed the ring generated $1 million USD a month.

Organized criminal groups are also believed to be behind the production and distribution of Internet pornography.

Identity Theft

The use of computers to store personal information and to conduct financial and business transactions contributed to a rise in identity theft crimes. While

HIDING IN PLAIN SIGHT

When the Mafia Commission case conviction of "Fat Tony" Salerno deprived Genovese Crime Family boss Vincent Gigante of his front man, Gigante developed a method of hiding in plain sight. Gigante is believed to have been the gunman in 1957's unsuccessful assassination attempt against Frank Costello.

After taking over as Genovese boss about 1981, he acted the role of a mentally ill street person, regularly walking the streets of New York's Greenwich Village in his bathrobe, mumbling to himself. Once, federal agents serving a subpoena reportedly found him standing in a shower stall holding an umbrella. When Gigante was charged with racketeering in the 1990s, mental health professionals testified that he was unfit for trial. New York Mafia informants eventually provided evidence that Gigante was in command of himself and of the crime family. Gigante pleaded guilty to an obstruction of justice charge in 2003, admitting that years of apparent mental illness was only a ruse.

Although reclusive, Vincent Gigante was considered one of the most cunning and clever big bosses, managing to contract murders at will, yet never be wiretapped.

He who is deaf, blind, and silent,

lives a thousand years in peace.

John Gotti (1940–2002), boss of the Gambino Crime Family.

identity theft is generally regarded as the act of a single criminal, the presence of organized crime has been detected in large-scale thefts of financial information from banks and retail computer systems.

Narcotics

The 1984 Pizza Connection Case had exposed a heroin smuggling ring dominated by Bonanno Family and associated Sicilian immigrants known as "Zips." Since the Bonanno Crime Family was decimated by successful prosecutions in this case, underworld leaders have shied away from open participation in narcotics trafficking. The drug trade, however, remains a cash cow for the Mafia, through its connections.

Human Trafficking

The Mafia is one of a number of international criminal organizations believed to be engaged in the practice of human trafficking, an emerging human rights issue of the new millennium. Tantamount to slavery, human trafficking involves the sale of human beings into criminal enterprises, primarily prostitution.

Information Age Rackets

As the world settles into the new millennium, the American Mafia of the Information Age is branching out into new rackets and adding new twists to old ones.

OPPOSITE Workers from the Teamsters Union picket and strike to stop shipments of cars to auto dealers in 1988.

Yakuza Internal Transformation

In the course of 300 years, the Yakuza have grown from street gamblers and local market racketeers to one of the most powerful organized crime groups in the world.

New Challenges

In their long history, the Yakuza have had their triumphs and setbacks. As they enter the new millennium, the Yakuza are confronted with a host of new challenges. They face a less tolerant public, tougher law enforcement measures, and fierce global competition. But the most serious challenge is their internal transformation.

The traditional Yakuza culture, morals, customs, and organizational structure are in danger of obsolescence. The fate and future of the Yakuza may well turn on how much they can retain their image of notable outlaws. The transformation worries traditional Yakuza bosses and the police alike.

BELOW Japanese soldiers assist in the clean-up after the gang-related gas attack on the Yokohama subway in 1995.

Protectors of Society

The traditional Yakuza take pride in distinguishing themselves from Italian or American Mafia. They do not see themselves as ordinary mobsters who will kill for profit. The true Yakuza are noble gangsters who respect morals. They take pride in being the descendants of the chivalrous commoners—the feudal time Robin-Hood-type heroes. The true goal of Yakuza is to take care of all society and stand up for the weak and the poor.

It is the Yakuza's traditional creed that it will not harm the ordinary people. Yakuza members who cause injury to ordinary people are subject to discipline and punishment. The image of the Yakuza as chivalrous gangster is best captured in the remarks of one Yakuza boss. As he put it, when walking on the street the Yakuza would give common people the sunny half of the street in winter and the shaded side in summer.

ABOVE Participants dressed as *samurai* in the Jidai Matsuri Festival. The October festival celebrates the feudal traditions of Japan. It's these traditions that keep the Yakuza in favor.

Fading Tradition

This Yakuza tradition, however, is fading. With the old bosses dead or in retirement, the Yakuza are taken being over by a new generation of bosses and these new bosses and their recruits are a different kind of Yakuza. They have less respect for the tradition and feel less restrained by the traditional code of conduct.

The new Yakuza members care less about the *oyabun-kobun* structure and are not willing to obey their bosses at every step. Unlike the old Yakuza, the priorities of the new Yakuza are no longer advancement within the Yakuza organization but are more concerned with accumulating great personal wealth. Few are ready to sacrifice their lives for the devotion to duty or go to jail for their bosses. Some young members have even betrayed their bosses and brothers to the police—an act unthinkable in the old Yakuza world. The ideal of chivalry means nothing to them.

In today's gang wars, the violence is no longer confined to gang members. Ordinary people, even police officers have fallen victim of the Yakuza shootings.

New Values

In the new Yakuza world, not only the Yakuza morals, but even the most common Yakuza traditions, tattoos, and fingercutting are fading away. The younger Yakuza are no longer interested in having full-body tattoos, for such tattoos cost a fortune. They opt for simpler and less costly designs and are also much less willing to perform the fingercutting ritual.

Cultural Status

Undoubtedly, even today, Japan's criminal underworld, the Yakuza—because of the influence of the Japanese culture—do have a noble side. No organized crime groups in any other industrialized nations can compare with the Yakuza in terms of the acceptance and tolerance they have gained from the public. And without question, the Yakuza's chivalrous side has contributed in no small measure to its status within Japanese society. Nonetheless, this chivalrous side is disappearing and perhaps with it the influence the Yakuza has in Japan.

2005 Kenichi Shinoda, boss of the Yamaguchi-gumi clan turns himself into police after losing an appeal against illegal gun possession.

2007 A senior member of Sumiyoshi-kai clan is shot and killed by a member of the rival gang Yamaguchi-kai in the center of Tokyo.

2007 The Nagasaki mayor is shot by a member of the Yamaguchi-gumi gang who was arrested at the scene.

2007 Surgery at UCLA to transplant four organs into a Yakuza gang boss, sparks debate about the ethics of wealthy foreigners buying into the US health system.

I had a hard time as the daughter of a gangster, but looking back I wouldn't have lived my life any other way. I am proud that my father was a Yakuza. I know his is a world that has no proper place for women. But I have his DNA.

Shoko Tendo, daughter of Yakuza boss Hiryasu Tendo, in an interview with *The Guardian* UK, 2007

Transformation

The transformation of the Yakuza is changing the face of organized crime in Japan. With the image of the noble outlaws on the way out and with the breakdown of the Yakuza internal lines of authority, the Yakuza have become much more violent gangsters, ready to take extreme action to get a quick result.

Firearms Smuggling

The highly vaunted ban on the possession of firearms has not stopped the smuggling of weapons. Just two decades ago, the police were content with the fact that, by and large, they had disarmed organized crime. Today, the Yakuza have become heavily armed gangsters. Guns are routinely used in gang wars, racketeering, and extortions. The police face an entirely different situation from the past and the Yakuza now bear more resemblance to mobsters of American Mafia.

Attitude Changes

The change in the Yakuza structure and the mode of operation has brought about a change in public attitude with the public becoming much less tolerant of the gangs. The Yakuza are not illegal in Japan and they may open their offices within the normal community, and residents have long accepted the fact of living side-by-side with gangsters. However, as the gangs take a violent turn and gang wars spill over onto the streets, many residents find the coexistence unbearable. In some instances residents even hear machine-gun firing and explosions. Angered by the gang violence, community residents have begun to file lawsuits to evict the Yakuza from the community.

With the diminished public tolerance, the lawmakers and the police have taken more aggressive measures to contain the Yakuza. Tougher anti-organized crime laws are being adopted and the police have stepped up the anti-Yakuza operations. It is not yet clear whether the more aggressive measures have reduced the strength of the Yakuza.

Regrouping

The tougher laws have brought down both the number of Yakuza groups and the number of Yakuza members. However, the anti-gang laws have prompted a Yakuza regrouping. Unable to stand the pressure brought to bear by the police under the new laws, many small Yakuza groups disbanded. But disbanding helped swell the ranks of big Yakuza syndicates.

BELOW Police collect evidence at the scene of a stabbing spree in Tokyo. The assailant, proclaiming he was a gangster, killed at least seven people and injured about twelve.

Freelance Criminals

The big organizations, more sophisticated and well financed, are now able to secure experts to help them withstand the challenges posed by the law and the police. Currently, more than 70 percent of the 85,000 Yakuza members belong to one of the three largest Yakuza syndicates. However, many former Yakuza members, though no longer belonging to any group, have not left the criminal underworld. They operate either as Yakuza associates or freelance criminals. These unorganized criminal elements are responsible for more crimes and arrests than the full-fledged Yakuza members. They are available for hire by corporations or individuals.

Global Competition

As the Yakuza enter the twenty-first century, the tough anti-gang measures are not their only concern. With fierce global competition, they need to restructure to regain the money-making momentum. The bigger and savvier Yakuza groups realize that the old schemes can no longer ensure a comfortable life. They must opt for crimes of greater sophistication and they are in the process of transforming themselves from street gangsters to economic, intellectual, and high-tech gangsters, and corporate and financial racketeers. In step with globalization of the economy, they have expanded overseas extending their operation to Korea, the Philippines, South-East Asian countries, and the United States.

Changing Image

In the new century, amid tougher anti-gang laws, increased police pressure, the very bad economic conditions, and the growing public disillusion with the gangsters, the Yakuza are undergoing a hard time. But the Yakuza are not on their way out and the Yakuza membership is still huge. The gangs are resourceful in coming up with new tactics to survive and remain active.

However, the Yakuza's future may well rely on how much good will they can retain from the public. The noble side of the gangsters secured them a unique place in Japanese society and earned them a distinction among organized crime groups in the world. Shedding the image of chivalrous gangsters may well spell their demise or at least further reduce their survival rate.

ABOVE Tetsuya Shiroo, a member of a gang affiliated with the Yamaguchi-gumi, shot the mayor of Nagasaki, Icco Ito, in 2007.

LEFT Perhaps the new image of Yakuza. Here a young couple include their children in the motorcycle gang activities.

Triads
Snakeheads and Tongs

2001 Head of the Supreme People's Procuratorate in China discloses that more than 2,500 officials had been linked to corruption by Triad gangs in 2000

2001 BBC News reports that around 50 Triad gangs are operating in Hong Kong

2006 Legal experts in China estimate there are over one million mobsters in the country

2006 Beijing's People's Court hears charges against the Hu brothers, suspected of illegal scrap metal dealing and sand quarrying, and connections to Triads

2007 Leading Hong Kong retailer Douglas Young is arrested for selling T-shirts and postcards depicting 14K Triad gang logos. Under Hong Kong law it's illegal to possess anything relating to Triads.

After the terrorist attacks of September 11, 2001, with the heightened need for more secure borders, the crime syndicates that were smuggling people across these borders were seen as a severe threat to the security of nations like the United States and Great Britain.

Terrorist Fears

These countries feared that among any refugees, there would be terrorists—extremists who could slip into the country unseen, and start their campaign of terror. Though this is not an unlikely scenario, most people that are smuggled across the borders by gangs of criminals are people who are anything but terrorists. Most of them pay thousands of dollars to make a trip that can take months and end with a job in a sweatshop.

Snakeheads

The smuggling of humans is a multi-billion dollar industry, generating tens of billions in profits each year, according to official reports by Europol. Chinese criminals, named Snakeheads, are very involved in the smuggling of people. Although these Snakehead gangs sometimes work closely with the Chinese Triads, most of the time they work alone. They are specialists in the process and profit-making of human trafficking.

One of the most famous Snakeheads is a woman by the name of Cheng Chui Ping. She lived in Manhattan's Chinatown, where she owned a shop and restaurant. People in the neighborhood called her "Sister Ping" and held her in high esteem because she brought Chinese people over from China, and treated them fairly. Ping was born in 1949 in Shengmei, in the Fujian province of China. During the 1970s, she and her

Chinese police storm a cargo ship in Fujian province suspected of carrying illegal immigrants by a human trafficking gang of Snakeheads.

LURE OF THE WEST

Each year thousands of Chinese desperately look for a better future and a decent job in what they see as the rich Western world. In order to get there, these people contact a smuggler, known as a Snakehead.

This Snakehead receives a down payment of several thousand dollars, and will receive the remaining amount ($25,000–$45,000 USD) when their client arrives at the promised destination. Since it is impossible for the smuggled person to have that much money upon arrival in the new strange country, the Snakehead gang allows him to work his debt off in one of their businesses.

husband moved to Hong Kong, where they opened up a convenience store. In the early 1980s, Ping arrived in the United States, opening a small variety store on Hester Street in New York. As her store became a meeting place for Chinese from the Fujian province, she started a remittance business, enabling emigrants to send money back to their families in China.

Her connections quickly got her involved in the smuggling business. At first she was actively involved in every step of the smuggling process, even accompanying illegal aliens on flights to the United States, but later she would subcontract her operations to other criminals, and groups like the Fuk Ching gang. As more people asked Sister Ping, and other smugglers, for their services, the Snakeheads started using large ships to smuggle people from China to the United States.

ABOVE Passengers from the *Golden Venture* freighter speak out about their legal status after spending four years in detention.

The Golden Venture

This is where Sister Ping's smuggling operations took a turn for the worse. In early June 1993, police officers found a large ship that had run aground near Queens, New York. People were jumping from the ship's deck, and when officers went to investigate further they found almost 300 Chinese inside. Many were in terrible condition after having lived on board for months with little to eat or drink. The ship's name was the *Golden Venture*, and authorities immediately began investigating who was behind this terrible crime. They quickly discovered that Sister Ping was involved, but before she could be apprehended she fled to Hong Kong. She continued her smuggling operations from her hometown, Shengmei.

Arrest

Since the United States does not have an extradition treaty with China, she was safe. But US authorities did not give up, and they eventually arrested her at Hong Kong airport. She was deported to the United States in 2003, and after a trial that lasted one month, she was found guilty of conspiracy to smuggle aliens, and several other crimes. On March 16, 2006, the judge sentenced her to 35 years in prison.

BELOW A young garment worker in a Hong Kong sweatshop wears a mask to protect her from dust.

World Market

The smuggling of Chinese continues to be the favorite criminal activity among the Chinese gangs. On January 23, 2009, 15 Snakeheads were given prison sentences of up to 11 years on charges of smuggling 111 persons to destinations ranging from Israel to the Republic of Korea. The gang was busted after an investigation that started in October 2007 and ended in July 2008. Human trafficking takes place to Australia where loads of "boat people" are apprehended every summer. In early 2009, one of these boats exploded killing and injuring a number of people on board.

THE POWER OF POLITICS

Despite China's harsh sentences for criminal activities, it seems that organized crime is regaining some of the influence it had before Mao's army forced them to go into hiding, or even flee mainland China. In the past few years there have been numerous stories indicating that Chinese wealthy businessmen and politicians have been involved in criminal activities. The lure of great wealth and a reputation as a tough guy seem to be too tempting.

In November 2007, hundreds of Chinese police armed with semi-automatic weapons raided a restaurant in Yangjiang, a city in the Guangdong province of China. Dozens of men, said to be Triad members, were arrested, including their leaders. And this is where the story becomes very interesting. The leaders arrested were Lin Guoqin and Xu Jianqiang. Lin is a local politician, also member of the People's Congress, and an important business man. Lin is alleged to have used intimidation to expand his business interests.

Though this type of behavior does not seem so strange to those who are familiar with the corruptive influence of crime groups on local politics, it is very surprising to see this type of behavior in China, where corrupt politicians are frequently sentenced to death. But organized crime is on the rise. According to the Xinhua news agency, Chinese authorities have broken up 4,000 crime groups since February 2006.

This highly colorful poster is displayed in China, advertising the police. It reads "Pintang Police at your service." China is intent on improving relations between citizens and the police.

The Untouchables

Since the Chinese Triads operate on a global scale, it is a necessity for authorities of different countries to work together in stopping these crime groups. China and the United States are an unlikely team, but in the case of "The Untouchables," they worked together perfectly.

The Untouchables were also known as the "125 Gang," named after the weight of their leader Kin Cheung Wong—275 lb (125 kg). Wong started his criminal career in New York's Chinatown. He was arrested for smuggling heroin, and after serving four years, was deported to China in 1994.

BELOW Chinese police question drug traffickers on a train from Kunming to Shanghai. Police found 14 oz (400 g) of heroin in the bras of the two girls.

The High Life

That wasn't the end of Kin Cheung Wong. Upon arrival, he started a nightclub, called the Huamei Entertainment Company, in the city of Fuzhou. It was a place where the extremely rich could enjoy a night out in style.

In this nightclub, he came into contact with very powerful men, chief among them the richest businessman in Fuzhou, Chen Kai. Wong allegedly used all his contacts to set up a very successful drug smuggling organization. From 2000 until 2003, authorities estimate that Wong's organization smuggled $100 million USD worth of heroin from the Golden Triangle to the United States and Canada.

I cannot say that I'm the good person. But I can tell you I'm not the bad person, either.

Raymond Chow, commenting on his gangster days in the *San Francisco Weekly*, 2007

Gang Caution

The group operated in extreme secrecy, and, thanks to corruption and substantial payoffs, managed to travel from one country to the other almost unnoticed. Wong's important connections allegedly went all the way up the political hierarchy, and reportedly included many high-ranking police officials. According to law enforcement sources in New York, their dealers there were also very careful, changing cars, clothes, and always watching out for the prying eyes of investigators.

International Sting

Wong himself was always very careful about where his drug deals took place, and whom he dealt with, but on May 16, 2003, he made a huge mistake when he was arrested while in possession of 77 lb (35 kg) of heroin. As he was escorted to prison, authorities in the United States, Canada, Hong Kong, and India arrested scores of members that had participated in this grand drug conspiracy. A Chinese court found Wong guilty, and sentenced him to death.

In the aftermath of the bust, scores of politicians and police officers were arrested. The case shook China to the core. Its president Hu Jintao personally sent 30 investigators to make sure that the case was handled properly.

When the dust settled, Chen, Wong's associate, was charged with bribing government officials, and running a brothel. For this last offence, Chen was given a death sentence. This brought closure to a case that illustrated how very much power organized crime in China has acquired in these past few decades.

ABOVE Coast guard and customs police practice maneuvers to intercept drug smugglers off the coast of Macau.

BELOW Once a form of punishment, tattoos are now becoming a popular form of artistry in China.

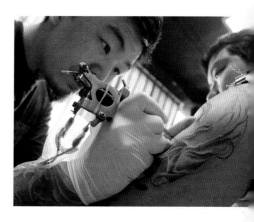

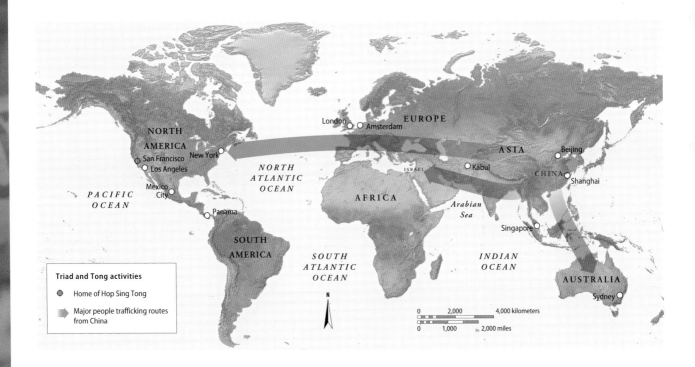

Triad and Tong activities

⊕ Home of Hop Sing Tong

➤ Major people trafficking routes from China

California Tongs

California has a large Chinese population, dating back to the nineteenth century, when the Chinese came to the United States looking for work. San Francisco, in particular, has always been a hotbed of Tong activity that continues to this day. The interesting part about the current-day Tong activities in San Francisco is the fact that one of these men, whom authorities say is a leader, is a former Tong leader-turned-informant. Raymond Chow had been the leader of the Hop Sing Tong, and served as an underboss to Peter Chong, who was the leader of the Wo Hop To Triad.

Amalgamation

During the early 1990s, the two men had plans to combine several American Tongs and Chinese street gangs into one big Triad, which was to be called Tien Ha Wui, or Whole Earth Association. But before they could achieve their goal, law enforcement indicted them on a host of racketeering charges. Chong managed to flee to Hong Kong in 1992, but was extradited to stand trial in the United States in 2000.

BELOW Police gather outside a Chinese restaurant in Chinatown, New York, after a gang related shooting in which eight people were injured.

He was convicted and sentenced to a prison term of 15 years. Chow's trial had already taken place in 1996 and had ended in a mistrial. But he was subsequently convicted of gun charges and given a 25-years-to-life sentence. Prison apparently didn't suit him, because he decided to cut a deal with the government, and testify against his former boss. As part of this deal, Chow was released from prison in 2003.

After his release, Chow went straight back to the streets of Chinatown, and, according to law enforcement, renewed his contacts with members of Asian gangs, including his former Hop Sing Tong underlings. The Hop Sing Tong was now led by Allen Ngai Leung. He arrived in California during the 1970s, at the age of 20. During the late 1970s, he became a member of the Hop Sing. As he became a successful businessman, he started playing

a bigger role within the Tong. When Chow was released from prison, an associate of his sent word to Leung that several young Hop Sing members needed money "to do business." When the Hop Sing Tong leadership voted against lending the younger members money, its front door was shot at by unknown assailants the next day.

Assassination

It was all too much for Leung, who decided to cooperate with authorities in solving this case. It was a dangerous move, and one that didn't end well. In February 2006 a gunman wearing a mask entered Leung's office and shot to him to death, while his wife watched in horror. No one has been charged with the murder, and though Chow is a suspect, he has not been indicted.

During Leung's funeral, hundreds of people came to pay their respects, among them a cabinet minister from Taiwan. Raymond Chow was also there, telling Chinese reporters he came to pay his respects to "Big Brother."

The Future

Throughout history, the Chinese Triads have shown they can cope with setbacks. Whether they are facing a brutal emperor, or a vicious communist dictator, they have proven they can make a comeback. They are deeply rooted in Chinese traditions, and are protected by their fellow Chinese all over the world. Their power and grip on the world economy stretches from Hong Kong and China to countries such as the United States, the Netherlands, and Great Britain, and Australia. It is safe to say that they should not be underestimated.

ABOVE The entrance to Chinatown in London. Almost every major city in the world boasts a Chinatown, most with considerable Triad influence.

Russian Mafia
Constant Presence

With criminal organizations controlling 40 percent of Russia's economy and more than 50,000 companies, and with 70 percent of businesses paying protection money to criminal organizations, it can be assumed that organized crime poses a threat not only to the prospect of a democratic Russia but also to global security and stability.

Criminal Numbers

Organized crime has been, and probably will remain, a powerful and dangerous constant in Russian life. There are no accurate figures on the numbers of criminal organizations and gang members in Russia. In the mid-1990s, the Russian Ministry of Internal Affairs estimated that there were 8,222 criminal organizations and a total of 32,068 known members. The numbers appear to have stabilized ever since. The recent estimate indicates that there are about 10,000 criminal organizations and about 30,000 gang members. There is no one Russian Mafia as such but about 30 to 50 powerful criminal organizations.

Free Structure

A notable characteristic of Russian organized crime is that the criminal underworld in Russia has never developed the traditions and mythology typical of traditional criminal organizations such as the Italian Mafia, the Chinese Triads, or the Japanese Yakuza.

Russian organized criminal groups are not organized in the classic pyramid structure. There are no godfathers sitting at the apogee of the gang hierarchy. Russian organized crime is not monolithic. Rather, it is highly diverse and fractured. There

BELOW Inmates of a high security prison in St Petersburg watch a New Year concert. The tattoos are losing favor with prisoners.

are powerful crime figures, including *vory v zakone*, but they are not godfathers. They possess great authority but have little direct power over other gang members.

Because of the respect they command, they often act as mediators and arbitrators of gangland disputes. Otherwise, they are just more powerful and influential gang members than the rank and file.

Russian gang members prefer greater autonomy. Anyone acting as a crime boss runs the risk of alienating his members if he treats them too much like subordinates. Alienated gang members may choose to leave the group and join a rival group, request a *vor* to mediate the dispute in order to maintain his autonomy, or simply have the crime boss assassinated.

Unpredictabilty

Diversity and loose organizational structure, combined with the lack of a tradition of honor, make Russian crime mobs more dangerous and less predictable. A kidnapping case in the United States serves to illustrate the point. A Russian organized crime group kidnapped five Russian immigrants and demanded ransom. The victims' families paid the ransom on time but never saw their loved ones return. After the gang members were captured, they confessed that they killed the hostages shortly after the abduction and they intended to kill them regardless of whether or not the ransom was delivered. Russian gangs are not associated with honor and respect. In the new millennium, it seems they are not restrained by any gangland laws.

We need to root out the practice of unlawful decisions "by request" or for money.

Dmitry Medvedev, President of Russia

2002 Russian legislators gain a 160 percent pay rise in an effort to keep them free from corruption and pay-offs by organized crime.

2005 The Federal Law on Government Protection of Victims, Witnesses, and Other Participants is approved, supposedly providing witness protection for those willing to report on organized crime. Insufficient funding makes its effect dubious.

2005 The director of secret police in Ukraine openly accuses Semyon Mogilevich, a known dealer in illegal oil and natural gas, of corruption in his company, Gazprom. Mogilevich was arrested in 2008.

GLOBAL CONNECTIONS

Russia's opening up to the world provides a unique opportunity for Russian organized crime to expand its operation globally. In the 1990s, desperate for money and an opportunity to make a living, many Russians moved abroad. Criminals followed the emigrants. Russian organized crime has ever since established its operation networks in more than 50 countries worldwide. Russian organized crime groups now work in collaboration with all major criminal syndicates in the world, including the Italian Mafia, the Japanese Yakuza, the Chinese Triads, and the Columbian drug cartels.

In collaboration with the Chinese Triads, the Russian Mafias are engaged in the hugely profitable enterprise of human trafficking. They have made Moscow a central distribution point for migrants and criminals seeking illegal entry to Western Europe and the United States.

Working together with the Japanese Yakuza, they have arranged for young women from Russia, former Soviet republics, and Eastern European countries to go to Japan to work as sex workers. The Russian gangs are key players in operating prostitution rings in Eastern and Western Europe.

Russian crime mobs have also cooperated with Columbian drug cartels and Mexican drug lords in international drug trafficking. A Russian crime boss even attempted to arrange a sale of an old Soviet submarine to the Columbian drug cartels to facilitate their drug trafficking operations to the United States.

Russian frontier guards assist in the destruction of illegal drugs that have been confiscated along the Tajik-Afghan border. Busts such as this have helped boost Russia's global crime-fighting reputation.

Sophistication

Despite the lack of a code of honor, Russian gangs suffer no deficiency in criminal sophistication and ambition. Many of today's Russian mobsters hold doctorates in physics, finance, mathematics, engineering, and computer science. Their high educational achievements enable them to engage in extremely sophisticated criminal enterprises. Russian mobsters are involved in all the typical gang crimes and in many aspects they surpass their criminal brothers in other countries.

Weapons of Mass Destruction

They deal in gambling, extortion, prostitution, kidnapping, contract killings, labor racketeering, counterfeiting, credit card fraud, loan sharking, money laundering, and trafficking in drugs, arms, and humans. The involvement of Russian organized crime groups in the smuggling trade is especially menacing because of their ability to have access to weapons of mass destruction.

In the 1990s, the Russian police thwarted more than 400 cases of attempted smuggling of nuclear material to foreign countries. The threat has by no means abated today. As long as there are demands from rogue states and terrorist organizations for weapons of mass destruction, there is a real possibility that Russian gangs may provide them access to such weapons.

Challenge

The Russian government in the recent years has made tremendous efforts to combat organized crime. The challenge is great. With organized crime so deeply embedded in government and business, any effort to combat organized crime would not be successful without thorough internal housecleaning. That will be a daunting task for any Russian government.

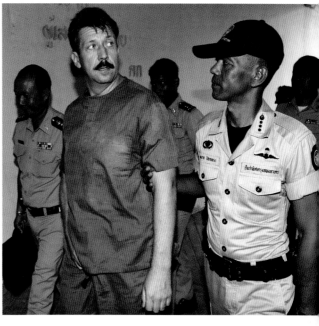

ABOVE Victor Bout, reportedly one of Russia's leading organized crime figures, is arrested in Thailand. Known as the "Merchant of Death," Bout was allegedly one of the world's foremost weapons traffickers.

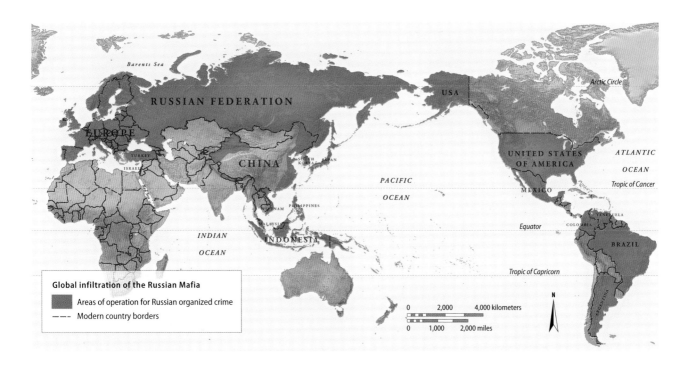

Global infiltration of the Russian Mafia

Areas of operation for Russian organized crime

--- Modern country borders

THE SOPRANOS
Mafia by Media

ABOVE Tony Soprano
(James Gandolfini) discusses a
"situation" over dinner.

In January 1999, America's HBO network launched a new drama series, *The Sopranos*, created by David Chase and centered on the fictional New Jersey Mafia *capo*, Tony Soprano (James Gandolfini)—at work, at play, and in therapy with Dr. Jennifer Melfi (Lorraine Bracco). The series went on to a six-season, 86-episode phenomenon that captured the imagination of viewers around the world.

"To blow up a store? You call that balls? Balls is you look a guy in the eye while you jam an icepick through his lung."

Butch (Greg Antonacci), Episode 77, *The Sopranos*

The Family

Wife Carmela (Edie Falco), teenage daughter Meadow (Jamie-Lynn Sigler), son Anthony 'AJ' Soprano Jnr (Robert Iler), and others in the Soprano family, all tend to create problems for Tony, who must avoid a plot to get rid of him by Uncle Junior (Dominic Chianese).

His inner circle also includes his mother Livia, sister Janice, second cousin Christopher Moltisanti, cousin Tony Blundetto, his calm and urbane New York counterpart Johnny Sack and his consigliore, Silvio Dante, who owns the Bada Bing club, where he regularly regales his associates with a legendary impression of Al Pacino.

The Humor

The series was marked by its intense scrutiny of life inside the family of a Mafia boss, and the extreme violence that occurs around him as part of his "work environment."

But the series was also popular for its dark, wry, and sometimes absurd, humor. One exchange (in episode 65) went like this:

"We're from Alcoholics Anonymous," Phil Leotardo (Frank Vincent)

"What's your names?" Joanne Moltisanti (Marianne Leone Cooper)

"Well, we're anonymous." Phil Leotardo

ABOVE The cast of *The Sopranos* with their Screen Actors Guild Awards. The show has been a continual award winner since season one.

The Style

The show's creator, David Chase, also wrote and directed many of the episodes; actor Steve Buscemi, who plays Tony Blundetto, also directed some episodes, as did acclaimed director Peter Bogdanovich, who plays the role of Dr Elliot Kupferberg, a "shrink's shrink" consulted by Dr Melfi.

The Detail

The original director of photography Alik Sahkarov and creator, David Chase, would break each scene down into shots, as if preparing to shoot a feature film. Wardrobe was another major element, and award-winning costume designer Juliet Polcsa was

meticulous about detail—she even dictated what socks the cast should wear. "Even if you can't see it on camera, the actor feels the difference," she maintained.

The Merchandise

Such was the impact of the show that a wide range of *Sopranos* branded merchandise was created for sale on the official *Sopranos* website, ranging from T-shirts, hats, accessories, to glassware, wine, office accessories, beer steins, and flip flops. For really keen fans, there are dedicated items branded with each of the various episodes.

OPPOSITE Paulie Walnuts (Tony Sirico) takes a hand to Christopher (Michael Imperioli).

Cartel Alliances
International Drug Trade

In the twenty-first century, the ongoing drug war in Mexico threatens Mexican as well as US national security. The situation in Mexico ranks with Iran as major US national security threats.

Colombia

In the twenty-first century Colombia still controls the wholesale distribution of cocaine on the US east coast. However, unlike the period from the 1970s to the mid-1990s, there is no monolithic cartel controlling the drug trade in Colombia. Today the trade is fragmented with different actors involved in various processes of production and distribution. The US Drug Enforcement Agency believes that there are hundreds of small autonomous groups in Colombia that facilitate and keep the wheels of the cocaine industry turning.

Plan Colombia

Plan Colombia, a program originally designed to provide the Colombian government needed resources to counter the growing insurgency, combat the illegal flow of drugs, and provide economic incentives to farmers for alternative crop development, came into force in 2000. Since that time the United States has spent over $6 billion USD in its effort to combat the production and distribution of illegal narcotics. However, efforts at bringing coca cultivation under control have largely failed.

> *In the last two or three years almost 100 percent of the gardens we've eradicated are Mexican drug cartel gardens, ... It's alarming if you think about it.*
>
> James Parker, US federal judge

Mexico's Drug Wars

The power of the cartels in Mexico is far-reaching and multi-dimensional. Citizens who live in areas dominated by drug traffickers live in fear of random acts of violence and a system that is unable or unwilling to enforce existing laws and establish social order. Most cocaine in the United States is trafficked through the US–Mexican border.

With the decline of the major Colombian cartels, an arrangement was established whereby Mexican drug trafficking organizations would receive a percentage of each shipment of cocaine. This provided Mexican cartels with an opportunity to become involved in the distribution process and become major players in trafficking Colombian cocaine to various global markets.

Moreover, since 2000, drug usage and addiction rates in Mexico have soared. In 2006, Felipe Calderon became President of Mexico and launched a nationwide campaign against the nation's ever expanding and powerful drug cartels.

Border Patrol

Much of the violence takes place between Ciudad Juarez and Nuevo Laredo, a US–Mexican border area that spans approximately 600 miles (960 km). Ciudad Juarez is one of the most violent cities in the country with a homicide rate in 2008 of over 1,600 people. Police in Ciudad Juarez have been so overwhelmed that the Mexican government has sent thousands of Mexican soldiers to the area to shore up security.

The United States has assisted Mexican authorities by providing intelligence assistance and state-of-the-art surveillance, drug monitoring equipment, and law enforcement training. Implemented in June 2008, this effort is known as the Merida Initiative.

Today, over 60,000 police and Mexican soldiers are in the fight against drug gangs who are vying for control over key drug transportation routes into the lucrative US market.

These cartels are well financed and well armed with sniper rifles, rocket launchers, Israeli Uzis, and AK47 assault rifles at their disposal. Much of this weaponry is shipped from the United States. The US cocaine market is a $38-40 billion USD a year industry. Mexican cartels are operative in major US cities and are allying with American drug gangs.

They are considered the principal organized crime threat in the United States.

OPPOSITE A Guambiano Indian collects resin from the poppy bulbs on her farm. Her town of Silvia, in Colombia, is government controlled while the surrounding hills are held by FARC forces.

MEXICAN MAFIA

La Eme, aka Mexican Mafia, is a Mexican-American prison gang that formed around 1957. It is allegedly involved in the trafficking of illegal drugs, specifically heroin. The group is predominant in the California prison system and has members on the street as well as in federal prisons throughout the United States.

The *Nuestra Familia*, aka Our Family, is another Mexican-American prison gang. They were formed in the 1960s and oppose and compete with *La Eme*. The *Nuestra Familia* are originally from northern California. The group became organized in the California state prison system and has members in the Colorado state prison system as well. They are allegedly involved in drug trafficking and numerous other violent activities.

The Mexican Mafia is one of the most feared gangs in the prison community. Their membership is marked by intricate tattoos of an eagle and a snake.

ABOVE A burqa-clad woman buys vegetables in the city of Herat, in western Afghanistan. Here, opium cultivation has dropped by 20 percent, unlike the southern regions where is still flourishes.

OPPOSITE Pakistani official stands guard as seized drugs are destroyed on International Anti-narcotics Day, in 2007.

International Alliances

Although criminal and terrorist groups both pose a danger to international security and are similar in many respects, they are inherently different types of organizations. Criminal activity is motivated by profit. Terrorist groups, while not being motivated by profit, may be willing to pursue any financial avenue or opportunity to ensure enough revenue to support the particular needs of recruitment, training, and logistical support, to further the objectives of their organization. When a relationship between criminal groups and specific terrorist organizations does exist, it is usually born of necessity and a shared need to further the objectives of both groups. For example, in the case of a state with weak, corrupt, or non-existent internal security, or law enforcement constraints, such as the situation in Afghanistan, terrorists in control of a certain territory may negotiate the movement of drugs by traffickers for arms or monetary imbursement.

Conversely, factors that may enter the decision of some terrorist groups to refrain from illegal activity, especially the drug trade, are increased susceptibility to military action or law enforcement, and loss of public and benefactor support among those who view this particular type of activity as a violation of some religious or social tenet.

Engaging in criminal activity to support operations and infrastructure while organized in the sense that there is a consistent pattern and *modus operandi* at work is not the same as establishing an ongoing operational alliance with groups such as the Albanian, Italian, or Russian Mafias. Colombian drug dealers have established formal alliances with Mexican, Dominican, Italian, and Russian criminal groups, providing new markets for Colombian narcotics and distribution channels to feed the growing drug demand in Europe, Russia, and the former Soviet satellite states. Equally discouraging is the fact that some of these alliances not only involve the distribution of dangerous narcotics and other illegal commodities but also supply weapons in exchange for drugs and provide opportunities for laundering the huge amounts of money earned by these criminal enterprises. There have also been reports that some former Russian KGB members were involved in some weapons-for-drugs exchanges. Evidence also exists that criminal groups operating out of Nigeria, have worked with Colombian cocaine and heroin drug criminals to traffic narcotics to the USA, Europe and South Africa.

The global trade in illicit narcotics is difficult to combat basically because it is a global trade. The demand for drugs exists in most countries throughout the world and is expanding as addiction levels rise constantly.

Drug cartels—approximate areas of influence

Alliance of several major organisations
Gulf cartel
Juarez cartel
Tijuana cartel
--- Modern country borders

UNITED STATES OF AMERICA
Los Angeles
San Diego
USA
Mexico
Dallas
New Orleans
Gulf of Mexico
Miami
Tropic of Cancer
MEXICO
CUBA
PACIFIC OCEAN
Mexico City
BELIZE
GUATEMALA
HONDURAS
NICARAGUA
COSTA RICA
N

0   250   500 kilometers
0   125   250 miles

AFGHANISTAN

The Opium Trade

In Afghanistan, a complex web of actors dominates the expanding opium trade undermining state institutions and the ability of the Kabul government to expand its reach nationally.

Opium Production

Opium production has risen steadily since the latter years of the Soviet-Afghan conflict (1979–1989). During the Taliban ascendancy beginning in November 1994, production peaked at over 3,400 tons. Following the Taliban-imposed ban in 2000, there was a rapid decline in opium cultivation to 185 tons. Much of this output was produced in territory held by the Northern Alliance, the group fighting the Taliban for control over the country.

While the ban eliminated a large percentage of opium cultivation in Taliban-held territory, it did not impact the trafficking of opiates. During their reign, Afghanistan's Taliban militia depended upon and derived revenue from the opium and heroin trade by imposing a tax on producers and distributors—peasant farmers, traders, and traffickers

Additionally, prior to 9/11, certain of the Taliban commanders and mullahs were directly involved in the trade. The Taliban was able to engender the support of various local commanders—warlords—by allowing them to continue involvement in the trade.

Following the October 2001 invasion by United States and coalition forces, opium production soared and has been increasing annually. This rise can be attributed to the initial defeat of the Taliban regime, the "power vacuum" that ensued, and the decision on the part of the USA to align with former warlords in the war against the Taliban and al-Qa'eda.

Southern Provinces

The nerve center of the drug trade and the region where security has been a major problem are the southern provinces where the insurgency and violence have not only been sustained but have increased in intensity and where production of opium is most profound. This is especially true of Helmand Province, the country's largest opium production area.

Today regional warlords, who allied with United States and coalition forces to oust the Taliban and al-Qa'eda, are in control of major portions of the country and are competing with each other for power and opium-generated wealth. Hence, political power in Afghanistan is concentrated in the hands of about a dozen regional warlords who command private armies and rule over opium-rich territory. This allows them to provide for their private militias, and fund projects designed to win public support which in turn increases their power base. The huge revenue generated by the opium trade also provides criminal actors with sufficient financial muscle to enter or otherwise influence the political process. This threatens and undermines the central government in Kabul and presents a number of security-related issues for international forces.

Corrupting Influence

The criminal pursuit of power and wealth creates a self-perpetuating situation whereby it becomes difficult for otherwise honest individuals to avoid the corrupting influence wrought by the huge profits available by illegal activity. This problem spawns and sustains corruption at the local as well as national level. While the fall of the Taliban created potential opportunities for development and reconstruction, much of this rebirth hinges on the ability of the Kabul government to curtail the increasing influence and power of local and regional warlords, their militias, and other armed factions. The rise of these regional commanders—warlords, private militias, criminal groups, and other armed factions—has indeed created fertile ground for the uninhibited cultivation of the opium poppy which in turn creates an environment which spawns instability violence, and corruption. The illicit narcotics industry not only serves the financial needs of many rural Afghans but also provides a source of revenue for the Taliban and their allies.

Afghanistan

▨ Helmand province—largest opium producer in Afghanistan

- - - - Modern country borders

0   250   500 kilometers
0   125   250 miles

OPPOSITE A man slices down the unripe opium seedpod to reveal the milky juice that is used to make opium.

BELOW Sayed Rahim walks on mounds of cotton he was unable to sell, resulting in him replacing his cotton crop with opium poppy.

Transnational Crime
Balkans, Africa, Australia

The twenty-first century has seen a change in the distribution of power among organized crime groups around the world. Apart from the surge in trafficking and terror in the Middle East and Afghanistan, there is increased focus on the Balkans and Africa.

Turkish Clans

Turkey, together with Lebanon, has long been one of the world's major opium-growing areas, with the illegal heroin and opium trade making the fortune and power of several Turkish clans that are still active today. The profits from this trade have allowed them to deeply penetrate into the Turkish ruling classes, both political and industrial, pouring wealth into the Turkish industrialization process.

When trouble arose along the eastern borders of Turkey, Turkish organized crime groups were forced to move their laboratories and logistics west—to Ankara, Istanbul, and even to Greece, Bulgaria, and the Balkans. Their know-how, reputation, and links to the Italian families, both in Italy and in North America, have seen Turkish families grow ever stronger on the international crime stage, organizing the heroin trade from the production zones in Afghanistan and the Golden Triangle to the consuming zones, mainly in Western Europe. Together with the political movement known as the "Grey Wolves"—an extreme right-wing political movement—Turkish crime families are often involved in crimes outside their country.

OPPOSITE Turkish demonstrators in Germany make the sign of the Grey Wolves, a group responsible for roughly 694 murders in the years 1974–1980.

THE BALKAN ROUTE

The so-called "Balkan Route" of the drugs trade began to operate effectively in the 1970s, when there was a massive increase in the number of trucks passing through what was then Yugoslavia. With the staging of the Olympic Games in Sarajevo in 1984, Yugoslavia was opened up even further to outside forces, with more and more trafficking of both people and goods occurring throughout the country. The Balkan Route radically changed the balance of power in the opium and heroin trade in Western Europe, controlled at the time by the Corsican networks through Marseilles. Three different routes have been used for drug trafficking by Turkish organized crime groups, together with Bulgarian and Yugoslavian groups—the north route, which passes by the Black Sea to Bulgaria then to Romania; the central route, which crosses Bulgaria and Serbia to Hungary; and the southern route, passing through Greece, Macedonia, and Serbia, through the city of Nis, then along the central route to Hungary.

Heroin wrapped in adhesive tape, seized by police along with five alleged traffickers and several weapons in Munich, Germany, 2009.

Carving Up the Market

In the early days of the Balkan Route, it was mainly former Yugoslavian nationals who were used as front men, ensuring the security of the drug trafficking, primarily through Serbia. Soon Serbian groups took power in countries where the Balkan Route ended—England, the Netherlands, Belgium, and part of France. During the 1970s and 1980s, however, markets in Germany and Switzerland remained predominantly in the hands of Lebanese and Turkish clans.

Blood alliances were also made at the time between Serbian and Italian families. Luigi Francesco Di Paolo, involved in the so-called "La Strega Massacre" in Milan in 1979, was the brother-in-law of Dragomir Petrovic, a chief of the clan established in Marseilles. Yet hostilities between different groups continued. An underground war took place in the late 1970s and early 1980s between the Italian clans and the Corsican and Yugoslavian clans to gain control of heroin trafficking.

Boom Time

With the war in Yugoslavia coming after the death of Tito, the criminal clans flourished and the markets for their services widened. In the classical drug trade, the 1990s saw an extraordinary blossoming of Croatian, Bosnian, and Serbian organized crime groups.

The Weapons Trade

BELOW How much is that machine gun in your illegal arms shop window? At a discreet distance from the capital, this Yemeni trader has a ready market.

While at first the drug trade attracted the main focus, the market for illegal weapons was such that a major trade soon developed, especially in Bosnia and Croatia in the early 1990s. The Italian clans played an important role, but the major actors were the Albanian clans. The insurrection of 1997 had seen almost all military stocks stolen and smuggled from Kosovo, Bosnia, and Serbia. Heavy weapons such as 10 ground-to-air missiles found in a cave near Gjirokaster, in Albania, were stolen from the army base of Arshi Lengo, south of Tirana. The illegal weapons and ammunition trade also became a way for state-owned companies in Montenegro, Bosnia, and Serbia to survive.

ARKAN Serbian Warlord

In the 1970s, the Serbian Mafia was called "Nasa Stvar" and moving up through their ranks was the famous Zeljko Raznatovic—"Arkan."

In 1969, at the age of 17, "Arkan" Raznatovic, who had been raised in a strict military family, was arrested for burglary. During his detention, he organized his own gang. In July 1972, Italian magistrates issued a warrant for his arrest for attempted theft and another, for the same reason, in September 1973. But Arkan was never arrested. In 1974, in a hold-up in Milan, Arkan escaped again. That same year in Sweden, Arkan was involved in series of hold-ups, the most famous being the Enselid Bank in Stockholm that brought him and his followers more than 80,000 Swedish kroner.

Arkan continued his criminal career across Europe, with arrests and spectacular escapes, coming increasingly into competition with Albanian clans, in particular Daut Kadriosvski, an alleged Albanian Mafia boss with contacts in Turkey and Germany.

During the war in Bosnia, Arkan set up a paramilitary brigade called "Arkan's Tigers" that was responsible for several crimes in former Yugoslavia. Its members set up crime businesses in Europe and the United States, using their strong connection with Arkan and his political allies and with the Italian clans already well established in all western countries.

Arkan was gunned down on January 15, 2000, at the Intercontinental Hotel in Belgrade. He was shot through the left eye and died two hours later in hospital. His assassination appeared to be a well-planned attack.

By this time, his friends were allegedly found in top criminal positions in different countries—Dragan Joskovic in Sweden, Ljubomir Magas in Germany (also a recognized member of the Zemun Gang), Slavko Labovic in Denmark, Veljko Krivokapic in Austria, and Sreten Jocic in Amsterdam. Most have now been arrested or killed.

Corruption, the greatest single bane of our society today.

Olusegun Obasanjo, former President of Nigeria

Serbian Gang Diaspora

In the early 1970s, the Serbs arrived in force in Milan, drawn partly by the ties that already existed between them and Italian families from Sicily and Calabria. In 1972, a Yugoslavian criminal gang was established in Milan, its main activities consisting of hold-ups, murders, and burglaries in Triest, Rome, and Milan.

In Serbia, organized crime groups were at their peak under the rule of Slobodan Milosevic. They focused on counterfeiting, narcotics dealing, car thefts, cigarette smuggling, racketeering, and murder—the recognized speciality of the Serbian groups. Alleged leading members at that time were Zeljko "Arkan" Raznatovic, Kristian Golubovic and Milorad Ulemek based in Belgrade, and Branislav "Dugi" Lainovic in Novi Sad. He was the chief of the paramilitary force called the "Srpska Garda," and was murdered in 2000 by a member of the Zemun Gang.

The Zemun Gang

In the 1980s, the Zemun Gang became the first recognized organized crime group in Serbia. It allegedly comprises more than 200 criminals boasting in excesss of 300 convictions in narcotics dealing and murder. Information available shows that Milorad Ulemek was one of the leading bosses of the Zemun Gang together with Dusan Spasojevic. Ulemek was detained and sentenced for the assassination of the Serbian Prime Minister, Zoran Djindjic. Other gang bosses were arrested by the Serbian police force in early 2000, but the gang is still very active today. At one time, Arkan was also a top member of the Zemun Gang.

Criminal War Heroes

The war in Yugoslavia saw the hardest Croatian criminals engaged to do the dirtiest jobs in army, police, and paramilitary operations. Returning home, they were allowed to continue their criminal careers with the silent approval of Croatian authorities.

Tomislav Mercep's units from Sisak (the "Wolves"), Tuta's Convicts' Battalion, and the military police in Gospic, Sibenik, and Split, were reportedly swarming with criminals, murderers, and war criminals who profited from plunder and the smuggling of arms, narcotics, stolen cars, and anything else that brought instant and easy profit. Promoted to the status of war heroes, many of them continued their criminal activities after the war. If or when they were caught in the act, they were punished only symbolically, though a few ended up in prison because they were so deeply involved in crime that even their contacts from the state and judicial authorities could not protect them.

The Croatian situation was similar to that in Serbia, with a connection existing between Serbian organized crime (mainly the Zemun Gang) and Croatian criminals, and a triangle between state authorities, private companies, and local criminal groups.

Muslim Bosnian Groups

Serbian and Croatian criminal groups have also largely taken over the illegal markets in Bosnia, sometimes working with, and sometimes fighting against, Muslim Bosnian organized crime groups. For example, the city of Mostar was regarded as one of the largest Balkan open markets for stolen cars—managed toward the end of the 1990s by an officer of the Croatian army and the local Mafia boss from the Muslim side.

In Bosnia and Herzegovina, Pale and Banja Luka have become major links along the routes for illegal goods, drugs, and weapons coming from Albania and Montenegro to both western and eastern countries.

OPPOSITE Key underworld witnesses took the stand in the trial of suspected assassins of reformist Serbian Prime Minister Zoran Djindjic.

BELOW Dejan "Bugsy" Milenkovic, an alleged former Zemun Gang member who helped authorities with inquiries into the murder of Zoran Djindjic.

FREDERIK DURDA

The existence of Albanian organized crime is not a new thing in the United States. After fleeing Albania for New York to escape a life sentence, Frederik Durda reportedly organized a drug and immigrant smuggling ring together with Skender Fici and Xhevdet "Joey" Lika, using a travel agency as a cover. But in 1980 this cover was blown, and Durda became the first Albanian national to be sentenced for drug trafficking.

Frederik Durda was a key link in organized cocaine trafficking from Colombia to Europe.

Albanian–Kosovar Families

The most spectacular rise among criminal gangs was that of the Albanian–Kosovar families. The first international Kosovo Mafia was founded by Mehmed Ali Karakafa who, in the early 1970s, organized a large heroin-smuggling operation from Turkey through Yugoslavia to Italy. The operation was conducted in association with his local partners, the Osmani brothers, Adnan and Fatmir, Latif Memeti, and Ismet Arifi.

Karakafa was a well-known criminal in the former Yugoslavia and was sentenced many times for drugs, gold, and ammunition smuggling. His group was also the first international Albanian organized crime group to have strong contacts with the Italian Mafia and with the Turkish organizations. In 1999 in Spain, the same group was supposedly financing Kosovo Liberation Army (KLA) operations from the Costa del Sol.

In the 1970s, some Albanians were also working for the Five Families of New York, acquiring experience in managing a criminal organization.

In 1999, Albanian Mafia boss, Nedmedin Zeka, running his operations from Bratislava, Slovakia, escaped from Prague, where he had been presiding over a large drug-dealing ring in the region of the former Czech Republic. In mid-1999, however, Hungarian police arrested Zeka and sent him to Italy for sentencing.

Another Albanian boss, Remzi Canaj, was arrested in the same period in the Netherlands, where he was in charge of the narcotics trade.

The Albanian-Italian Connection

Albania was relatively closed to foreigners until the death of its leader Enver Halil Hoxha in 1985, which liberated the country and generated massive turmoil. From the criminal point of view, it meant the sudden invasion of Italian *Mafiosi*. The two countries have always been very close, both geographically and historically. In 1939, Italian troops invaded Albania prior to World War II. Around 1980, it is thought that Albania began to play

BELOW Albanian leader Enver Hoxha, whose assassination in 1985 proved pivotal to the development of organized crime in his country and in the region.

a major role in the Balkan Route and, in 1982, a significant number of Italian criminals flew to Albania to escape police operations that were being conducted against a heroin-smuggling network.

When the country opened up in 1986–1987 after the death of Hoxha, the migration of Albanian nationals to Italy and Greece increased. Goods from Western Europe began flooding the country, and the people were exposed to western television. During the decade following Hoxha's death, Albanians become more and more integrated into the western economy, often through people-smuggling networks with links in Italy and Greece, used to supply labor for agriculture and construction.

As Italian television was easily received in Albania, most of the coastal population quickly learned the language, and during the early 1990s some Albanians began to ask that Albania be made an Italian province. During this period, the wealthy mayor of Bagheria in Sicily, Michelangelo Aiello, was strongly supporting the establishment of commercial relationships with Albania.

The Mafia clans from the Puglia region and the Albanian criminals reinforced their link in a meeting held in Milan in 1987. Convened by an alleged figure of Italian organized crime, Dora Vendola, reportedly boss of the Sacra Corona Unita clan, this meeting dealt with cigarette and narcotics smuggling between the Balkans and Italy.

ABOVE A Spanish Civil Guard officer with booty seized in an operation against organized crime that netted 16 suspects and goods valued at two million euros.

PYRAMID SCHEMES IN ALBANIA

It is hardly surprising that the five most important investment pyramid companies, based on the classical Ponzi scheme—Vefa, Silva, Cenaj, Gjallica and Kamberi—were established in the city of Vlora, opposite the Italian coast. These companies were funneling almost 90 percent of the $300 million USD that was sent to the country by the Albanian diaspora. The investment opportunities were also used by residents, retired people, national companies, state-owned companies, and others who invested their own savings and pension funds.

In 1997, the first pyramid investment company to collapse was Sudja. The Albanian Government of Sali Berisha arrested a 30-year-old woman and froze the funds, an amount of $1.5 billion USD, of two other companies named Xhaferri and Populli. In total, Albanians had invested between $7 and 9 billion USD in these kinds of funds. At the beginning of 1997, the country was in panic. All investors were fleeing, sometimes with money, sometimes without. The Albanian police have stated that the day after the crash of the first pyramid scheme, one boat left the port of Vlora for Italy with $130 million USD on board. To avoid prosecution, Durin Pogani, owner of the company Pogani, fled to Australia, where he still lives.

ABOVE Destined for burning anyway, these contraband cigarettes are slated for destruction. Cigarettes are especially lucrative in times of unrest and war.

Mafia On the Move

The relocation of Italian Mafia bosses stepped up a pace after 1992, a year that saw the brutal assassinations of anti-Mafia judges, Giovanni Falcone and Paolo Borsellino. The state's response to these outrages was so strong and determined that it came close to defeating the Sicilian clans. To avoid arrest, many Mafia bosses, mainly from Sicily, fled to Albania, establishing themselves in ports such as Durrës and Vlora, then moving on to Montenegro together with Camorra bosses escaping the clan wars between the Cutolo NCOs and the other traditional families.

Tobacco Road

As always, war opened new opportunities for the very lucrative trade of cigarette smuggling. From a base in Switzerland, at least seven top Italian bosses, most of them connected with the Camorra and the Sicilian clans, dealt directly with the tobacco companies. But they also began to create new entities in Serbia, Kosovo, Macedonia,

and Montenegro in order to move the cigarettes directly from the Netherlands to the Balkans, then back to Europe by boat through the Strait of Otranto. The business was so lucrative that it became one of the main sources of income for the Montenegrin and Albanian governments. The whole traffic was managed by Italians, using Albanian and Montenegrin nationals as a workforce.

Dirty Laundry

During the years 1990–1997, illegal money began to pour into Albania and Montenegro, along with a need to have it laundered. Despite the UN embargo on former Yugoslavia countries during the war, money came in from a wide variety of sources: Drug trafficking, weapons dealing, people smuggling, cigarette smuggling, and oil smuggling to name a few. The need to have this money cleaned led to the rise and subsequent collapse of the infamous "pyramid" schemes that were to wreak such financial, political, and social havoc in Albania and other Balkan states.

ABOVE When Albania's banking sector collapsed due to an organized pyramid investment scam In 1997, many honest Albanians lost their entire life savings.

Albanian Insurrection

The collapse of the pyramid investment companies ruined the country and ignited the Albania insurrection of 1997 which caused more than 2,000 deaths. During the insurrection most of the Albanian army weapons stockpiles were stolen, to be sold over the following years to Kosovo clans, Italian clans, Bosnian clans, and others. The heavy weapons trade network reached into the Asia, Russia, Colombia, and other conflict areas. Almost 60 percent of Albania's small weapons were recovered in later years, primarily due to the arms-for-money program set up by the Albanian government, with a massive amount of aid from the international community.

ABOVE X-ray machines have recently been used by police in the United Kingdom to detect people-smugglers.

A Criminal Corridor

The modification of smuggling routes to Montenegro and Albania due to the war, and the economic problems affecting the Yugoslavian populations of Kosovo and Macedonia, combined to create a "criminal corridor" managed primarily by Kosovo families along the new route from Turkey—through Bulgaria or Greece, Macedonia, Kosovo, Bosnia, Montenegro, and Albania—to Italy.

The insurrection of 1997 also had a massive impact on immigration and people smuggling. The flood of Albanians and Kosovars fleeing their homes to Italy reached its peak with the arrival of overcrowded boats along the coast of Puglia in Italy in 1998. The Italian prime minister declared such arrivals "no longer tolerable."

KANUN—FAMILY CODE

Family rules in Albania and Kosovo make clans virtually immune to internal betrayal and ensure strong adherence to internal rules when a conflict arises between two families. This internal rule is referred as the "Kanun," the medieval code of conduct of the populations of Albanian origin. It also sets out the vendetta code between and within families.

According to scholars, the "Kanun" is a Greek word translated into Albanian by Turkish invaders—the code dates from about the fifteenth century. It includes not only the rules of vendetta by blood, but also a complete set of civil and penal procedures that have been applied through the centuries. The power of the Kanun in modern times is reflected in figures from European Union and Albanian government sources, which show that the number of murders directly linked to Kanun vendettas have been declining, from 45 in 1978 to only 12 in 2002. Often a family under vendetta chooses to change its life dramatically, sometimes moving to a completely closed environment—seclusion. In 2002, more than 140 families were living in closed environments in Tirana, 98 in Durrës, 111 in Vlora, 62 in Berat, and 33 in Lushnja.

Pashke Sokol Ndocaj and her uncles. Since the death of her father and brothers, Pashke has lived as a man in the ancient traditions of Avowed Virgins of Albania, where women renounce their former sex and "become" men to head the family.

Albanian "Fares"

With their stranglehold on the trafficking of drugs, cigarettes, people, weapons, and other commodities, and their agreements with Italian clans and Turkish families, the Albanian clans have grown rapidly in power worldwide. Formed from the Turkish and Italian clans' workforce, the "fares"—Albanian Mafia—have become a very real new transnational criminal power within just a few years, ruling two countries—Kosovo and Albania— directly, and controlling Montenegro and Macedonia through the diaspora.

AlbaKos Abroad

Italian magistrates have identified some Albanian/Kosovo bosses who have successfully established their operations in the Milan area, controlling cocaine trafficking, dealing, and prostitution. Other evidence shows the Albanian/Kosovar Mafia to be strong in the United Kingdom where they allegedly control prostitution in Soho, London.

Police have found evidence of links between AlbaKos (Albanian/Kosovar) clans and Chinese bosses in the business of people smuggling, and also evidence of Albanian clans providing killers for Italian clans.

International Approval

Almost all Kosovar bosses have strong connections to Switzerland, where Kosovars constitute the second-largest established foreign community. The knowledge that their political struggle against Serbian invaders was supported not only by NATO but by the whole international community, and particularly by the United States, which has established one of its largest foreign military bases in the region, has left the clans and their members basking in the glow of international approval, allowing them to develop their activities worldwide in relative safety.

2002 Two Serbian journalists are arrested after publishing articles on organized crime in the country.

2007 Six Italians are shot in Germany in a feud between organized crime gangs.

2009 Prosecutors drop corruption charges, linked to a multi-billion dollar arms deal, against ruling party president Jacob Zuma in South Africa.

2009 Somali pirates hijack a tugboat with 16 crew members, in the Gulf of Aden.

OPPOSITE A small boat heads for a watery grave at an isolated Albanian port, its smuggling days over, its cargo long gone.

Rapid Expansion

The steady growth in trafficking, like the proliferation of power and wealth among the various families, provides ongoing fuel for Kanun-style vendettas. The 1990s and early 2000s saw the AlbaKos clans involved in almost all kinds of organized criminal activity, not only in their own region, but worldwide. The amazingly rapid expansion of the AlbaKos' organized crime structures is certainly due to the massive wave of migration that accompanied and followed both the Albanian insurrection and the war in the Balkans. Specialists say that, at that time, more than 10,000 people per month were fleeing from Albania and Kosovo, mostly to Western Europe and North America.

BELOW Macedonian police arrest Stanislava Cocorovska-Poletan, alleged organizer of a record cocaine shipment from Venezuela to Macedonia.

Albanians In Between

In 2003–2004, the American FBI established a list of 15 organized crime families operating in Albania, managing criminal markets, legal markets, and politics. According to the FBI, these families are structured in more or less the same way as the Italian crime families. Most law enforcement agencies are constantly searching for information about such crime families but the connection they continue to maintain with the political establishment does not make it easy. The FBI claimed that, in 2004, the Albanian crime families were acting as mediators between Afghan and Turkish opium producers and the global heroin market, with roughly 80 percent of the entire heroin trade passing through Albania.

Who's Who

The same FBI sources mention Daut Kadriovski as the major crime boss in Albania. When Kadriovski was arrested in Germany in 1985, authorities confiscated his villas, his yacht, and his cars. He managed to escape his trial, allegedly by bribing officials, and flew to the United States in 1993 were he was in close contact with the Italian crime families in New York and Philadelphia. Further reports indicate his strong involvement with the Gambino-affiliated family of Nardino Colotti.

But Kadriovski is not alone in the organized crime panorama. Other reports and intelligence sources mention Albanian organized crime bosses such as Mehmed Haidini, Princ Dobrolishti, Ismail Lika, Alex Rudaj, and Victor Hoxha.

Intelligence Reports

In Kosovo, documents dated 2005 and 2006 from German intelligence, the United Nations, and KFOR (the Kosovo Force) have linked several leading political figures to organized crime activities ranging from weapons and drug dealing to money laundering and blackmail.

Today, almost all intelligence agencies around the world recognize the AlbaKos Mafia groups as the most serious source of potential danger from organized crime. Truly international, ruthless, boasting an extensive arsenal of weapons, contacts, workforce, and experience, they have grown in only 20 years to a position that enables them to challenge all other transnational organized crime groups. Rather than do so, however, they try to work with them. The only national groups who seem, so far, a little reluctant to make such contacts are the Russian organized crime groups. But the recent flood of Russian money into Montenegro can be interpreted in two ways, as a re-entry of Russian power to the region, or affirmation of a strong alliance.

OPPOSITE Heads of Enver Hoxha, the Prime Minister whose legacy of isolation and fear of the outside world has been overturned by organized crime groups.

BELOW KFOR soldiers search the Serb quarter of Mitrovica for weapons during the 1999 Kosovo war. The town became a symbol of Kosovo's ethnic divisions.

ABOVE Australian criminal and convicted drug trafficker Tony Mokbel, a fugitive until recaptured in Athens in 2007, is now best known for his missing hairpiece.

RIGHT Sydney Airport became a crime scene on March 22, 2009 when up to 15 members of an Australian motorcycle gang bludgeoned a rival to death while horrified passengers looked on. Faced with a public outcry, the state government responded by boosting anti-gang squad numbers from 50 to 125.

Australia

Despite the fact that Australia was colonized by convicts from Britain and their jailers, its geographic position protected it from the influence of organized crime for over a hundred years after settlement. However, the influx of immigrants, particularly after World War II, brought various criminal organizations to its shores.

Multicultural Crime

In Australia, the 'Ndrangheta clans are often referred to as "The Honoured Society." One preeminent member of this Italian-based organization was Robert Trimbole, who has been directly linked to the disappearance of politician Donald Mackay in Griffith, NSW, in 1977, after he had identified Trimbole and his associates to police as large marijuana traffickers, leading to their arrest.

Almost all major Chinese Triads are present in Australia. Although they previously acted as "soldiers" for the Chinese clans, Vietnamese gangs have become international and are also present in Australia. Japanese organized crime groups—Yakuza—are deeply involved in illegal activities in the country. A 1994 media report stated that one of the largest Japanese crime syndicates, the Yamaguchi-gumi, owned at least three "corporate" holiday villas on the Queensland Gold Coast.

Underworld War

Australian organized crime attracted worldwide attention with the Melbourne gangland killings between 1995 and 2006, when 34 criminal figures were murdered. Opposed to the 'Ndrangheta families were the Moran family, the Carlton Crew, the Radev Clan, the Sunshine Crew, and the Williams family, along with Greek families such as that of Tony Mokbel.

Since then, the grip of the 'Ndrangheta families on Italian-Australian organized crime has grown, with the arrest in 2008 of Francesco Madafferi and 20 other affiliates, and the seizure of ecstasy tablets, cocaine, and more than 30 million Euros in cash. Among those arrested were the alleged bosses of a crime family from Griffith and the Lebanese Mafia, and a suspected drug baron from a motorcycle gang. The presence of organized crime groups from all parts of the globe has thus become very strong in Australia, with gangs working together on international trafficking as well as on various other criminal activities and investments.

UNDERBELLY

Real Life Underworld

With a timeline of roughly a decade from the mid-late 1990s, *Underbelly* began as a one-off 13-part TV drama series telling the story of the Melbourne underworld's war highlighting the infamous Carlton Crew criminal gang. The book *Leadbelly* by John Silvester and Andrew Rule, covering the infamous gangland killings of 1998 and beyond, provided much of the groundwork.

Public Outcry

The escalating murders—often in the open, on the street—eventually triggered a public outcry and a political imperative to lock up the villains. They also made for riveting television, as the series charted the rise and demise of jailed Carl Williams (Gyton Grantley), a leading figure in the gang wars.

Some other real-life characters who have become part of Melbourne folklore are Alphonse Gangitano (Vince Colosimo), Roberta Williams (Kat Stewart), Mick Gatto (Simon Westaway), Mario Condello (Martin Sacks), Lewis Moran (Kevin Harrington), Mark Moran (Callan Mulvey), Jason Moran (Les Hill), Tony Mokbel (Robert Mammone), and Judy Moran (Caroline Gillmer), the Moran family matriarch.

Prequel

Following the success of the original series, a second series was made in 2009—*Underbelly: A Tale of Two Cities*. As most of the characters portrayed in the original series were now either dead or in jail, the second series became a prequel, covering the years between 1976 and 1987, starting with the murder of anti-drugs campaigner Donald Mackay. Characters include Chris Flannery (Dustin Clare), known as Mr Rent-A-Kill, and Terry Clark (Matt Newton), known as Mr Asia.

BELOW Vince Colosimo fails to act the part for once as he poses with police at the launch of *Underbelly*, 2008.

Africa

Organized crime did not really develop in Africa until the rise of the Nigerian groups in the 1980s. With decolonization making Africa the playground of state interests, little room was left for other actors, especially illegal actors. Nevertheless, the local conflicts that occurred post-independence in most of the current African nations provided many opportunities for illegal trafficking, especially of weapons and ammunition.

During the Algerian war, the French army fought against private weapons traffickers. South Africa, ruled by apartheid and at war with all its neighbors, desperately needed foreign help to curb the international embargo. Central Africa was at war, as were the Saharan countries. But at the same time that all these countries were involced in local conflicts, they were also involved in the international trade of natural resources. The presence of these resources in the midst of regional instability provided more and more opportunities for organized crime groups to penetrate different countries, acting directly by smuggling and trafficking—people, drugs, and weapons—and indirectly by laundering money, and finding support in high places.

Indian and Asian immigration to the eastern coasts of Africa—Tanzania, Kenya, Mozambique, South Africa, and Madagascar—has also allowed organized crime to gain power and local support through an ever-growing and wealthy diaspora.

419 Plus

Among native Africans, what we can call "organized crime" comprises mainly the Nigerian groups which act both inside Africa and internationally. Although they may not be structured as rigidly and hierarchically as some other criminal groups, Nigerian criminal organizations are recognized by intelligence agencies worldwide as a reality. They did not gain significant power until the early 1980s, but they have been involved since the 1970s in massive international monetary scams—now known as 419 scams after the section number of the Nigerian criminal law that applies to them—and in extortion, racketeering, insurance scams, prostitution, and drug smuggling.

ABOVE A confiscated elephant tusk is marked to show where and when it was seized. Illegal ivory trafficking remains an ongoing problem in parts of Africa.

BELOW A black marketeer paddles empty fuel drums across Warri Harbor, Nigeria. The tanker may be abandoned, but the black market is flourishing.

PIRACY

Another criminal enterprise that has recently grown in importance, especially for the Yoruba clans, is the stealing and dealing of oil. Sometimes criminals "kidnap" oil tankers in the Guinean Gulf waters and the channels along the Nigerian south coast, sometimes they puncture the pipelines, stealing gallons of crude oil that are then sold on the

black market locally and in the region. When the oil price was high, some of this stolen oil made its way onto international grey markets. Somalia currently leads the pack when it comes to oil piracy, kidnapping tankers along the coast. Often the crew are held to ransom along with the oil. The United States government under President Obama seems determined to halt the rise of piracy, and a 24-nation response group has been set up by the United Nations to counter Somali piracy and hostage taking.

Captain Richard Phillips (right), held hostage for four days by pirates off the coast of Somalia, was rescued by US naval forces.

Family and Tribe

Nigerian criminal groups are not organized like other such groups around the world, their structures being determined instead by family and tribe. Nigerian territory is divided into more than 75 different tribal languages. The southern and western tribes are considered the wealthiest, due to their oil resources.

Nigerian Diaspora

The power of the Nigerian groups comes first of all from the large-scale emigration that has seen Nigerian communities settling in almost all countries of the world, especially the industrialized world. The Nigerian diaspora has established itself in India, Pakistan, Thailand, South America, the United States, and more recently in the United Kingdom where Nigerians represent one of the largest black communities. Their connections have enabled them to oversee and manage new routes for cocaine from Latin America to Europe, passing through Africa, as well as heroin routes from Pakistan and India to Western Europe and the United States.

BELOW The Crime Wall, a memorial to those who have died as victims of crime in South Africa, which has one of the highest crime rates in the world.

Jobs For the Jobless

Along with drug smuggling, the Nigerian organized crime groups have been involved since the late 1980s in people smuggling. Organizing the transfer, first of Nigerians, but soon of all the region's emigrants to Western Europe, they manage the trafficking routes from sub-Saharan Africa to the Mediterranean coasts, and the air routes to "friendly" European airports. With the help of local contacts—both Nigerian and European organized crime groups— they also find work for the immigrants, who are used clandestinely for almost any kind of labor—mainly construction, agriculture, and local dealing, though the Nigerian organized crime groups also run brothels, alone or with other crime groups, providing prostitutes through the same people-smuggling networks.

Campus Cults

One of the most remarkable developments of organized crime in Nigeria is called the "confraternity." Originally based on university campuses, the confraternity began to move into the wider community around 1950.

The most renowned confraternity—Pyrates Confraternity—is said to have been founded as a social group by six friends from the University College in Ibadan which at that time was associated with the University of London. Among them was the future Nobel prize-winning writer Wole Soyinka. For almost 20 years, the Pyrates were very popular on university campuses, using the mythology of piracy and its symbols, and adopting well-known pirate names such as Long John Silver.

The confraternity concept exploded after the civil war in 1969, and in the 1980s the original group expanded into more than 300 groups. Thus began the transition toward violent crime and Mafia-style activities.

In the 1990s, as the movement spread beyond the universities, it turned to Mafia-style activities at an international level, with the majority of confraternities engaged in activities such as armed robbery and kidnapping. Cult members may also get money from political racketeering. The exact death toll from confraternity activities is unclear, but one estimate made in 2002 was that 250 people had been killed in campus cult-related murders in the previous decade. These figures are insignificant compared to those from cult activities in 2008 and 2009 in Benin City, the Edo state capital, with over 40 cult-related deaths recorded monthly.

Cyber Crime

The Nigerian scams are well known to almost anybody in the industrialized world. Who has not received an email stating that a large sum of money is theirs if they will only supply their banking details? Scammers send spam-like emails to a set of addresses grabbed from different directories, asking for account details in France, Switzerland, Germany, Italy, the United States, Japan, Australia. Some get lucky.

The creativity in the stories made up to scam people is quite impressive. Most people ignore the emails, but a few do not, hoping that this might be the opportunity of a lifetime. The game is based on the mass effect and has worked for years, with an estimated annual total of $1–2 billion USD profit.

The networks behind such internet scams are not all based in Nigeria. The Nigerians have had many imitators in Senegal, Ivory Coast, Togo, Sierra Leone, Benin, and Congo, sometimes with a direct link to one or more Nigerian networks.

The know-how of Nigerian networks is quite impressive. Occasionally someone caught in the scam goes to Africa at the invitation of the network and is shown large sums of cash which is really fake money, just to induce him to pay more and more in "entry fees." A number of years ago, certain individuals—among them two Swiss businessmen—made the trip to Lagos in order to find out what was going on. They have since disappeared.

OPPOSITE Militants patrol the river in the oil-rich Delta region of southern Nigeria. Attacks in the region have helped to raise world oil prices and cut Nigeria's output.

OPPOSITE BOTTOM Christian Julian Irwin, 48, is believed to have fallen victim to a Nigerian internet scam. He went missing in Nigeria after a frantic phone call saying people and dogs were chasing him.

BELOW A confiscated drug-smuggling submarine at Colombian coast guard headquarters. The smugglers went free when the evidence sank without trace.

Nigerians Abroad

The largest of the businesses in which Nigerian clans are active is heroin and cocaine smuggling from Latin and Central America to Europe and the United States. Nigerian clans are deeply involved in the traffic, working together with Colombian cartels and Italian clans, and sometimes even Albanian clans. They supervise the smuggling via mules from Africa to Europe, playing on the different legislations and with an intimate knowledge of the level and kind of controls in the various European airports.

In Europe, they can rely on a complete logistical network aimed at recuperating the drugs and dealing them on the streets, often using Nigerian, Sierra Leone, Togo, Liberian, Benin, and other sub-Saharan refugees. The presence of Nigerian smuggling in the United Kingdom is probably quite a significant one, with strong bases and a reliable support network bound by a common language.

A Triangle of Association

In the twenty-first century, organized crime encompasses all forms of trafficking and all types of commodity—people, cigarettes, drugs, weapons, cars, or human organs. And in each organized crime group a triangle of association can be found between the local clans, the local authorities, and the corporations.

The Money Trail
Tracking the Profits

Organized crime exists for profit. And the huge profits made from organized crime and Mafia activities have to be hidden and then distributed in such a way that authorities are unaware or unable to trace their sources or their owners.

Money Laundering

Money laundering is the term used for the filtering of illegal funds or profit through various legal or illegal enterprises, and/or countries, in an endeavor to avoid income tax and the notice of authorities. It also includes the generation of assets, other than money, through illegal acts. Although often thought to have originated with Al Capone, with him hiding money in laundromats, the term "money laundering" wasn't actually used until the Watergate Scandal in the United States in 1973.

The act of money laundering is a worldwide epidemic, done by both individuals and criminal organizations. It has been estimated that money laundering accounts for as much as 5 percent of the entire world's gross domestic product, which is about $1.5 trillion USD. Some businesses are better than others when trying to hide the

origin of illegally obtained money. Generally, most types of businesses that deal with a high cash flow, and have products and/or services that can be easily managed or manipulated, are ideal. Money is laundered through various methods. However, there are some traditional businesses that have been used for decades to disguise or hide financial gains.

Bars and Clubs

Depending on the liquor laws of a country, bar receipts are an ideal way to hide money. Receipts can state that two bottles were sold, when really only one bottle was sold. Now the bar has an extra bottle of vodka and has to do something with it. The choices available now involve moving the extra alcohol out of the bar and reselling it, redirecting it to another establishment, or sending it out as a gift.

Bigger profits are available if the criminal organization not only owns the bar but also the company that supplies the bar with alcohol. In this case, the criminal organization can make false invoices for orders and payments between the supply company and the bar to channel the money.

Cover or admission charges to an establishment are another way to funnel money. Say only 200 individuals enter that night at $20 each. The establishment will claim on receipts that throughout the night 500 individuals paid a cover charge. These 300 extra charges means that $6,000 of illegal money can now be funneled into the establishment and appear to be from the cover charge. If the establishment is open five nights a week, that is $30,000 per week that will appear to be from a legitimate source. Anything like this—a service and not a product—is great for organized crime as there is no left-over legitimate product to draw suspicion or give them concern.

Tighter controls on the issuing of liquor licenses and stricter accounting requirements have put bars and clubs under much closer scrutiny by authorities.

ABOVE The happy hour rush is on. Men crowd into this "speak-easy" to purchase illegal alcohol during Prohibition in the USA in the 1920s.

ABOVE LEFT The inner workings of a bank can be seen in this massive vault deep within the building with a series of combinations, doors, locks, to secure the contents.

Dry Cleaners and Cash Businesses

Dry cleaners and businesses taking small individual sums of money but with a high cash flow are the easiest enterprises in which to conceal income and launder money. How much of their chemicals are actually being used, or how many items are actually being processed is difficult to define. It is easy to say that 10 shirts were cleaned when in fact only five were cleaned and then funnel in dirty money for those five shirts.

Large Corporations

Brokerage firms and casinos are also great fronts since there is so much money being dealt with and shifted around that it is difficult to keep track of it all. The idea is just to blend or mix in the dirty money with the clean money.

Shell Companies

Shell companies do not have any assets or do any business and are thus are perfect as fronts for individuals wishing to hide their identity or their financial gains. The ideal front for this type of operation is a consulting company that has no product to keep records of other than the service of giving time and advice that is easily manipulated by the criminal organization.

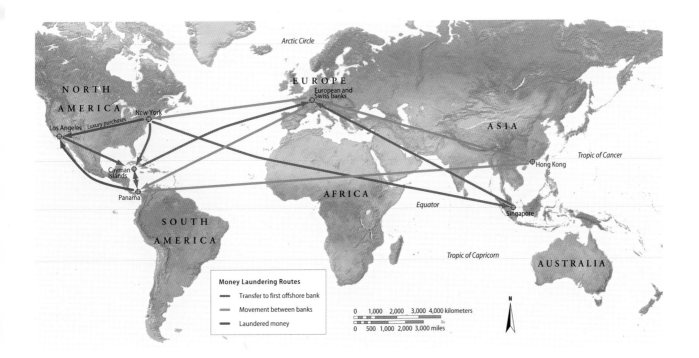

Money Laundering Routes
—— Transfer to first offshore bank
—— Movement between banks
—— Laundered money

0   1,000 2,000 3,000 4,000 kilometers
0   500 1,000 2,000 3,000 miles

Offshore Methods

In the new millennium, criminal organizations have been forced to develop more sophisticated methods of hiding money as governments and agencies become more adept and successful in their detection and tracing methods.

Banks

If an organized crime group has influence or control over the banks in which they make the initial deposits, the danger of being caught carrying out illegal transactions is not as much of a concern. For instance, Russian criminal organizations are known for controlling banks, which allows them to make transfers and deposits very easily. However, if a criminal organization does not have any influence or control over a bank, it is necessary to move the money through various entities until the trail is lost.

The first transaction is usually to offshore accounts such as the Cayman Islands or Singapore. Deposits are most often made into multiple accounts. Once in the first offshore bank, it becomes much easier as the country of original jurisdiction has no more authority. Transfers are then made from the Cayman Islands, or wherever, to Swiss bank accounts, other European bank accounts, or also to Panamanian bank accounts. Deposits are also often double backed between these different "off-shore" banks, creating an even more confusing web for authorities to track.

The purchase of expensive items such as yachts, cars, jewelry, and real estate helps conceal the money, as well as infusing the money back into financial institutions of the original country, investing in stocks, bonds, mutual funds, and legitimate businesses. Any money drawn out by the organization by this stage should be clean enough to avoid detection.

To spend without gaining suspicion is not always easy because the government will be curious how individuals who are in control of five dry cleaners are able to own multiple homes, cars, boats, jewelry, and enjoy lavish vacations. Traveling and spending the money overseas in other countries and leaving it there is a popular method of concealing money.

BELOW Called the "Mafia Banker," Michele Sindona stands trial in Milan after his company failed, ruining thousands of Italians. Evidence found he had a system allowing the Mafia to launder and traffic money through his company.

PROVING IT!

Forensic Science and Organized Crime

Organized crime covers a wide range of activities, from drug dealing to loan sharking to murder. There are now many rapidly evolving forensic disciplines that can be applied to attack these activities.

ABOVE High tech CCTV cameras installed across the UK have helped curb street crime and control larger operations by organized crime groups. This is the surveillance headquarters in Manchester, UK.

Forensic Accounting

Forensic accounting is a legal discipline that embodies accounting, auditing, and other investigative techniques in litigation. This method may be used in such diverse cases as copyright infringement, fraud, or the laundering of illegal funds.

Paperwork

Not all the work is boring paperwork. In 1978 FBI agents set up a dummy corporation "Abdul Enterprises, Ltd." with a phony sheik as a front man who was seeking political favors in return for cash. The scam was so convincing that it lead to the conviction of a US Senator, six members of the US House of Representatives, and several minor political functionaries. This success lead to Congress forcing the Justice Department to issue "guidelines" to provide stricter "oversight" to such future undercover actions.

In 2006, the Gambino Crime Family ran afoul of the US "Racketeer Influenced and Corrupt Organizations Act" of 1970 (RICO) that allowed for criminal and civil liability for organizations that included bribery, theft, fraud, embezzlement, and money laundering in their activities. In 2008, the FBI and US attorneys served further indictments against six members of the New York family.

> *Forensic science is the link between the criminal and the crime.*
>
> Ken Goddard, author

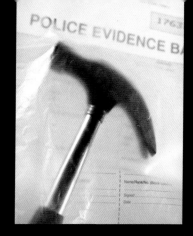

ABOVE The success of forensic science requires the scrupulous gathering of evidence without contamination. Experts isolate different items in bags or other sealed containers to avoid mistakes.

Surveillance

Surveillance of suspects has become increasingly more complex with the development of small video cameras and listening devices. Electronic eavesdropping became even more sophisticated with the use of cell phones or disposable phones.

Forensic Chemistry

The trace components of seized drugs can be used to infer the process used to prepare and purify the drugs, or, if diluted or "cut," what materials were used. The analysis by gas chromatography and mass spectrometry of a millionth of a gram can give all the components in a mixture and its percentage in the mixture. Light isotope analysis can identify the region where a plant was grown. Counterfeit pills may be examined by pill ballistics to compare the dies used to make the pills.

Homicide

The traditional handling of a homicide in the Mafia has been for a person simply to disappear. The man who killed John Gotti's son in a New York auto accident just disappeared and was never found, but an alleged bomber in Philadelphia who reportedly killed a rival with a nail bomb was found dead with a firecracker in his mouth. Point made. The Bureau of Alcohol, Tobacco, and Firearms handles many of the bombings in the United States, particularly those involving terrorists or organized crime.

BELOW Ultra-violet light is used to read DNA strands at this laboratory.

Forensic Anthropology

Bodies, even if long dead, need to be identified by forensic anthropologists. Examination of the bodies for cause of death is done by the medical examiner. If there are any useful bullets found, then the Firearms Identification Unit will examine them and try to link them to other cases or, if lucky, to a known firearm. The Criminalistics or Trace Laboratory analyzes any trace materials encountered in an investigation.

US Secret Service

Extortion and kidnapping often involve documents and the Documents Unit of a police laboratory would handle comparison of papers, inks, and handwriting or printing. They may handle and identify counterfeit tax stamps that are used on stolen cigarette packs, which have been a staple of organized crime for decades. The US Secret Service maintains a large and modern laboratory to investigate counterfeit currency and tax stamps, as well as threats against federal officials.

DNA

DNA analysis has revolutionized the field of Forensic Science in ways never expected. Links between many different kinds of evidence and crime scenes can be made now by looking for traces of sweat, saliva, blood, and other body materials. DNA analysis can be especially useful in the cases involving the occasional sausage-style disposal of bodies. One forensic case in Philadelphia came with the question, "Who was in the sausage?"! Who indeed!

OPPOSITE Mong Lar in Burma is an Asian Las Vegas, crowded with casinos and brothels. It is also the center of money laundering for drug traffickers.

BELOW Colombian drug cartel leader, Diego Sanchez, on the FBI's "Ten Most Wanted" list, is extradicted to the USA.

Law and Punishment

The United Nations Office on Drugs and Crime (UNODC) believes that up 70 percent of all governments do not have laws and policies that are capable of dealing with money laundering. Even if countries do have the legislation, most often white-collar crimes are punished far less severely than other crimes.

The United States passed the Racketeer Influenced and Corrupt Organization Act—RICO—that has been a helpful tool in the fight against organized crime. RICO covers 35 different crimes and being found guilty of any two within a 10-year period can make this act applicable to an individual. Within the 35 crimes are the bread-and-butter of most organized crime groups such as drug trafficking, extortion, gambling, bribery, embezzlement, money laundering, kidnapping, and much more. The punishment for an individual who is convicted of this act can be 20 years in prison and or a $25,000 USD fine. Through RICO, law enforcement agencies have been able to investigate and arrest individuals based on their possessions, and conduct civil forfeiture, sometimes referred to as asset forfeiture. RICO was meant to be a tool to be specifically used against organized crime. However, law enforcement has seen fit to apply it to others outside the typical criminal organizations such as corrupt police organizations, motorcycle clubs, Major League baseball, anti-abortion activists, and those with no links to any type of organized crime.

However, as long as there are countries not participating in the enforcement of policies for money laundering, criminal organizations will have someplace to go.

ROADBLOCKS AND REWARDS IN THE MONEY TRAIL

1913 Sixteenth Amendment to the US Constitution—levy income tax—creates the need for money laundering in the USA.

1919 Eighteenth Amendment to the US Constitution begins Prohibition, creating a new racket for organized crime. It also created more law enforcement against organized crime.

1929 The Great Depression means criminal organizations are among the few businesses surviving, as countries around the world suffer. They are the only ones providing services people really want for prices they can afford.

1933 Prohibition is repealed with the ratification of the Twenty-first Amendment to the US Constitution, causing organized crime groups to find new sources of revenue.

1945 The end of World War II increases the fight against crime on the home front of many countries.

1951 The Revenue Act in the USA establishes wage excise and occupational taxes. It is later repealed as unconstitutional, but it forces out bookmakers for over 15 years.

1970 Racketeer Influence and Corrupt Organization (RICO) Act in the USA is passed.

1974 Basel Committee on Banking Supervision creates a discussion among the economic powers on money laundering.

1982   The USA Organized Crime Drug Enforcement Task Force causes a disruption in organized crimes endeavors in drugs, weapons, and white-collar crimes such as money laundering.

1988   United Nations Convention against Illicit Traffic in Narcotic Drugs and Psychotropic Substances is passed and is the first attempt to provide comprehensive measures against money laundering on a global level.

1989   Fall of the Berlin Wall and communism throughout the Soviet Union creates many opportunities for private individuals to take advantage of the new capitalist markets available to them in those countries. Many new eastern European and Russian crime groups are started.

1989   Financial Action Task Force (FATF) is created to combat money laundering and terrorist activities on an international level with 34 countries as members.

1995   The Egmont Group—an international gathering of non-law enforcement financial intelligence units—collects financial information about dealings that are suspicious, with six countries currently participating.

1997   Committee of Experts on the Evaluation of Anti-Money Laundering Measures & the Financing of Terrorism (MONEYVAL) is created to evaluate the member states on the compliance of anti-money laundering measures.

2001   The USA Patriot Act enables law enforcement to arrest members of organized crime groups as "domestic terrorists" with the new expanded definition.

THE GLOBAL FINANCIAL CRISIS

Generally in states of economic turmoil, organized crime groups and their interests thrive, as the industries they run do well when people are at their lowest and most desperate. However, the global financial crisis of this millennium has created some turmoil for criminal organizations.

ABOVE Wall Street big shot, Bernard Madoff, enters federal court charged with securities, mail, and wire fraud, as well as money laundering.

Legitimate Cover

Over the years organized crime groups have become more vested and infused with legitimate business markets so when legitimate business is in trouble, the black market will be in trouble as well. Investments in the stock market by organized crime are just as affected as legitimate business. In times of economic downturn, criminal organizations also have a difficult time explaining how their legitimate front businesses remain viable in a recession when there is no obvious cash flow to sustain them.

Criminal Conundrum

An economic downturn poses a unique problem to the money launderers as well. First, if the economy is in a recession, people often resort to the services provided by the criminal organizations, and if people are spending money on drugs, gambling, and prostitutes, then they are not going to have as much money to go to restaurants and bars which are often the criminal organizations' legitimate interests that aid in funneling illegal money. Most likely in these situations organized crime groups will store much of their illegal cash. This, in itself, is a problem, because large sums of cash are hard to hide and move. The biggest problem in a deep recession, however, is that crime groups are not able to spend large sums of money without drawing suspicion.

BELOW Colombian entrepreneur, David Guzman, is arrested in Panama. He is accused of using his business to acquire million-dollar resources from clients in a money laundering scheme.

The Future

The advent of advanced computer technology will only benefit criminal organizations. It is true that law enforcement agencies will have access to the same technology, but criminal organizations have existed for over a century now and they are still very strong. There is no reason to believe they will disappear anytime soon. Criminal organizations will grow, shrink, and change but they will always adapt to the situation before them.

OPPOSITE October 24, 2008. A trader on the New York Stock Exchange reflects on the day's trades as the DOW drops over 300 points.

A CENTURY OF MAFIA
AND ORGANIZED CRIME

People and events are placed within their years of prominence

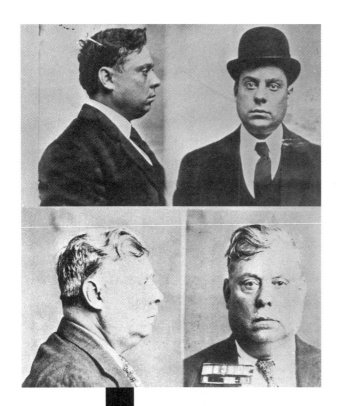

IGNAZIO SAIETTA
(LUPO THE WOLF)

Born 1877, Corleone, Sicily
Died 1947, Atlanta, USA, natural causes
Hitman; Black Hand leader; extortion

JAMES COLOSIMO

Born 1877, Calabria, Italy
Died 1920, Chicago, USA, shot
Gambling; prostitution; racketeering

JACK ZELIG

Born 1888, New York, USA
Died 1912, New York, USA, shot
Monk Eastman Gang; murderer

OWNEY MADDEN (LEFT)

Born 1891, Leeds, UK
Died 1965, Arkansas, USA, natural causes
Boxing promoter; murderer; street fighter;
speak-easy owner; Cotton Club owner

291

CALOGERO "DON CALÒ" VIZZINI

Born 1877, Sicily
Died 1954, Sicily, natural causes
Sicilian boss of bosses during World War I;
fraud; corruption; murder

MONK EASTMAN
(EDWARD OSTERMAN)

Born 1873, New York, USA
Died 1920, New York, USA, shot
Eastman Gang; war with Five Points Gang;
assisted Tammany Hall
(*Shown*–funeral)

< 1914

1920 >

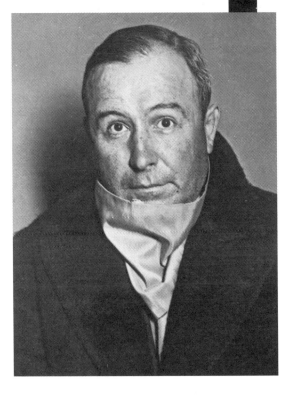

JOHNNY TORRIO

Born 1882, Irsina, Italy
Died 1957, Chicago, USA, natural causes
Gambling; prostitution

< 1920

THOMPSON SUBMACHINE GUN

Invented 1919 by John T. Thompson
Known as "Tommy gun"
Weapon of choice for American Mafia
through first half of twentieth century
(*Shown*–John Thompson with Tommy gun)

DUTCH SCHULTZ

Born 1902, New York, USA
Died 1935, Newark, USA, shot
Bootlegging; numbers
(*Shown*–Dutch Schultz's body in morgue)

JOE ADONIS

Born 1902, Campania, Italy
Died Rome, Italy, natural causes
Ran empire from restaurant in Brooklyn;
enforcer for Frankie Yale
(*Shown*–Joe's Restaurant at the time of Willie
Moretti's death in 1951)

GEORGE CLARENCE "BUGS" MORAN (LEFT)

Born 1893, St Paul, USA
Died 1957, Chicago, USA, natural causes
Bootlegging; battle with Johnny Torrio;
fierce temper

1925 >

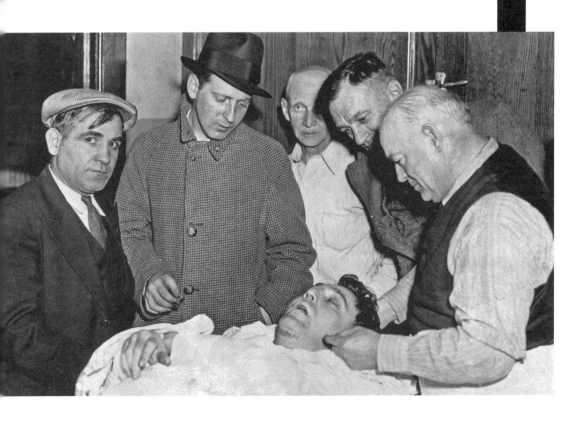

CHICAGO CRIME COMMISSION

Founded 1919 by business leaders
to combat organized crime
Still fosters cooperation with law enforcement
(*Shown*–1927 Committee examining
various gangster weapons)

MAFIA TRIAL

Date 1928, Palermo, Sicily
(*Shown*–153 members of Andaloro-Ferrarello
gang await trial in Sicily)

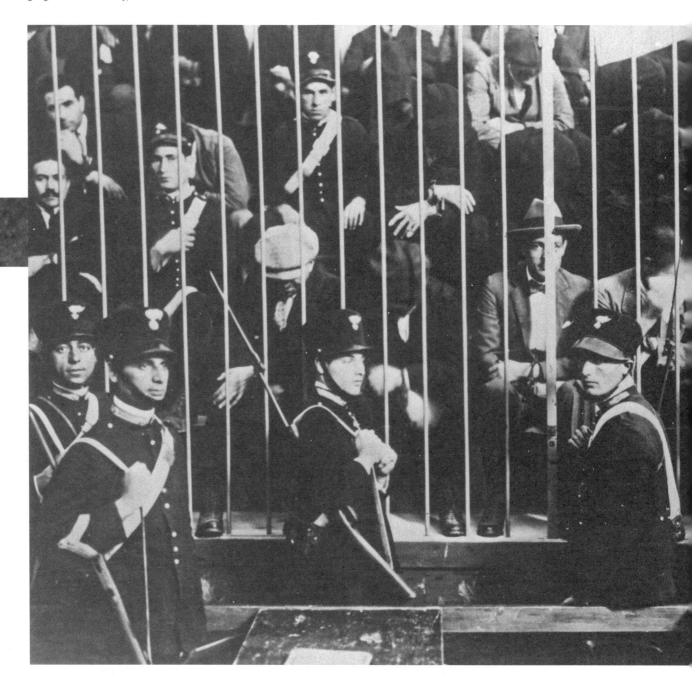

< 1927

1928 >

FRANK COSTELLO

Born 1891, Calabria, Italy
Died 1973, New York, USA, natural causes
Luciano Crime Family; Castellammarese War;
racketeering; casinos

ALPHONSE "AL" CAPONE

Born 1899, New York, USA
Died 1947, St. Louis, USA, natural causes
bootlegging; tax evasion
(*Shown*–Al Capone signing $50,000 USD
bond on income tax indictment, 1931)

LOUIS "LEPKE" BUCHALTER

Born 1897, New York, USA
Died 1944, New York, USA,
by federal execution
Murder, Inc.; hitman

< 1929

F. B. I. - N. Y.
LOUIS BUCHALTER
60-302-N2660
AUG 23 1939

CHARLES "LUCKY" LUCIANO

Born 1897, Sicily, Italy
Died 1962, Naples, Italy, natural causes
Boss of Genovese Crime Family;
chairman of The Commission;
international heroin trafficking

ST VALENTINE'S DAY MASSACRE

Date February 14, 1929
Place Chicago's North Side
(*Shown*–Bodies of men shot against wall
on orders of Al Capone)

JOE "JOE THE BOSS" MASSERIA

Born 1887, Marsala, Sicily

Died 1931, New York, USA, shot

Genovese Crime Family;

Castellammarese War

(*Shown*–Place of death, Coney Island)

KANSAS CITY MASSACRE

Date June 17, 1933, Union Station,

Kansas City, USA

(*Shown*–Bodies of two slain officers

gunned down by Mafia hitmen)

JOSEPH BONANNO

Born 1905, Castellammare del Golfo, Italy
Died 2002, Tucson, USA, natural causes
Alleged Bonanno Crime Family;
Castellammare War; Banana War

1931

1933 >

301

ALBERT ANASTASIA (LEFT)

Born 1902, Calabria, Italy
Died 1957, New York, USA, shot
Alleged Murder, Inc.; contract killer; enforcer
for Luciano

MURDER, INC.

Established to perform murders
for the American Mafia
Victims included Dutch Schultz,
witnesses, and informants
(*Shown*–hitmen Harry Malone (left) and
Frank Abbandando in court)

< 1935

ELIOT NESS

Born 1903, Chicago, USA
Died 1957, Pennsylvania, USA,
natural causes
Prohibition agent; responsible for
conviction of Al Capone

1940 >

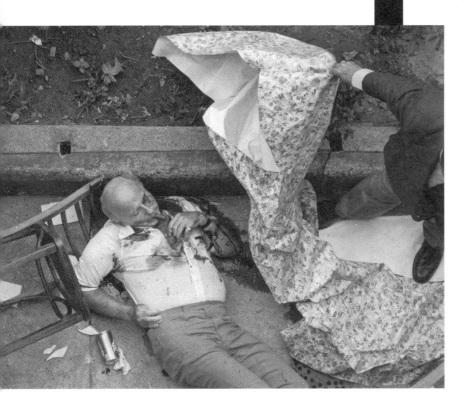

CARMINE GALANTE

Born 1910, New York, USA
Died 1979, New York, USA, shot
Alleged Bonanno Crime Family; hitman
for Vito Genovese

MEYER LANKSY

Born 1902, Grodno, Poland
Died 1983, Miami Beach, USA,
natural causes
Developed The Commission;
gambling; established casinos in Cuba

LOUIS CAPONE (LEFT)

Born 1896, Chicago, USA

Died 1944, New York, USA, by federal execution

Murder

MENDY WEISS (RIGHT)

Born 1906, Chicago, USA

Died 1944, New York, USA, by federal execution

Murder

SALVATORE GIULIANO

Born 1922, Sicily

Died 1950, Sicily, shot

Bandit; separatist; kidnapping

(*Shown*–death scene)

PURPLE GANG

Founded 1910, Detroit, USA

Murder; extortion; bootlegging

(*Shown*–member Harry Fleischer on arrest)

MICKEY COHEN

Born 1913, New York, USA
Died 1976, Los Angeles, USA,
natural causes
Chicago Outfit; race wires; casinos;
tax evasion

J. EDGAR HOOVER

Born 1895, Washington DC, USA
Died 1972, Washington DC, USA,
natural causes
Head of FBI through eight presidencies

VIRGINIA HILL

Born 1916, Alabama, USA
Died 1966, Koppl, Austria, apparent suicide
Girlfriend of "Bugsy" Siegel; witness
at Kefauver hearings; denied any
knowledge of organized crime

ALEX "LOUIS" GREENBERG

Born ?

Died 1955, Chicago, USA, shot

Friend and backer of Al Capone;

allegedly extorted money from Frank Nitti

(*Shown*–giving evidence before Senate Committee)

McCLELLAN COMMITTEE

Date 1957

Televised hearings into Teamsters Union's

misuse of funds and labor racketeering

(*Shown*–John F. Kennedy and Robert

Kennedy at hearings)

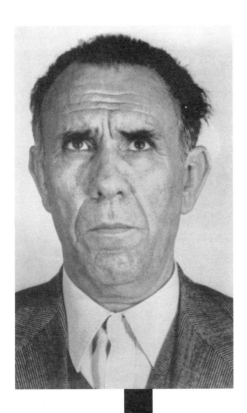

GAETANO BADALAMENTI

Born 1923, Cinisi, Sicily
Died 2004, Massachusetts, USA,
natural causes
Alleged Sicilian Mafia Commission; Pizza
Connection; drug trafficking

VITO GENOVESE

Born 1897, Naples, Italy
Died 1969, Springfield, USA, natural causes
Genovese Crime Family; Castellammarese
War; Apalachin meeting

JOHNNY STOMPANATO

Born 1925, Illinois, USA
Died 1958, Beverly Hills, USA, stabbed
Bodyguard of Mickey Cohen; boyfriend of
Lana Turner; stabbed by Cheryl Crane
(Turner's daughter) after a struggle
(*Shown*–Lana Turner (second left), Johnny
Stompanato (center), Cheryl Crane)

< 1957

CARLO GAMBINO

Born 1902, Palermo, Italy
Died 1976, New York, USA, natural causes
Gambino Crime Family; Castellammarese War;
The Commission

JOSEPH GALLO

Born 1929, New York, USA
Died 1972, New York, USA, shot
Alleged hitman; racketeer

JACQUES ANGELVIN (FRONT RIGHT)

Born 1914, Marseille, France

Died 1978, Cannes, France, natural causes

Actor; alleged heroin trafficking

GAMBINO CRIME FAMILY

Heirarchy chart of leading American Mafia
crime family that still exists

< 1962   1963 >

RICHIE ROBERTS

Born 1929, New York, USA

Still living

Policeman and later defense attorney;
involved in case against
Harlem boss, Frank Lucas

THE CARLO GAMBINO FAMILY

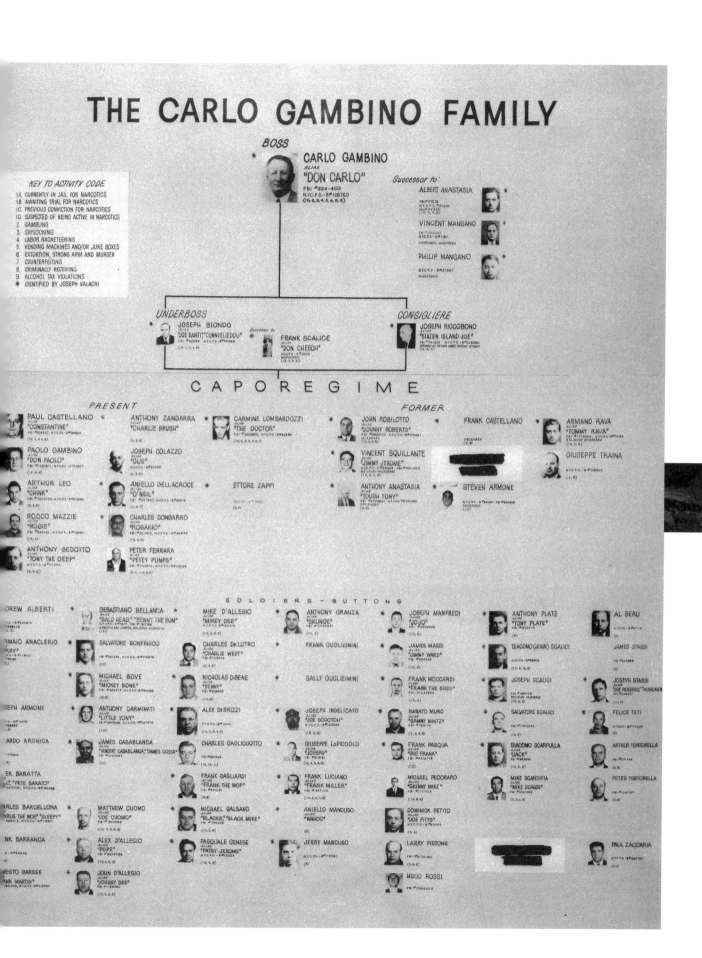

FRANK LUCAS

Born 1930, La Grange, USA
Still living
Alleged international narcotics trafficking

RONALD AND REGGIE KRAY

Born 1933, East London, UK
Died Ronnie 1995; Reggie 2000,
London, UK
gangsters; racketeers; protection; murderers
(*Shown*–Ronnie and Reggie with their mother
and grandfather)

CARMINE TRAMUNTI
(COVERING FACE)

Born 1910, New York, USA
Died 1978, New York, USA, natural causes
Alleged Lucchese Crime Family

SALVATORE RIINA

Born 1930, Corleone, Sicily
Still living
Arrested 1993, still in prison
Alleged Corleonesi; hitman

1970 >

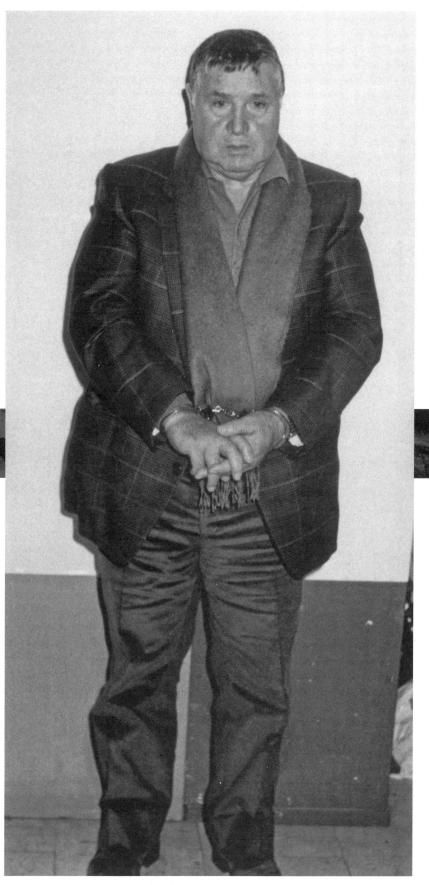

PAUL CASTELLANO

Born 1915, New York, USA

Died 1985, New York, USA, shot

Alleged Gambino Crime Family; racketeering

1975   1976 >

JIMMY HOFFA

Born 1913, Indiana, USA

Disappeared 1975, Bloomfield, USA

Teamsters Union boss; bribery

YOSHIO KODAMA

Born 1911, Nihonmatsu, Japan

Died 1984, Tokyo, Japan, natural causes

Alleged Yakuza boss; Lockheed scandal

JOHN ROSELLI

Born 1905, ?
Died 1975, Miami, USA, strangled,
shot, mutilated
Chicago Outfit; worked for Capone; allegedly
involved with CIA in plot to kill Castro

BARON EDUARD JOHN EMPAIN

Kidnapped January 23, 1978, Paris, France
Released March 26,1978, Paris, France
Kidnapped by group including Colombian
drug cartel and Italian Mafia member,
Georges Bertoncini

< 1976

1978

ALDO MORO

Born 1916, Puglia, Italy
Died 1978, Rome, Italy, kidnapped and murdered
Ex-prime minister of Italy; held in captivity for
54 days by Red Brigades, then murdered and body
dumped in car in Rome
(*Shown*–tribute poster)

LOCKHEED SCANDAL

Date 1950s to 1976
Bribes paid by Lockheed Corporation
to secure Japanese contracts
to build aircraft.
(*Shown*–Japanese Prime Minister,
Kakuei Tanaka, after being charged
with bribery, 1976)

DRUG BUST

Crashed 1981, Florida, after pursuit
by US Customs
Loaded with 800 lb (365 kg) of Jamaican
marijuana from cartel in South America

Date December 23, 1984
Killed 16 people, hundreds injured
Train 904 exploded approximately 25 miles (40 km)
from Bologna, in one of Italy's longest tunnels.
Right-wing terrorists allegedly conspired with Mafia
and Camorra to carry out bombing

ANTHONY "FAT TONY" SALERNO (LEFT)

Born 1911, New York, USA
Died 1992, Springfield, USA, natural causes
Alleged Genovese Crime Family; gambling;
numbers; loan sharking; protection

1981   1985 >

ENRIQUE LEHDER RIVAS

Born 1950, Armenia, Colombia
Still living, in US federal prison
Alleged co-founder of Medellin Cartel;
drug trafficking

MASS TRIAL

Date 1985
Place Naples, Italy
Charges brought against 640 members of
Camorra, all apparently working under
boss Don Cutolo.

RACKETEER INFLUENCED AND CORRUPT ORGANIZATIONS ACT (RICO)

Date 1970

US federal law providing for the arrest and charging of individuals who have committed any two of 35 designated crimes over a 10-year period. Used by DA Rudolph Giuliani in Mafia Commission Trial, 1986 (*Shown*–Rudolph Giuliani at press conference, 1986)

PABLO ESCOBAR

Born 1949, Antioquia, Colombia
Died 1993, Medellin, Colombia, shot in gun battle with Colombian Drug Enforcement team
Drug lord

1989 >

DRUG WAR IN COLOMBIA

Began after 1989 assassination of Luis Carlos Galan by Medellin Cartel. Andean Strategy developed in response, with deployment of US military advisors and troops to stem narcotics trafficking to the USA
(*Shown*–car bomb, Bogota, Colombia, 1989)

<1989

1990>

INVASION OF PANAMA

Date 1989
Operation *Just Cause* to depose dictator Manuel Noriega, who was later tried on eight counts of drug trafficking, racketeering, and money laundering.
(*Shown*–devastation from US bombing, El Chorrillo, Panama)

JOHN GOTTI (LEFT)

Born 1940, New York, USA
Died 2002, natural causes
Gambino Crime Family; racketeering, murder, gambling, extortion

THE MOB CREW

US gang, allegedly known for involvement
in organized crime
(*Shown*–TMC member with weapon and money)

PAKISTANI ANTI-NARCOTICS TASK FORCE

Established 1995 to combat trafficking of
narcotics across the Pakistan border.
(*Shown*–Anti-Narcotics Task Force members
guarding drug traffickers caught
on border of Afghanistan and Pakistan)

GIOVANNI FALCONE

Born 1939, Palermo, Sicily
Died 1992, Palermo, Sicily, car bomb
Italian magistrate fighting Mafia in Italy;
assassinated in car bomb
(*Shown*–aftermath of car bomb)

JOHN GOTTI, JR (CENTER FRONT)

Born 1964, New York, USA
Still living, in federal prison
Son of John Gotti

2000 >

AFGHAN NORTHERN ALLIANCE

Established 1996 to combat trafficking of narcotics across the Afghan border. (*Shown*–Afghan Northern Alliance members displaying seized heroin from village of Khadja-Bakhoutdin)

< 2001

US DRUG HAUL

Date April 7, 2003
Discovery by US Drug Enforcement officers
of cocaine paste processing plant in
Huallagua Valley, Peru
(*Shown*–lab workers under arrest)

PIRACY

Date December 17, 2002
Yemeni and Somali pirates under guard after
arrest by the Indian Navy for attempting to
take over an oil tanker in the Gulf of Aden

BERNARDO PROVENZANO

Born 1933, Corleone, Sicily
Still living—in prison after 42 years on the run
Alleged Corleonesi; murder; extortion

VIKTOR BOUT

Born 1967, Dushanbe, Soviet Union
(now Tajikistan)
Still living—arrested in 2008
Alleged international arms trafficker

DORA AKUNYILI

Born 1954, Nigeria
Still living
Director General of National Agency for
Food and Drug Administration Control in
Nigeria to 2008. Worked for eradication
of counterfeit drugs by organized crime.

DRUG TRAFFICKING

Date July 31, 2007
LAPD and federal authorities arrest
gang members and seize drugs and
weapons in south Los Angeles.
(*Shown*–officers displaying some
of the weapons seized)

2007 >

ANTHONY DOYLE

Arrested Chicago 2005
Ex-Chicago Police Officer.
Charged in the Family Secrets trial with
passing information to the Chicago Outfit

MONGOLS MOTORCYCLE GANG

Founded 1969, California, USA
Alleged drug dealing; murder; money
laundering; extortion
(*Shown*–"Wanted" poster of gang
members, October 2008)

< 2007   2008 >

JESUS "THE KING" ZAMBADA GARCIA

Arrested October 22, 2008, Mexico City,
Mexico
Alleged Mexican drug lord, Sinaloa drug
cartel

RICARDO GUTIERREZ "RICKO"
Sergeant-at-arms Highland Park Chaper - DRUGS

WILLIAM CRAGG OWENS "TARGET"
President Oxnard Chapter DRUGS

JO...

Ser
Des
LAN

SAM TREVINO "WAPO"
President Henderson Chapter

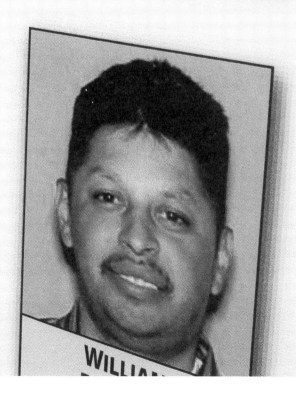

WILLIA...

NASER ORIC

Born 1967, former Yugoslavia

Still living

Arrested 2008, Sarajevo, Bosnia
and Herzegovina

Alleged racketeering; weapons trafficking;
extortion

BENEDETTO CAPIZZI

Born ?, Sicily

Still living

Alleged elected boss of Sicilian Mafia in 2008

(*Shown*–arrest in 2008)

< 2008

2009 >

LA FAMILIA MICHOACANA

Drug Cartel based in Michoacana, Mexico
Alleged drug trafficking; extortion; involved in
bloody war with opposing cartels, particularly
the Zetas
(*Shown*–mass arrest of 44 members
during family baptism in Morelia, Mexico,
on April 18, 2009)

Glossary

actor/s participant, participants, or group involved in a particular action or plan

arson deliberate lighting of fire for the purpose of destroying property for profit or revenge

book betting racket usually involving sporting events and run by a bookmaker

bookmaker person who runs a betting operation, usually involving sporting events

bootlegging illegally producing, buying, and selling of liquor during Prohibition in the USA

capo boss of a Mafia crime family

contract order issued for the murder of a specific person, usually with a fee for the service

crime family body of individuals, not necessarily related, who together form a group for the purpose of illegal profit from various enterprises, also illegal

Carabinieri Italian police

Cosa Nostra another name for the Mafia. Often used in the USA but originated in Sicily

crew group of individuals who work under a *capo* or boss

counterfeiting illegal printing of fake currency (money)

dice gambling game involving the throwing of dice and betting on the numbers that turn up

embezzlement the illegal taking or stealing of money by fraud

extortion the gaining of profit by threats or violence

fence individual who knowingly buys and sells stolen goods

fix deal made with law enforcement authorities to ignore criminal activity

forgery making or adapting items or documents in an attempt to deceive for profit

fraud deliberately misrepresenting a situation to make a profit

kangaroo court illegal process of judgment where the perpetrators are not legally trained and the verdict is flawed

hangout establishment used for a gathering or meeting

hitman person who kills someone, usually for a fee

identity theft legal use of someone's identity through fake documents, usually with the intent of taking money from bank accounts

interdiction legal prevention, such as an embargo

jurisdiction the geographic area that a legal court or country controls under its laws

loan shark a person who loans money at such exorbitant rates that the principal can never be repaid.

local offices of a trade union that have voting power but no actual membership

made formally inducted into a crime family or Mafia group, usually with some initiation ceremony

Mafioso Italian word for member of a criminal organization or Mafia. Plural—*Mafiosi*

money laundering process of moving profits, funds, or cash/money from one location to another, or through different enterprises, with the intention of not paying income tax on the funds, and hiding the (often illegal) origin of the funds

numbers form of lottery where people bet money on what numbers will be drawn

outfit criminal slang for a crime family

pickpocket person who steals directly from the pocket or purse of another person

racketeering engaging in illegal enterprises such as fraud, extortion, or prostitution

rat person who reports the criminal doings of another to either the crime family or the authorities

RICO Racketeer Influenced and Corrupt Organizations Act is a United States federal law providing for the arrest and charging of individuals who have committed any two of 35 designated crimes over a 10-year period. It was enacted in the United States in 1970 and used to arrest many Mafia members

scam fraudulent business scheme

Secret Service usually refers to the US Secret Service who were initially engaged to fight counterfeiting and other federal crimes. The Secret Service is now mainly responsible for the protection of the president of the United States and all politicians in the USA as well as those visiting from other countries

skim siphoning funds from a legal business enterprise, or hiding money to avoid the paying income tax

slot machines machines where coins are inserted in a slot as a bet that a series of numbers or images will appear. Often called one-armed bandits or poker machines

speak-easy establishment where illegal liquor was sold during Prohibition

subpoena order issued by a court, ordering the appearance of a witness in court

teamster/s member of the International Brotherhood of Teamsters, a labor union in the United States. Jimmy Hoffa was the president of the Teamsters

traffic/trafficking illegal transport and sale of items such as illicit drugs, humans, weapons, and tobacco

turncoat person who betrays his criminal group or friends by changing his alliances

vor/vory Russian gang member/members (often prisoner/prisoners) known for their violence and tattoos

wire electronic device hidden on a person in order to transmit secret conversations or information back to authorities

wire service originally a telegraphic service for transferring information about sporting results and allowing betting to take place across the country before the results were posted legally

Witness Protection Program federal service provided by most countries for the protection of witnesses whose lives are in danger by giving evidence. Their identity is suppressed and they are moved to a "safe house" for an indeterminate time

Index

Garrido, Felix, 198
Garrone, Matteo, 216, 217
Gazprom, 247
Gendarmeria Reale, 19
Geneva Convention for the Suppression
   of the Illicit Traffic in Dangerous Drugs, 95
Genovese, Frank, 39
Genovese, Michael, 127
Genovese Crime Family, 143, 214, 232,
   234, 235
Gentile, Nick, 39
Georgia (country), *280*
Gerlinger, Albert, *95*
German gangsters, 59
German immigrants, 56
Germany, 38, 41, 162, 222, 223, 260, 271, 285
Ghost Shadows, 165
Giancana, Sam, 142
Giardini family, 38
Gigante, Vincent "the Chin", *142*, 143,
   235, *235*
Girotti, Vera, 113
Giuffré, Nino "Little Hand", 208
Giuliani, Rudolph, *135*, 142
Giuliano, Nunzio, *219*
Giuliano, Salvatore, 38, 42, *43*, 44, *44*, 45
Gjallica, 266
Glasgow, UK, 197
Glick, Allen, 141
global competition, 239
global economy, 8
global financial crisis, 286, *287*
global organized crime, 175, 248
global security threat, 8–11
   see also transnational organized crime
Global Strategies Group, 128
globalisation, 8, 158–67, 197, 204, 205, 222–3
Godfather trilogy, The, 132–3, *132*, *133*,
   137, 207
Golden Triangle, 158, *158*, 162, 242, 258
Golden Venture, 241, *241*
Goldwater, Barry, *127*
Golubovic, Kristian, 262
Gong, Eddie, 164
Gong Li, 161, *161*
Gorbachev, Mikhail, 168, 172
Gordon, Waxey, 65, *65*
Gotti, John J. "Teflon Don", 128, 143, 224, 225,
   225, 226, *226*, 283
Gotti Jr, John, 128, 225, *225*
Grand Hôtel et des Palmes, 116, *116*
Grantley, Gyton, *273*
Grau, Ramon, 130
Great Britain *see* United Kingdom
Great Depression, 284
Greco, Louis, 229
Greco, Salvatore, 117
Greco family, 38
Greece, 258, 265, 268
Green Dragons, 165
Green Gang, 79, 81
Grey Wolves, 258, *259*
Guadalajara cartel, 188
Guam, 198
Guangdong, China, 26, 78, 160, 162, 242

Guangzhou, China, 28, *79*
guapos, 14–15
Guarduna, 14–15
Guerrero, Wilson, 185
gulags and prisons, *31*, 84, *84*, *85*, 86, *86*, 87,
   90, 91, *91*, 173, 175, *246*
Gulf cartel, 188
Gulf War (first), 190
Gully Posse, 199
Gulmares, Cristina de Almedia, 113
guns *see* arms trafficking
gurentai, 76
Guzik, Jake "Greasy Thumb", 64
Guzman, David, *286*

H

Hague Commission, 95
Haidini, Mehmed, 271
Han Yong-wan, *159*
Harding, Warren, 54, 129
Harriman, Edward H., *103*
Harrison Narcotic Act (US), 95, 97
Hart, Dickie, 193, 195
Hartnett, Gabby, *64*
hashish, *163*
Hathaway, Ann, 214
Hatoyama, Ichiro, 71
Havana, 69, 127, 130, 131, *131*
Heaven and Earth Society *see* Tiandihui
Helmand Province, (Afghanistan), 257
Hennessy, David, 22, 23, 48
Hennessy, Mike, 22
hermano mayor, 14
heroin, 35
   American Mafia &, 112, 116, 125, 227, 235
   Latin America, 92, 97, 183, 184, 185, 188,
      252, 253, 254
   Sicilian Mafia &, 112, 116
   transnational organized crime groups &,
      258, *258*, 260, 264, 265, 267, 270, 277
   Triads &, 158, 159, 162–3, 166, 242, 243
Herzegovina, 263
Heung Chu, 83
Higgins, Charles "Vannie", *47*
hijacking, 104, 194
Hill, Billy, 192, *192*, 194
Hill, Henry, 226
Hill, Maggie, 107
Hill, Virginia, *68*, 69
Hines, Jimmy, 47
Hing Ah Kee Kwan, 83
Hitler, Adolf, 41, 162
hitmen, 105
Hoffa, James Riddle "Jimmy", 126, 138, *138*,
   139, 141, 230–1, *231*, *234*
Holland *see* Amsterdam; Netherlands
Hong Kong, 78, 79, 81, 83, 159, *160*, 162,
   241, *241*
Hong Kong banks, 281
Hong Kong Triads, 82–3, 159, 160, 162, 166,
   240, 243, 245
Honoured Society, The, 272
Hoover, J. Edgar, 124, 126, 127, 128, 129, *129*

Hop Sing Tong, 244, 245
Horitaka, *110*
horseracing, 107
Hoskins, Bob, 67
Hotel and Restaurant Employees and
   Bartenders International Union, 234
Hoxha, Enver Halil, 264, *264*, 265, *270*
Hoxha, Victor, 271
Hsing Chung Hui, 78
Hu brothers, 240
Hu Jintao, 243
Huang Chih-jung "Pock-marked Huang",
   80–1
human trafficking
   Africa, 274, 275
   American Mafia &, 48, *49*, 235
   Balkan Route, 258, 268, 269
   Jamaican Posses &, 199
   Russian Mafia &, 248, 249
   snakeheads &, 240–1, *241*
   transnational organized crime &, 8, 258,
      269, 277
   Yakuza &, 148
Hung Ching, 165
Hung Society *see* Tiandihui
Hungary, 258

I

Ianniello, Matthew "Matty the Horse", 232
identity theft, 234–5
Ignatz Florio Cooperative Association
   Among Corleonesi, 51
Iler, Robert, 251
immigrants, 20, *23*, 46, *46*, 49
   see also African immigrants; Chinese
   immigrants; Indian immigrants; Irish
   immigrants; Italian immigrants; Jewish
   immigrants; Polish immigrants
Imparato, Gianfelice, 216, *217*
Imperioli, Michael, *250–1*
Inagawa, Hideki, 147
Inagawa, Kakuji, 147
Inagawa, Toi, 147
Inagawa-kai, 75, 110, 147
Inca tradition, 95
Indelicato, Anthony, 143
India, 243, 275
Indian immigrants, 103, 274
indigenous Andean populations, 94, *94*, 95,
   96–7, *96–7*, *99*, 180, *252*
Indochina war, 190
Indonesia, 98, 148
Industrial Revolution, 103
industriante, 220
informants
   American Mafia, 54–5, 129, 134, 141, 142,
      226–7, 228, 229
   'Ndrangheta, 220
   Sicilian Mafia, 113, 118–19, 120, 123, 205,
      208, 210
   Triad, 244, 245
Information Age, 224–35
Inquisition, 15, 18–19

Russian Mafia *(contd.)*
  constant presence of, 246–51
  crime superpower, 168–79
  global foundations of, 35
  industry &, 171
  international drug cartel alliances of, 254
  mother cult of, 88
  movies about, 176–7, *176, 177*
  multinational crime &, 110–11
  origins of, 30–1, 86, 285
  peasant outlaws of, 30–1
  rackets of, 31, 84, 87, 178–9, 169, 170, 171,
    173, 247, *247*, 248, 249
  rise of, 178
  sophistication of, 249
  tattoos of, 86, 89, *89*, 91, 174, *246*
  tsarist rule &, 30–1
  vory v zakone, 84–91, *89*, 110, 172–3, 174–5,
    177, 246, *246*
  weapons-for-drugs exchanges &, 254
  weapons of mass destruction &, 249
  women &, 88

S

Sabini, Charles Ullano "Darby", 107
Sabini brothers, 107
sack murders, *50*, 51
Sacra Corona Unita clan, 265
Sage, Walter, *35, 141*
Sahkarov, Alik, 251
Sakhalin, (Siberia), 31
Saietta, Ignazio *see* Lupo, Ignazio "the Wolf"
St Clair gang, 107
St Louis, 59
St Petersburg, (Russia), 31
St Valentine's Day Massacre, 48, *49*, 60, *60*,
  61, 102, 104, 106
sake, 144–5, *144*
Salerno, Anthony "Fat Tony", 143, 235
Salvati, Joseph, 229
samurai, 24–5, *24*, 72, *145*, 156, *237*
San Franscisco, 244
San-ho Hui, 78
San Luca, Calabria, (Italy), 223
Sangiorgi, Ermanno, 19
Sant' Anastasia, 212
Santino, Umberto, 17
Santoro, Salvatore, 143
sarakin, 145
Sasakawa, Ryoichi, *152*
Saviano, Roberto, 216, *216*, 217
Sayed Rahim, *257*
Scalise, Frank, 126–7
Scalish, John, 127
Scarfo, Nicky, 225
Scarpa, Gregory, 226
Schevenigen, (Netherlands), *162–3*
Schiro, Cola, 62
Schultz, Dutch, 59, 65, *65*, 105, 107
Schwimmer, Reinhart, 48
Scopo, Ralph, 143
Scorsese, Martin, 233

Scott, Ridley, 155
Scottish gangsters, 197, 198
Second Five Ancestors, 29
Second Opium War, 28
Second World War *see* World War II
secret societies, 30, *30*, 31
Senaloa cartel, 188
Sendero Luminosa, 181
Senegal, 276
separatism, 41, 42
Serbia, 262, 266
Serbian organized crime groups, 258, 260,
  261–2, *261*
Serpico, Camille, 214
Setola, Giuseppe, *213*
sex industry
  Russian Mafia &, 248
  Yakuza &, 76, 148, *148*
  see also brothels; prostitution
sex tours, 148
Shan Chu, 83
Shanghai, (China), *26*, 79, 80, 81
Shanghai Convention, 95
Shanghai massacre, *80*
Shanghai Triad, 161, *161*
Shao Lin monastery, 28, 29
Sheeran, Frank "the Irishman", 138, 230–1
shell companies, 280
Shengmei, 241
Shing Triad, 82
Shining Path, *see* Sendero Luminosa
Shinoda, Kenichi, 237
Shiroo, Tetsuya, *239*
shogunate, 24, 25
Shower Posse, 198, 199
shtetls, 103
Shui Bao, 165
Shun Chi, 28
Siberian gulags/prisons, *31*, *84*, *91*
Sicilian land reform, 114, 115
Sicilian Mafia
  bourgeoisie, 115
  Camorra compared to, 212–13
  Commission, 117, 118
  communism &, 39, 41, 44, 112–13
  fascism and power of, 36–45
  gang warfare &, 113, 117, 118, 122–3
  global foundations of, 34
  globalisation &, 204, 205
  land &, 18, 19, 114
  mass trials, 112, 119–20, *119*
  new wave of, 204–11
  origins of, 15, 16–19
  parliamentary commission on, 117
  political power of, 112, 115, 205, 210
  rackets of, 19, 36, 39, 112, 113, 114, 115, 116,
    117, 118, 122, 205, 207, 208
  relocation of, 266
  separatism &, 41, 42
  status of, 17
  structure of, 10, 117, 119
  tax collection by, 19
  value of organized crime of, 205
  weaponry of, 117, *117*

World War II &, 38, 39, 40, 41, 116
  see also informants
Sicily, 15, 18, 19, 20, 21, 34, 36, 38, *38*, 39, *39*,
  40, 41, *41*, 42, *42*, *45*, 48, 50, 53, 60, 61, 110,
  110–11, 114, 115, 129, 139, *144*, 235, 207,
  211, 265 *see also* World War II
Siegel, Benjamin "Bugsy", 48, 68, 69, *69*, 131
Sierra Leone, 276
Sigler, Jamie-Lynn, 251
Silesi, Joseph, 127, 131
Silu, China, 28
Silva, 266
Sinatra, Frank, 194, *226*
Sindona, Michele, *281*
Singapore, 162, 281
Sirico, Tony, *250–1*
SISDE (Service for Information and the
  Safeguard of Democracy in Italy), 210
Sister Ping *see* Cheng Chui Ping
skimming, 140, 141
Skolimowski, Jerzy, 177
slave labor, 190
  see also human trafficking
Slidell, John, 46
slot machines, 124, 125, 140, *140*
Slovakia, 264
Smiley, Allen, 69
Smith, Charles Martin, 66
snakeheads, 240–1
Social Democratic Labor Party (Russia), 31
socialism, 41, 44, 113, 120
sokaiya, 153
Solzhenitsyn, Alexander, *87*
Somali pirates, *9*, 269
Sopranos, The, 250–1, *250–1*
South Africa, 192, 254, 269, 274, *275*
South America, 148
  drug cartels of, 180–9, *184*
  drug seizures in, *182*, 183, *183*, *188*
  drugs trafficking &, 221, 223
  immigration to, 275
  kidnappings in, 186–7, *186*
  'Ndrangheta &, 221, 223
  see also Latin America
South Korea, 157
Southeast Asia, 98, 158, *158*
Southampton (UK), 166
Southern Society, 30
Southside Posse, 199
Soviet Mafia *see* Russian Mafia
Soviet Union *see* Russia; USSR
Soyinka, Wole, 276
Spain, 264, *265*
Spangler Posse, 199
Spanish colonial rule, 96–7, 212
Spanish Inquisition, 15, 18–19
Spanish Mafia, 14–15
Spasojevic, Dusan, 262
spies, American Mafia, 227, 229
Spilotro, Anthony, 141
Srpska Garda, 262
Stack, Robert, 66, *66*
Stalin, Joseph, 31, 84
Stardust Casino, Nevada, 140, 141
Statute of Limitations (USA), 225

Contributors

Jonathan Carlozzi

Jonathan has a graduate degree from California State University, Sacramento, where his studies focused on security, history, criminology, and the relationship between modern culture, the media, and crime. Jonathan has presented papers at conferences on the relationship between communication technology and crime, as a member of the Western Society of Criminology. He is currently teaching at John Jay College of Criminal Justice, New York, where his research deals with technology and crime, the history of the criminal justice system, and white collar crimes.

Nicolas Giannakopoulos

Nicolas is a renowned expert in transnational organized crime structures. From 1996 to 2000, he was in charge of a national research program financed by the Swiss Confederation entitled "Swiss Corruption and Organised Crime." His research programs include money laundering analysis, organized crime policy, corruption, and focusing on the creation of models and tools that help analysts work. In 2000, Nicolas co-founded the company Inside.CO SA in Geneva (CH) together with six other specialists, creating a unique international quality standard to protect private companies from organized crime networks infiltrations and influences.

David Hompes

David, who publishes under the name of Amoruso, is a freelance journalist living in the Netherlands. He has been studying organized crime for almost a decade. In the summer of 2001, he published the website "Gangsters Inc." which features articles about organized crime groups from around the globe. His work can also be found in *The Encyclopedia of International Organized Crime* that was published in 2005. He is a regular contributor to the American crime magazine *Mob Candy*.

Thomas Hunt

Thomas is a writer and researcher of organized crime history, specializing in the American Mafia. He is editor and publisher of *Informer: The Journal of American Mafia History*. He publishes websites and moderates Internet forums on the subject. He co-authored, with Martha Macheca Sheldon, the award-winning *Deep Water: Joseph P. Macheca and the Birth of the American Mafia*. He also has written and co-written articles for the *On the Spot Journal of Crime and Law Enforcement History*. He serves as editor for organized crime and crime publications categories of the Internet's Open Directory Project.

Lorenzo Picchi

Lorenzo is currently working on his Ph.D. at the University of Florence. He teaches history of the Italian Mafia at Fairfield University, University of New Haven, Richmond University, and George Mason University, all in Florence. He has held several conferences in universities including Yale, Rutgers, and De Paul. His research includes the history of the Mafia from 1992 to 2006; the rise of agrarian fascism in Tuscany; the Italian front in World War I through the letters and the diaries of the soldiers, and the role of the Masonic Lodges in influencing Italian politics from the end of World War II up until the present day.

Frank Shanty

Frank is co-founder and Director of Research for the Cobra Institute, a terrorism and counterterrorism research firm in Abingdon, Maryland, USA. Frank has recently completed his doctoral dissertation: "The Nexus between International Terrorism and Drug Trafficking from Afghanistan (1979-2006)" at the University of South Australia. He has co-authored two published studies on terrorism and has served as general editor and contributing author on *Encyclopedia of World Terrorism*, Vol. 4, M.E. Sharpe Publishers, and *Organized Crime: From Trafficking to Terrorism*, ABC-CLIO Publishers, 2007. Frank has practical experience in law enforcement, training in hazardous material incident management, and first responder training. He has done extensive research in the area of transnational organized crime, illicit trafficking in conventional small arms and light weapons, i.e. Chemical, Biological, Radiological, and Nuclear (CBRN) weapons and matériel. Frank is listed on the United Nations Terrorism Prevention Branch–Roster of Experts.

Charles Tumosa

Charles received a Ph.D. in Chemistry from Virginia Polytechnic Institute and State University in Blacksburg, VA in 1972 and then spent 17 years as Head of the Criminalistics Laboratory of the Philadelphia Police Department in Philadelphia, PA analyzing evidence in crimes of violence. He then went to the Smithsonian Institution in Washington, D.C. where he established an analytical laboratory and did research in the Materials Science of cultural materials for 16 years. At present he teaches Trace Evidence, Instrumental Analysis, and Forensics and Art in the Forensics Studies Program at the University of Baltimore, MD.

Andrew Urban

Andrew is the publisher and editor of an award-winning online weekly movie magazine. Specializing in film journalism, Andrew was Australian bureau chief for London-based film trade publications from 1985 to 1994. He was channel host for the World Movies subscription movie channel in Australia, and with his partner Louise Keller, he co-produced and hosted *Movies This Week*, a short movie review TV program. Andrew has presented several contemporary movie appreciation courses at Sydney University's Centre for Continuing Education. In January 2007, Andrew was commissioned by the Australian Film Television and Radio School's Centre for Screen Business to produce an extensive, ongoing series of in-depth on-camera interviews with film and TV industry practitioners, for the CSB website.

Yue Ma

Yue Ma is a faculty member in the Department of Law and Police Science at John Jay College of Criminal Justice in New York. He received his Ph.D. from Rutgers University. He also holds a J.D. from Rutgers University Law School and an LL.M. from University of Minnesota Law School. Yue Ma is interested in the comparative study of legal and criminal justice issues. He has published articles exploring a wide range of legal and criminal justice issues in the transnational context, including the impact of international human rights law on criminal justice, comparative analyses of prosecutorial discretion, plea bargaining, the law of interrogation and judicial supervision of prosecutorial decision-making. Yue Ma is also interested in exploring issues related to organized crime.

Picture Credits

THE ART ARCHIVE

27 bot The Art Archive / British Museum / Eileen Tweedy; 81 bot right The Art Archive / Kharbine-Tapabor

CORBIS

1 center © Corbis Australia; 2-3 © Corbis Australia; 4-5 center © Corbis Australia; 6 center left © Corbis Australia; 6 center right © Corbis Australia; 7 center left © Corbis Australia; 7 center right © Corbis Australia; 8 bot left © Corbis Australia; 9 center right © Corbis Australia; 9 top © Corbis Australia; 10 bot left © Corbis Australia; 10 top right © Corbis Australia; 11 bot right © Corbis Australia; 12-13 © Corbis Australia; 14-15 top © Corbis Australia; 15 bot right © Corbis Australia; 16 top © Corbis Australia; 17 bot right © Corbis Australia; 18 bot right © Corbis Australia; 18 top left © Corbis Australia; 19 bot right © Corbis Australia; 20 bot left © Corbis Australia; 20 top left © Corbis Australia; 21 top © Corbis Australia; 22 top © Corbis Australia; 023 bot left © Corbis Australia; 23 center right © Corbis Australia; 24 bot left © Corbis Australia; 25 bot right © Corbis Australia; 26 bot left © Corbis Australia; 27 top right © Corbis Australia; 29 top left © Corbis Australia; 30 bot left © Corbis Australia; 31 top right © Corbis Australia; 32-33 © Corbis Australia; 34 center left © Corbis Australia; 34-35 bot © Corbis Australia; 37 bot right © Corbis Australia; 37 top © Corbis Australia; 38 bot right © Corbis Australia; 39 bot right © Corbis Australia; 39 top right © Corbis Australia; 40 bot left © Corbis Australia; 40 top left © Corbis Australia; 41 bot right © Corbis Australia; 42 top © Corbis Australia; 42 top right © Corbis Australia; 43 top © Corbis Australia; 43 bot © Corbis Australia; 44 center © Corbis Australia; 44-45 top © Corbis Australia; 46 top © Corbis Australia; 47 bot left © Corbis Australia; 47 center right © Corbis Australia; 47 top right © Corbis Australia; 48 center left © Corbis Australia; 48-49 top center © Corbis Australia; 49 center right © Corbis Australia; 50 bot left © Corbis Australia; 50 top © Corbis Australia; 51 bot left © Corbis Australia; 52 top © Corbis Australia; 53 bot right © Corbis Australia; 53 top right © Corbis Australia; 54 bot left © Corbis Australia; 54 center left © Corbis Australia; 55 top © Corbis Australia; 56 bot © Corbis Australia; 56 top left © Corbis Australia; 57 top right © Corbis Australia; 58 top © Corbis Australia; 59 bot left © Corbis Australia; 59 bot right © Corbis Australia; 59 top right © Corbis Australia; 60 bot left © Corbis Australia; 60 top left © Corbis Australia; 60-61 top center © Corbis Australia; 61 bot right © Corbis Australia; 62 top © Corbis Australia; 63 bot right © Corbis Australia; 63 top right © Corbis

Australia; 64 top © Corbis Australia; 65 center right © Corbis Australia; 65 top right © Corbis Australia; 68 bot left © Corbis Australia; 68 top © Corbis Australia; 69 center right © Corbis Australia; 70 bot left © Corbis Australia; 70 top © Corbis Australia; 71 bot left © Corbis Australia; 72 bot left © Corbis Australia; 73 bot right © Corbis Australia; 73 top © Corbis Australia; 74 top © Corbis Australia; 75 bot right © Corbis Australia; 75 top right © Corbis Australia; 76 bot right © Corbis Australia; 76 top left © Corbis Australia; 77 top © Corbis Australia; 78 bot left © Corbis Australia; 78 top left © Corbis Australia; 79 top © Corbis Australia; 80 bot © Corbis Australia; 81 top left © Corbis Australia; 82 top © Corbis Australia; 83 top right © Corbis Australia; 84 bot left © Corbis Australia; 86 top right © Corbis Australia; 87 bot right © Corbis Australia; 88 top © Corbis Australia; 89 bot right © Corbis Australia; 90 bot left © Corbis Australia; 90 top © Corbis Australia; 91 bot left © Corbis Australia; 92 bot left © Corbis Australia; 93 bot © Corbis Australia; 93 top right © Corbis Australia; 94 top left © Corbis Australia; 94 top right © Corbis Australia; 95 center right © Corbis Australia; 96 bot © Corbis Australia; 97 bot center © Corbis Australia; 97 center © Corbis Australia; 99 right © Corbis Australia; 100 center right © Corbis Australia; 100 top left © Corbis Australia; 101 top © Corbis Australia; 102 bot © Corbis Australia; 103 top right © Corbis Australia; 104 bot left © Corbis Australia; 104 top © Corbis Australia; 105 bot left © Corbis Australia; 105 top right © Corbis Australia; 106 bot © Corbis Australia; 107 bot right © Corbis Australia; 107 top right © Corbis Australia; 108-109 © Corbis Australia 110 center left © Corbis Australia; 110-111 bot © Corbis Australia; 112 bot right © Corbis Australia; 113 bot right © Corbis Australia; 113 center left © Corbis Australia; 114 top left © Corbis Australia; 114 top right © Corbis Australia; 115 bot right © Corbis Australia; 115 top © Corbis Australia; 116 top © Corbis Australia; 117 bot right © Corbis Australia; 117 top right © Corbis Australia; 118 bot left © Corbis Australia; 118 center left © Corbis Australia; 119 top © Corbis Australia; 120 bot left © Corbis Australia; 121 © Corbis Australia; 122 bot left © Corbis Australia; 122 top right © Corbis Australia; 123 top © Corbis Australia; 125 bot right © Corbis Australia; 125 top © Corbis Australia; 126 center left © Corbis Australia; 126 top right © Corbis Australia; 127 bot © Corbis Australia; 128 top © Corbis Australia; 129 center right © Corbis Australia; 129 top right © Corbis Australia; 130 bot © Corbis Australia; 130 top left © Corbis Australia; 131 bot right © Corbis Australia; 132 top © Corbis Australia; 134 center left © Corbis

Australia; 135 bot right © Corbis Australia; 135 center right © Corbis Australia; 135 top © Corbis Australia; 136 bot left © Corbis Australia; 137 bot right © Corbis Australia; 137 top © Corbis Australia; 138 bot © Corbis Australia; 138 top left © Corbis Australia; 139 bot right © Corbis Australia; 139 top left © Corbis Australia; 140 top © Corbis Australia; 141 bot right © Corbis Australia; 141 top right © Corbis Australia; 142 top © Corbis Australia; 143 bot right © Corbis Australia; 143 center right © Corbis Australia; 144 top left © Corbis Australia; 145 top © Corbis Australia; 146 bot left © Corbis Australia; 147 bot right © Corbis Australia; 147 top © Corbis Australia; 148 bot left © Corbis Australia; 150 bot right © Corbis Australia; 150 top left © Corbis Australia; 151 top © Corbis Australia; 152 top left © Corbis Australia; 152 top right © Corbis Australia; 153 bot right © Corbis Australia; 154 bot © Corbis Australia; 156 top right © Corbis Australia; 157 bot right © Corbis Australia; 158 bot left © Corbis Australia; 159 bot © Corbis Australia; 159 top right © Corbis Australia; 160 top © Corbis Australia; 161 top right © Corbis Australia; 162-163 top center © Corbis Australia; 163 top right © Corbis Australia; 164 top left © Corbis Australia; 164 top right © Corbis Australia; 165 bot right © Corbis Australia; 166 bot right © Corbis Australia; 166 top left © Corbis Australia; 167 top © Corbis Australia; 168 bot right © Corbis Australia; 169 top left © Corbis Australia; 169 top right © Corbis Australia; 170 top © Corbis Australia; 171 bot right © Corbis Australia; 172 top left © Corbis Australia; 173 top right © Corbis Australia; 174 bot left © Corbis Australia; 174 top © Corbis Australia; 175 top right © Corbis Australia; 178 bot left © Corbis Australia; 178 top right © Corbis Australia; 179 bot © Corbis Australia; 179 top right © Corbis Australia; 180 top © Corbis Australia; 181 top right © Corbis Australia; 182 bot © Corbis Australia; 182 top left © Corbis Australia; 183 bot right © Corbis Australia; 183 top left © Corbis Australia; 184 center left © Corbis Australia; 184 top left © Corbis Australia; 187 bot right © Corbis Australia; 187 top © Corbis Australia; 188 bot right © Corbis Australia; 188 top left © Corbis Australia; 189 © Corbis Australia; 190 center left © Corbis Australia; 191 © Corbis Australia; 199 bot right © Corbis Australia; 192 bot right © Corbis Australia; 193 bot right © Corbis Australia; 194 top left © Corbis Australia; 195 top © Corbis Australia; 196 bot © Corbis Australia; 197 bot right © Corbis Australia; 197 top left © Corbis Australia; 198 top © Corbis Australia; 199 top right © Corbis Australia; 200-201 © Corbis Australia; 202-203 top © Corbis Australia; 203 bot right © Corbis Australia; 204 bot left © Corbis Australia; 207